Performance

JAA ATPL Training

This book has been written and published to assist students enrolled in an approved JAA Air Transport Pilot Licence (ATPL) course in preparation for the JAA ATPL theoretical knowledge examinations. Nothing in the content of this book is to be interpreted as constituting instruction or advice relating to practical flying.

Whilst every effort has been made to ensure the accuracy of the information contained within this book, neither Jeppesen nor Atlantic Flight Training gives any warranty as to its accuracy or otherwise. Students preparing for the JAA ATPL theoretical knowledge examinations should not regard this book as a substitute for the JAA ATPL theoretical knowledge training syllabus published in the current edition of "JAR-FCL 1 Flight Crew Licensing (Aeroplanes)" (the Syllabus). The Syllabus constitutes the sole authoritative definition of the subject matter to be studied in a JAA ATPL theoretical knowledge training programme. No student should prepare for, or is entitled to enter himself/herself for, the JAA ATPL theoretical knowledge examinations without first being enrolled in a training school which has been granted approval by a JAA-authorised national aviation authority to deliver JAA ATPL training.

Contact Details:

Sales and Service Department
Jeppesen GmbH
Frankfurter Strasse 233
63263 Neu-Isenburg
Germany

Tel: ++49 (0)6102 5070
E-mail: fra-services@jeppesen.com

For further information on products and services from Jeppesen, visit our web site at: www.jeppesen.com

JA310109-000
ISBN 0-88487-359-5
Printed in Germany

PREFACE

As the world moves toward a single standard for international pilot licensing, many nations have adopted the syllabi and regulations of the "Joint Aviation Requirements-Flight Crew Licensing" (JAR-FCL), the licensing agency of the Joint Aviation Authorities (JAA).

Though training and licensing requirements of individual national aviation authorities are similar in content and scope to the JAA curriculum, individuals who wish to train for JAA licences need access to study materials which have been specifically designed to meet the requirements of the JAA licensing system. The volumes in this series aim to cover the subject matter tested in the JAA ATPL ground examinations as set forth in the ATPL training syllabus, contained in the JAA publication, "JAR-FCL 1 (Aeroplanes)".

The JAA regulations specify that all those who wish to obtain a JAA ATPL must study with a flying training organisation (FTO) which has been granted approval by a JAA-authorised national aviation authority to deliver JAA ATPL training. While the formal responsibility to prepare you for both the skill tests and the ground examinations lies with the FTO, these Jeppesen manuals will provide a comprehensive and necessary background for your formal training.

Jeppesen is acknowledged as the world's leading supplier of flight information services, and provides a full range of print and electronic flight information services, including navigation data, computerised flight planning, aviation software products, aviation weather services, maintenance information, and pilot training systems and supplies. Jeppesen counts among its customer base all US airlines and the majority of international airlines worldwide. It also serves the large general and business aviation markets. These manuals enable you to draw on Jeppesen's vast experience as an acknowledged expert in the development and publication of pilot training materials.

We at Jeppesen wish you success in your flying and training, and we are confident that your study of these manuals will be of great value in preparing for the JAA ATPL ground examinations.

The next three pages contain a list and content description of all the volumes in the ATPL series.

ATPL Series

Meteorology (JAR Ref 050)

- The Atmosphere
- Wind
- Thermodynamics
- Clouds and Fog
- Precipitation
- Air Masses and Fronts
- Pressure System
- Climatology
- Flight Hazards
- Meteorological Information

General Navigation (JAR Ref 061)

- Basics of Navigation
- Magnetism
- Compasses
- Charts
- Dead Reckoning Navigation
- In-Flight Navigation
- Inertial Navigation Systems

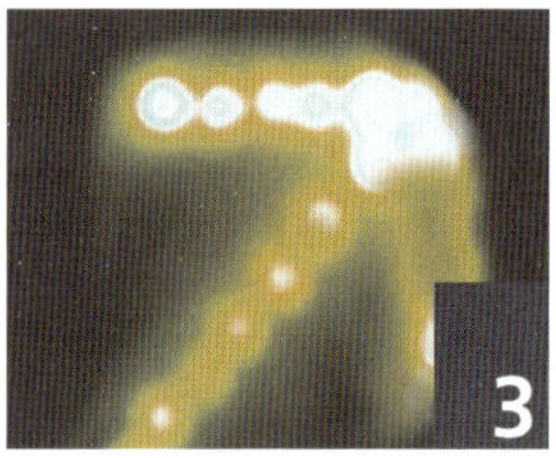

Radio Navigation (JAR Ref 062)

- Radio Aids
- Self-contained and External-Referenced Navigation Systems
- Basic Radar Principles
- Area Navigation Systems
- Basic Radio Propagation Theory

Airframes and Systems (JAR Ref 021 01)

- Fuselage
- Windows
- Wings
- Stabilising Surfaces
- Landing Gear
- Flight Controls
- Hydraulics
- Pneumatic Systems
- Air Conditioning System
- Pressurisation
- De-Ice / Anti-Ice Systems
- Fuel Systems

Powerplant (JAR Ref 021 03)

- Piston Engine
- Turbine Engine
- Engine Construction
- Engine Systems
- Auxiliary Power Unit (APU)

Electrics (JAR Ref 021 02)

- Direct Current
- Alternating Current
- Batteries
- Magnetism
- Generator / Alternator
- Semiconductors
- Circuits

Instrumentation (JAR Ref 022)

- Flight Instruments
- Automatic Flight Control Systems
- Warning and Recording Equipment
- Powerplant and System Monitoring Instruments

Principles of Flight (JAR Ref 080)

- Laws and Definitions
- Aerofoil Airflow
- Aeroplane Airflow
- Lift Coefficient
- Total Drag
- Ground Effect
- Stall
- C_{LMAX} Augmentation
- Lift Coefficient and Speed
- Boundary Layer
- High Speed Flight
- Stability
- Flying Controls
- Adverse Weather Conditions
- Propellers
- Operating Limitations
- Flight Mechanics

Performance (JAR Ref 032)

- Single-Engine Aeroplanes – Not certified under JAR/FAR 25 (Performance Class B)
- Multi-Engine Aeroplanes – Not certified under JAR/FAR 25 (Performance Class B)
- Aeroplanes certified under JAR/FAR 25 (Performance Class A)

Mass and Balance (JAR Ref 031)

- Definition and Terminology
- Limits
- Loading
- Centre of Gravity

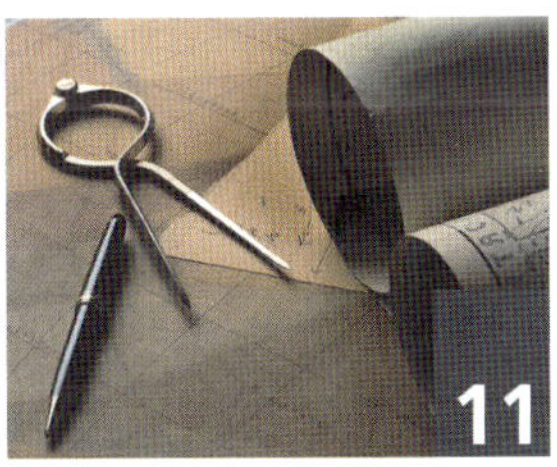

Flight Planning (JAR Ref 033)

- Flight Plan for Cross-Country Flights
- ICAO ATC Flight Planning
- IFR (Airways) Flight Planning
- Jeppesen Airway Manual
- Meteorological Messages
- Point of Equal Time
- Point of Safe Return
- Medium Range Jet Transport Planning

Air Law (JAR Ref 010)

- International Agreements and Organisations
- Annex 8 – Airworthiness of Aircraft
- Annex 7 – Aircraft Nationality and Registration Marks
- Annex 1 – Licensing
- Rules of the Air
- Procedures for Air Navigation
- Air Traffic Services
- Aerodromes
- Facilitation
- Search and Rescue
- Security
- Aircraft Accident Investigation
- JAR-FCL
- National Law

Human Performance and Limitations (JAR Ref 040)

- Human Factors
- Aviation Physiology and Health Maintenance
- Aviation Psychology

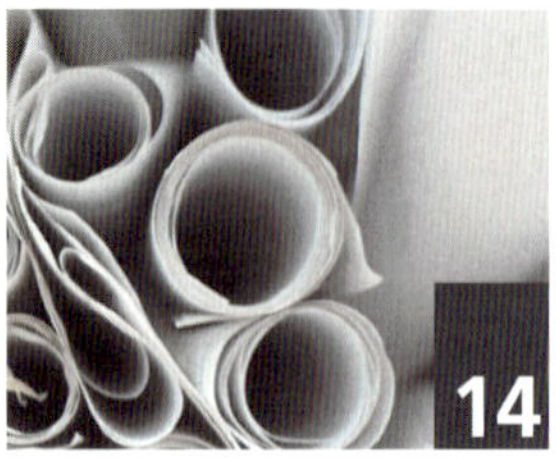

Operational Procedures (JAR Ref 070)

- Operator
- Air Operations Certificate
- Flight Operations
- Aerodrome Operating Minima
- Low Visibility Operations
- Special Operational Procedures and Hazards
- Transoceanic and Polar Flight

Communications (JAR Ref 090)

- Definitions
- General Operation Procedures
- Relevant Weather Information
- Communication Failure
- VHF Propagation
- Allocation of Frequencies
- Distress and Urgency Procedures
- Aerodrome Control
- Approach Control
- Area Control

CHAPTER 1

Fundamental Mathematics

CHAPTER 2

Fundamental Principles of Flight

CHAPTER 3

Thrust and Power

CHAPTER 4

Regulations and Aerodromes

CHAPTER 5

Take-Off

CHAPTER 6

Climbing

CHAPTER 7

Descending and Gliding

CHAPTER 8

The Cruise

CHAPTER 9

Landing

CHAPTER 10

Class A Take-Off

CHAPTER 11

Additional Take-Off Techniques

CHAPTER 12

The Initial Take-Off Climb

CHAPTER 13

Enroute

CHAPTER 14

Landing

CHAPTER 15

JAR Performance Class B Aeroplanes

CHAPTER 16

Single Engine Piston (SEP1)

CHAPTER 17

Multi-Engine Piston (MEP1)

CHAPTER 18

JAR Performance Class C Regulations

Chapter 1
Fundamental Mathematics

INTRODUCTION

Aircraft performance does not involve complex mathematics, only simple equations and the application of trigonometry. This chapter reviews fundamental mathematics to enable rapid progress in the main performance chapters.

EQUATIONS

THE PRINCIPLE OF AN EQUATION

An equation is a method of showing that the outcome of two things is the same, or equal.

For example:

10 = 5 x 2 (The outcome of the left-hand and right-hand side is the same.)

Equations are useful because they can be used to show the relationship between factors which vary.

For example, there are 2.2 pounds (lb) in one kilogram (kg). This is shown in the following equation:

lb = kg x 2.2

Any value of mass in kilograms can be put into the equation and its mass found in pounds.
For example, what is the mass of an 8 kg object in pounds?

lb = 8 kg x 2.2 = 17.6 lb

TRANSPOSING EQUATIONS

Because both sides of an equation must be equal, if something is done to one side of the equation the same must also be done to the other.

ADDING AND SUBTRACTING

T = D + p (Thrust equals drag plus part of weight.)

The above equation shows the relationship between the forces along the flight path in a climb. However, it is only used as an example to find D in this case.

To get D by itself on the right-hand side of the equation, p must be subtracted (– **p**) from BOTH sides of the equation.

T – **p** = D + p – **p** (The + p and – **p** on the right-hand side equal 0 and **cancel out**.)

T – p = D

Some people think of this as "when you change sides of an equation, change the sign".
That is, + p became - p when it changed sides.

MULTIPLYING AND DIVIDING

An equation that is used in performance is:

$F = m \times a$ (Force equals mass times acceleration.)

To find acceleration, divide both sides by mass (**m**).

$$\frac{F}{m} = \frac{m}{m} \times a$$

The m/m on the right-hand side now equals 1 and cancels out.

This is often called **cross multiplying** because the mass appears to have moved from the top to the bottom when it moved from the right to the left side of the equation.

$$\frac{F}{m} = m \times a$$

In the same way, to find **a** in the following equation:

$$\frac{a \times b}{c} = \frac{d}{e}$$

$$a = \frac{c \times d}{b \times e}$$

In what appears to be a cross multiply, both sides are actually multiplied by $^{c}/_{b}$.

COMBINING MULTIPLYING, DIVIDING, ADDING, AND SUBTRACTING

An equation discussed in Chapter 5 is:

$$\text{Angle of climb} = \frac{T - D}{W}$$

(Angle of climb equals thrust minus drag divided by aeroplane weight.)

To find T in the above equation:
First multiply by W

$$\text{Angle of climb} \times W = T - D$$

Then add drag **D** to both sides of the equation

$$(\text{Angle of climb} \times W) + \mathbf{D} = T - D + \mathbf{D}$$

$$(\text{Angle of climb} \times W) + D = T$$

CHANGING VARIABLES ON DIFFERENT SIDES OF AN EQUATION

Chapter 3 introduces the lift equation:

$\overset{\uparrow}{L} = \frac{1}{2} \rho TAS^2\ S\ \overset{\uparrow}{C_L}$ (Where TAS is true airspeed, S is wing area, and C_L is the coefficient of lift, which for the moment can be thought of as angle of attack)

This equation tells us that lift increases if the coefficient of lift increases. Lift would also increase if the TAS or wing area were to increase.

CHANGING VARIABLES ON THE SAME SIDE OF AN EQUATION

Again using the lift equation:

$$L = \frac{1}{2} \rho\ TAS^2\ S\ C_L$$

For straight and level flight, lift must remain the same to equal the aeroplane's weight. Therefore, if the TAS is reduced, one of the other variables on the same side must increase. Since S, the wing area, cannot be changed, the wing's angle of attack must be changed, which increases the coefficient of lift, C_L.

$$L = \frac{1}{2} \rho\ \underset{\downarrow}{TAS^2}\ S\ \overset{\uparrow}{C_L}$$

From flying experience, you know that when slowing down in level flight, the aeroplane's nose is raised, which increases the angle of attack and, therefore, coefficient of lift.

PROPORTIONAL AND INVERSELY PROPORTIONAL

Sometimes it is only necessary to understand the relationship between factors and not have to calculate a value. In this case, the expressions proportional or inversely proportional are often used.

PROPORTIONAL

If two factors are proportional, it means that if one factor increases, so does the other. Factors are always proportional if they are on different sides of an equation and both terms are on the top or the bottom.

In the lift equation, $L = \frac{1}{2} \rho\ TAS^2\ S\ C_L$

Since L and S are both on the top, on either side of the equal sign, they are proportional:

Lift is proportional to wing area ($L\ \alpha\ S$).

This means that if wing area doubles, lift doubles.

Lift is also proportional to C_L ($L\ \alpha\ C_L$).

This means that if the coefficient of lift doubles, the lift doubles.

However, lift is proportional to true airspeed squared ($L\ \alpha\ TAS^2$). Therefore, if the TAS doubles, the lift increases by 2^2, which means that lift is 4 times greater.

INVERSELY PROPORTIONAL

If two factors are inversely proportional, it means that if one factor increases, the other decreases. Factors are always inversely proportional if they are on the same side of an equation (and both on the top or bottom).

In the lift equation, $L = \frac{1}{2} \rho\ TAS^2\ S\ C_L$, as TAS^2 ,S , and C_L are all on the same side (and on the top as there is no bottom line), so any two will be inversely proportional to each other.

For example, TAS^2 is inversely proportional to C_L.

SQUARE AND SQUARE ROOT

The lift equation includes the term TAS^2. This means TAS squared, which is TAS times TAS.

Another numerical example would be 4^2, which equals 16. Although you can find it by entering 4 x 4 in the calculator, it would usually be found by entering 4 and then pressing the square button (normally x^2).

For example, if the TAS is trebled, lift increases by 3^2, which is 9. A factor that increases with the square of itself gets very big with only a small increase in size. If TAS were to increase to 5 times its initial value, lift would become 5^2, which is 25 times bigger.

The square root of a number is a different number, which when multiplied it by itself equals the first number.

The symbol for square root is √. Therefore, the √ 9 is 3, because 3 x 3 (or 3^2) is 9.

INDICES

Another way of expressing the values in an equation is by the use of indices.
Obviously, TAS^2 means squared, but what about TAS^{-2}?

The negative sign in the superscript means divided by; hence TAS^{-2} is $1/TAS^2$.

The SI unit for speed is **m/s**, which is often written as **ms^{-1}**. Likewise, acceleration, which is m/s^2, is ms^{-2}.

GREATER THAN AND LESS THAN

Sometimes, it is enough to know which of two results is greater or less. In this case, because they are not equal, the equal sign is not used. When the left side is greater or the right side is smaller, the sign is >. Similarly, when the right side is greater or the left side is smaller, the sign is <.

A numerical example is $5 + 7 < 15 - 2$. This is because 12 is smaller than 13. It is often used to describe two factors in a certain situation, such as in a climb $T > D$ (thrust is greater than drag).

PERCENTAGES

A percentage is a way of describing the comparative sizes or fractions.

The whole of something is 100%. It can be thought of as the whole of something being divided into 100 parts. All of it is, therefore, all 100 of the 100 parts or 100%. Half of it is 50% or 50 of the 100 parts.

If something increases by 10%, it has increased by an extra 10 parts of the original and is now 110 parts or 110% of the original size.

If the original airspeed was 90 kt, an increase of 10% is 9 kt. The new airspeed which is 110% of its original size is:

$$\frac{110}{100} \times 90 \text{ kt} = 1.1 \times 90 \text{ kt} = 99 \text{ kt}$$

Similarly, if something reduces by 20%, it is getting smaller by 20 parts. Therefore, it is now 100 – 20 parts = 80 parts or 80% of its original value. Relating this to an actual speed, 80% of 100 kt is:

$$\frac{80}{100} \times 100 \text{ kt} = 0.8 \times 100 \text{ kt} = 80 \text{ kt}$$

In performance, percentages are often used to describe the effect of a factor on a distance or gradient (e.g. wet landing distance compared to dry). The distance needed to land and stop on a wet runway is greater than on a dry runway. The percentage increase, which is discussed later, is 15%. This means that if the original dry landing distance (100%) is 2000 ft, on the wet runway it is:

$$\frac{115}{100} \times 2000 \text{ ft} = 1.15 \times 2000 \text{ ft} = 2300 \text{ ft}$$

SQUARING SMALL PERCENTAGE CHANGES

Airspeed often has a square effect on other variables, such as take-off distance.

Another chapter shows that take-off distance is proportional to the take-off speed squared. If the take-off speed increases by 10%, it is now 1.1 times its original speed. This means that the take-off distance is now $1.1 \times 1.1 = 1.1^2 = 1.21$ times its original length.

The take-off distance is now 21% longer, which is approximately 20% longer. It is important to recognise that for small percentages, the effect of squaring a percentage increase looks like a double (i.e. a 10% increase in speed results in approximately a 20% increase in take-off distance, or a 5% decrease in speed results in the take-off distance decreasing by approximately 10%).

TRIGONOMETRY

Trigonometry is the relationship between an angle in a right-angled triangle and the ratio of the length of two of its sides. It is useful because the angle can show the relationship to the size of two forces.

NAMES OF THE SIDES OF A RIGHT-ANGLED TRIANGLE

Before sine, cosine, and tangent (which refer to angles) are introduced, learn the names of the sides of a right-angled triangle.

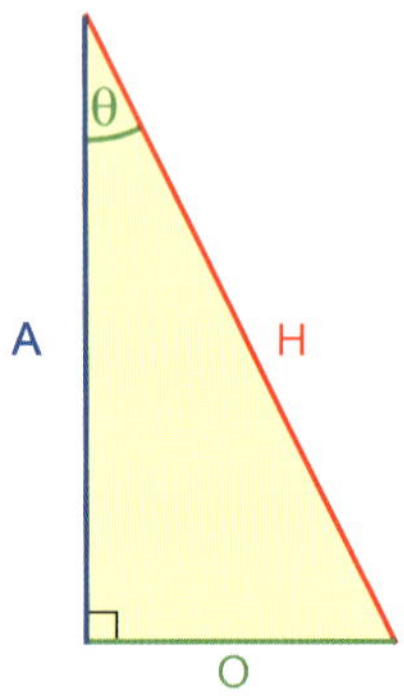

The longest side of a triangle (which is always the side opposite the right angle) is called the hypotenuse, or **H** for short.

The triangle side that is opposite to the angle θ is known as the Opposite, or **O**.

The third side of the triangle, which is next to or adjacent to one side of the angle (the hypotenuse is on the other side), is known as the Adjacent, or **A**.

THE EQUATIONS OF TRIGONOMETRY

An easy way to remember the relationship between the sin, cos, and tan of an angle and the appropriate sides is the made-up word:

SOHCAHTOA (phonetically sounds like sow/ca/toe/a)

This word splits into the three trigonometric functions (sin, cos, and tan), giving the relationships between the angle and the appropriate sides.

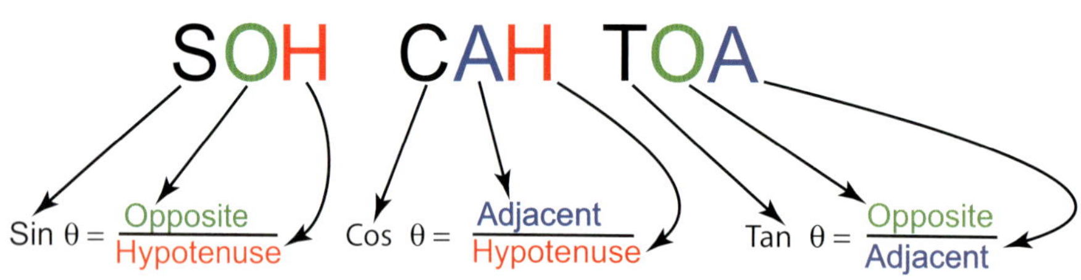

$$\text{Sin } \theta = \frac{\text{Opposite}}{\text{Hypotenuse}} \qquad \text{Cos } \theta = \frac{\text{Adjacent}}{\text{Hypotenuse}} \qquad \text{Tan } \theta = \frac{\text{Opposite}}{\text{Adjacent}}$$

TRIGONOMETRY AND THE CALCULATOR

1) TO FIND AN ANGLE GIVEN TWO SIDES

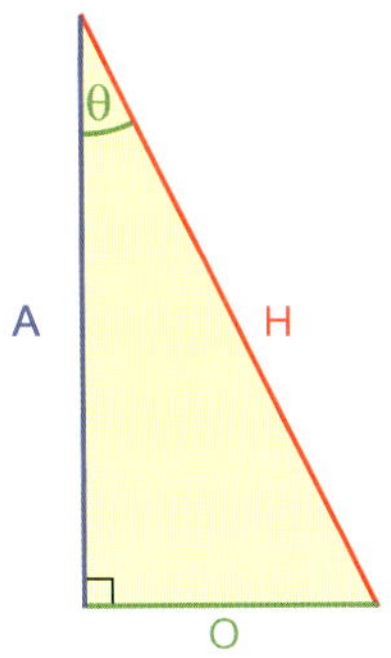

In the triangle, the opposite side is 2 cm long and the hypotenuse is 4 cm long.

Therefore,

$$\text{Sin } \theta = \frac{2 \text{ cm}}{4 \text{ cm}} \quad \text{or} \quad \frac{1}{2} = 0.5$$

The angle that has a sin of 0.5 is always 30 degrees. It can be found by entering 0.5 in the calculator and then pressing the inverse button (inv or -1) followed by the sin button.

2) TO FIND A SIDE GIVEN ONE SIDE AND ONE ANGLE

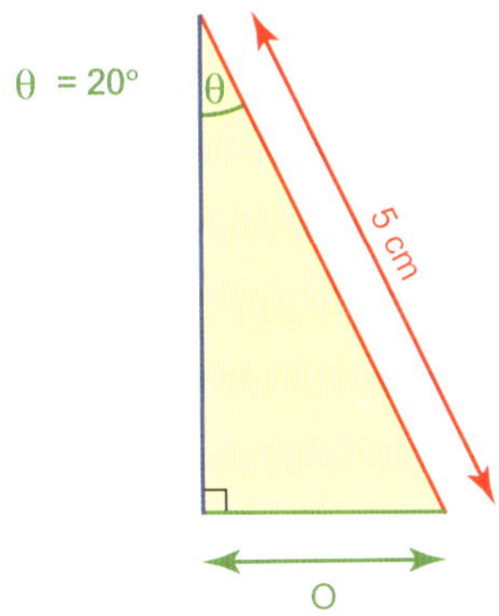

In this triangle, the angle is 20° and the hypotenuse 5 cm long.

The length of the opposite side is found using tan.

$$\text{Sin } \theta = \frac{\text{Opposite}}{\text{Hypotenuse}} = \frac{O}{H}$$

Therefore,

$$\text{Sin } \theta \times H = O$$

$$O = \sin 20° \times 5 \text{ cm}$$
$$= 0.342 \times 5 \text{ cm}$$
$$= 1.71 \text{ cm (approximately)}$$

The length of side A is found in a similar way.

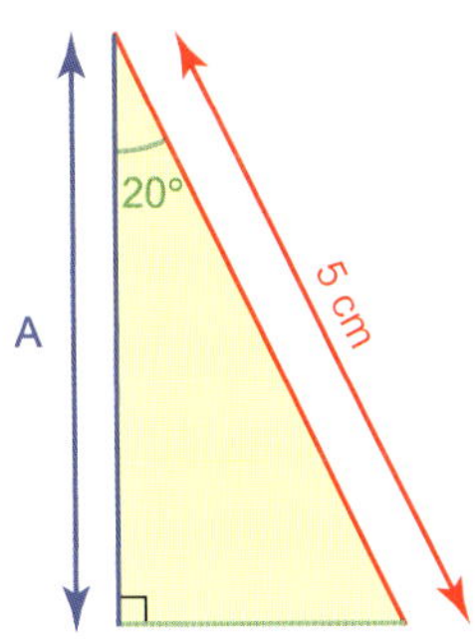

$$\text{Cos } \theta = \frac{A}{H}$$

$$A = H \cos \theta$$
$$5 \times \cos 20°$$
$$5 \times 0.94$$
$$4.7 \text{ cm}$$

TRIGONOMETRY IN PERFORMANCE

In performance, the angle is normally the angle between forces (such as L, D, T, or W) or speeds, while the sides are the magnitudes of these forces or speeds.

Chapter 2
Fundamental Principles of Flight

This chapter is to support the main performance chapters.

INTRODUCTION

Aircraft performance is an applied subject based on principles of flight. To enable rapid progress in the main performance chapters, this chapter reviews two main areas: aeroplane speed and the forces acting on an aeroplane.

PRESSURE

The starting point for aeroplane speed is pressure. This is because some aeroplane speeds, although called speed, are actually pressures.

Pressure is the force exerted over an area:

$$\text{Pressure} = \frac{\text{Force}}{\text{Area}}$$

Its SI units are Nm^{-2}, Pascals, or millibars.

STATIC PRESSURE

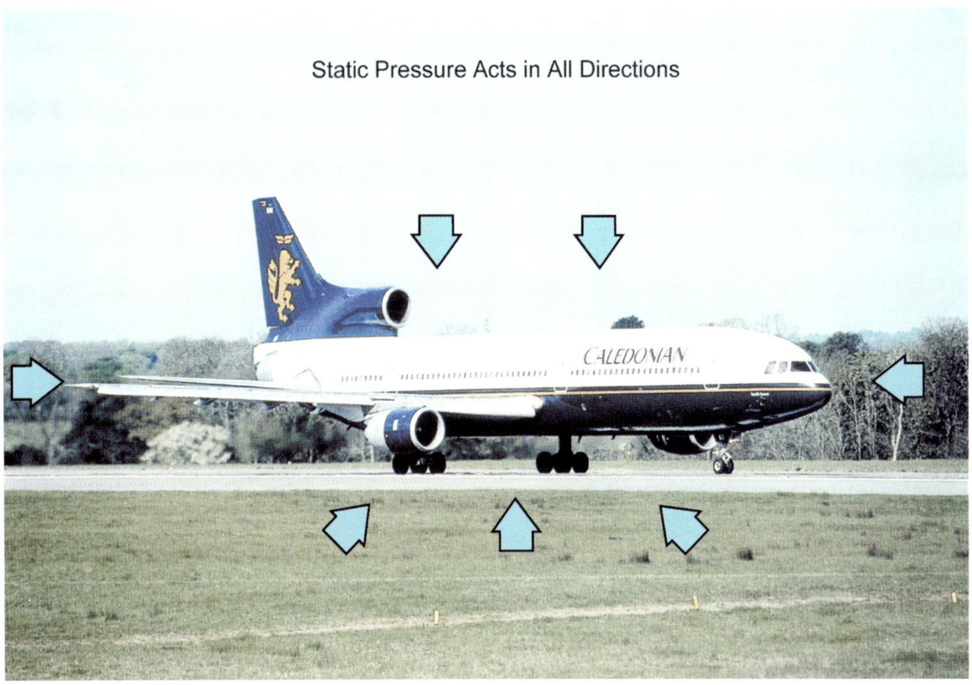

Static Pressure Acts in All Directions

The atmosphere is composed of molecules, which have mass and are attracted by gravity to the Earth. The lower an object is in the atmosphere, the greater the mass of atmosphere above it, and, therefore, the greater the weight pressing down on it. However, because the atmosphere is also pressing down on the air next to it, it experiences an equal pressure from all directions. This pressure is always acting on the object and is called static pressure.

DYNAMIC PRESSURE

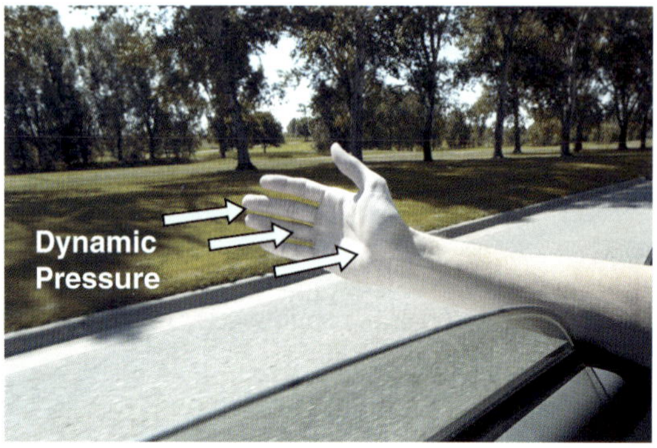

Whenever there is relative movement between an object and the air it is in, there is also dynamic pressure. This pressure only acts in one direction, which depends on the direction of motion. When you hold your hand out of a moving car window, you feel this dynamic pressure pushing your hand backward. This dynamic pressure increases when the car accelerates. This is because the kinetic energy of the air acting on your hand is increasing. The kinetic energy of the air also increases if the density of the air increases. Dynamic pressure increases as relative speed increases, but it also increases as the air density you are passing through increases.

Dynamic pressure = $\frac{1}{2} \rho V^2$

The above equation shows that dynamic pressure is proportional to air density (ρ) and proportional to speed squared (V^2). Dynamic pressure ($\frac{1}{2} \rho V^2$) is common to all aerodynamic forces and determines the air loads imposed on a moving aeroplane.

TOTAL PRESSURE

The total pressure around a body must be constant. Therefore, if the speed of an airflow increases, the dynamic pressure increases and the static pressure must decrease.

Total pressure = Dynamic pressure + Static pressure

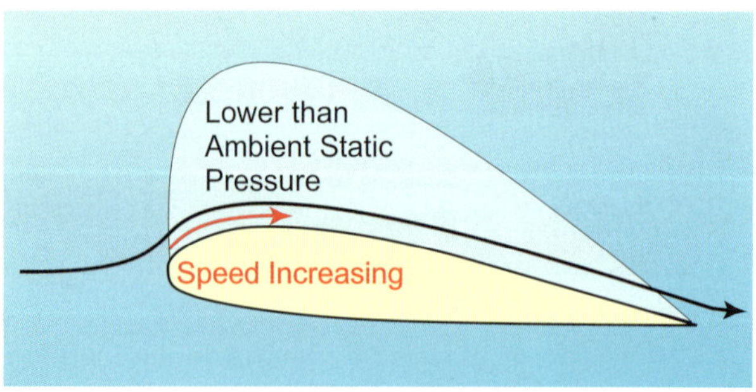

The above diagram shows airflow over a wing. Since the speed of the airflow over the upper surface has increased, so must the dynamic pressure. However, because the total pressure remains constant, the increase in dynamic pressure must produce a reduction in static pressure. The reduced static pressure above the wing is the main source of lift.

AEROPLANE SPEEDS

INDICATED AIRSPEED (IAS)

IAS is the speed shown on our airspeed indicator. It is not actually a real speed but an indication of dynamic pressure. This is because lift depends on dynamic pressure. Increasing dynamic pressure results in reducing static pressure and producing lift.

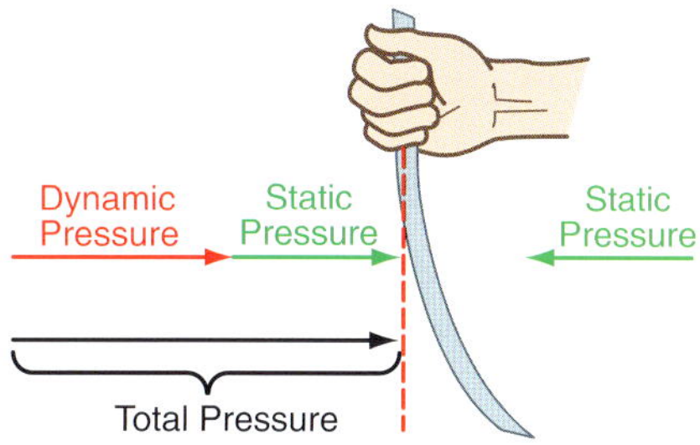

The diagram above shows a ruler (held at the top) in an airflow. The amount by which the ruler bends is a measure of IAS. The faster the airflow, the more the ruler bends and the higher the IAS. The ruler is actually bending with dynamic pressure, because it has total pressure (dynamic and static) acting on its face and only static pressure on its back.

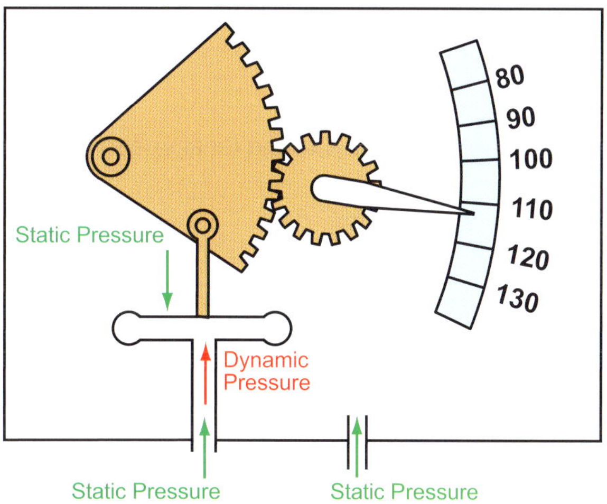

This is also the principle of an airspeed indicator in which total pressure from the Pitot tube feeds into the airspeed capsule and static pressure feeds into the instrument case surrounding the capsule. The capsule, therefore, expands in proportion to the dynamic pressure.

CALIBRATED AIRSPEED (CAS)

CAS is IAS corrected for position and instrument errors. It is a slightly more accurate IAS. Because larger modern aircraft have air data computers that remove the instrument and position error, the display of speed on these aeroplanes is CAS. Almost all the V speeds used in performance (such as V_R and V_1) are CAS. The only exception is V_{mo}, which is the maximum operating speed of a large aeroplane. Because this is a very fast speed and the air is compressing, V_{mo} is an Equivalent Airspeed.

EQUIVALENT AIRSPEED (EAS)

EAS is CAS corrected for compressibility, and is the most accurate of the indicated airspeed family. IAS, CAS, and EAS are all measures of dynamic pressure. However, EAS is the most accurate.

TRUE AIRSPEED (TAS)

TAS is the actual speed of the aeroplane through the air. It is a real speed, not a dynamic pressure. However, TAS, EAS, IAS, and dynamic pressure are related by air density (ρ).

$$\text{Dynamic pressure} = \tfrac{1}{2}\,\rho V^2 = \tfrac{1}{2}\rho TAS^2 \,\alpha\, EAS^2$$

To be exact, EAS should be in the above equation. However, during these performance notes CAS is used, which would be read on a transport aeroplane.

$$\text{Dynamic pressure} = \tfrac{1}{2}\,\rho V^2 = \tfrac{1}{2}\rho TAS^2 \,\alpha\, CAS^2$$

The above equation shows that to maintain the same CAS when climbing (air density reducing), the TAS must increase.

$$\tfrac{1}{2}\underset{\downarrow}{\rho}\overset{\uparrow}{TAS^2} \,\alpha\, CAS^2$$

MACH NUMBER (M)

Mach number is not a speed but a ratio of TAS to the local speed of sound (LSS).

$$\text{Mach number} = \frac{TAS}{LSS}$$

The local speed of sound varies with air temperature. As altitude increases, the air temperature normally decreases and the speed of sound decreases. This means that if an aeroplane climbs at constant Mach number, its TAS decreases.

$$\text{Mach number} = \frac{\overset{\downarrow}{TAS}}{LSS\ \downarrow}$$

In jet transport performance, Mach numbers are used enroute and during the upper parts of the climb and descent.

THE FORCES ACTING ON AN AEROPLANE

During flight, the forces acting on an aeroplane are lift, drag, and weight, plus in powered flight, thrust. Thrust is examined more closely in the next chapter. In this section, weight, lift, and drag are reviewed. Then the relationship of lift, weight, thrust, and drag in different phases of flight is discussed.

WEIGHT

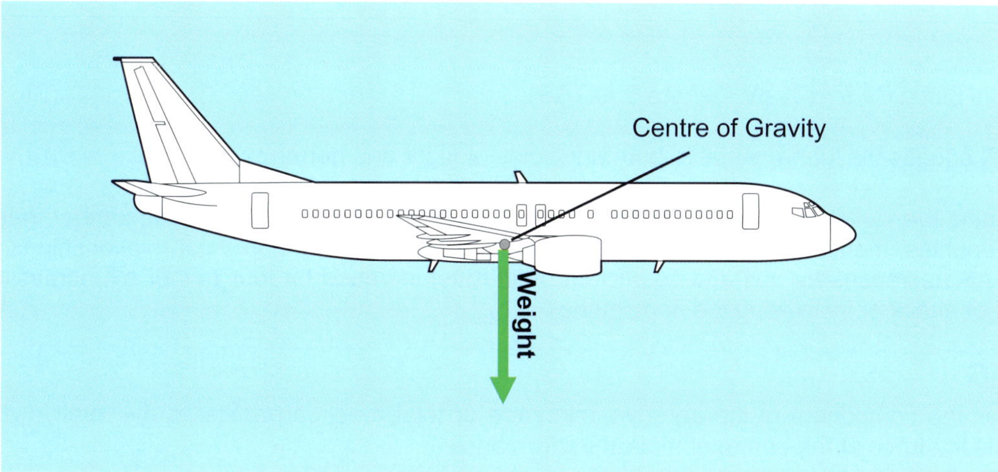

An aeroplane has mass, which when acted on by gravity produces the force weight. The weight of an aeroplane always acts vertically straight down from the aeroplane's centre of gravity.

The acceleration due to gravity, **G**, is considered to be constant in these ground school studies. The value of G to be used is 9.81 m/s^2, which is sometimes rounded to 10 m/s^2.

An aeroplane mass of 60 000 kg has a weight of 60 000 kg x 9.81 ms^{-2} = 588 600 N.

LIFT

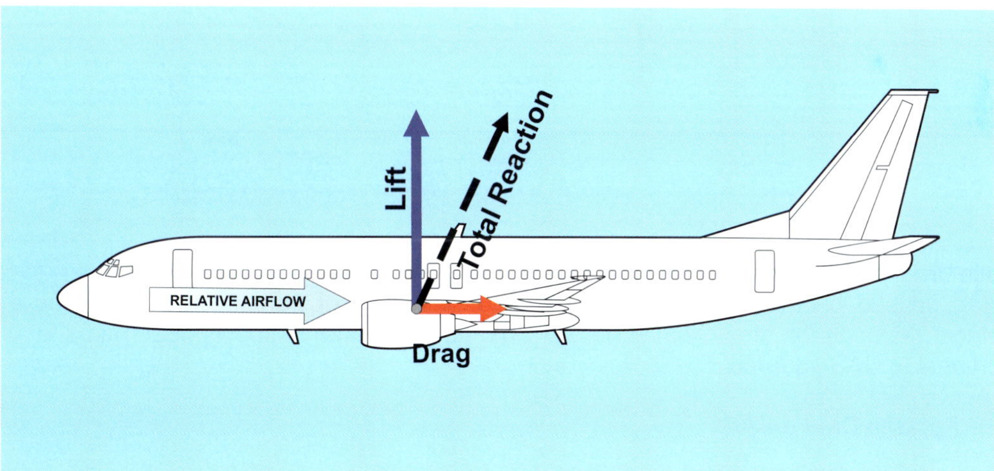

The pressure distribution around a wing (of area S) has a total reaction or net aerodynamic force on the wing, which acts from the centre of pressure.

As shown in the above diagram, lift is the component of this force that is perpendicular to the relative airflow. The relative airflow is always along and opposite in direction to the flight path of an aeroplane and is only horizontal in straight-and-level flight.

The size of the lift force depends on the CAS squared, the wing area, and the wing's coefficient of lift. This is shown in the equations below:

$L \alpha CAS^2 S C_L$ or $L = ½ \rho V^2 S C_L$

Since $CAS^2 \alpha ½ \rho V^2$ (where V is TAS)

The lift equation is fundamental to both principles of flight and performance.

Changing the variables in the lift equation was covered in the math chapter. Remember that if the CAS doubles, the lift becomes four times greater (2^2). Another fundamental relationship is that if the CAS decreases by half, the coefficient of lift must increase by four (either by increasing the angle of attack or increasing the flap setting).

DRAG

Drag is the component of the aerodynamic force or total reaction parallel to the relative airflow. Drag is the force at the centre of aircraft performance.

PARASITE DRAG

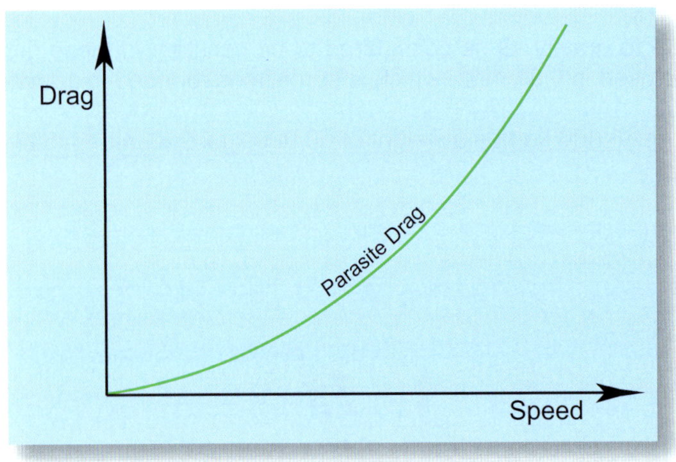

Parasite drag is the drag caused by the relative motion of the aeroplane wing to the air, excluding the drag caused because lift is being produced. The size of parasite drag (Dp) for a given aeroplane depends on the CAS squared. The above diagram shows that parasite drag is proportional to CAS squared.

Parasite Drag α CAS^2

This means that at low calibrated airspeeds, there is little parasite drag, but there is a large amount of parasite drag at high calibrated airspeeds.

INDUCED DRAG

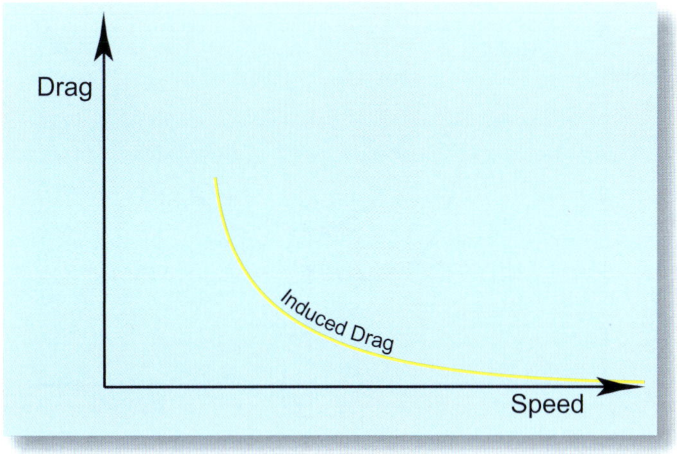

Induced drag is caused by the production of lift. The above diagram shows that induced drag is inversely proportional to IAS squared. This means that for a particular wing, the induced drag is greatest at the stalling speed.

$$\text{Induced drag} \propto \frac{1}{CAS^2}$$

TOTAL DRAG

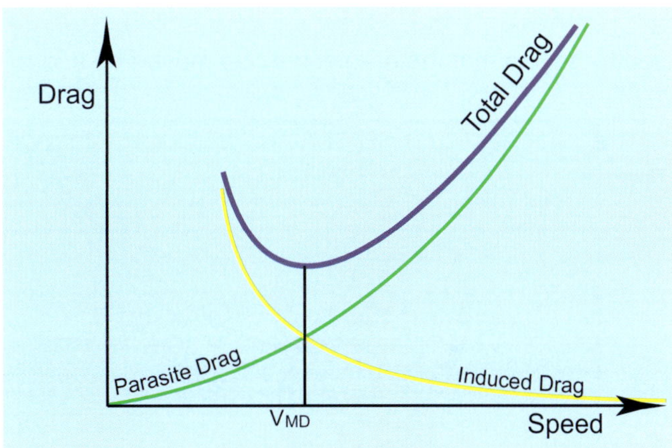

The total drag acting on an aeroplane in flight is the sum of parasite drag and induced drag. The above diagram shows the induced drag (yellow) and the parasite drag (green). At any given CAS, the total drag (shown in blue) is the induced drag added to the parasite drag.

In the diagram, the total drag is smallest at a medium speed, not at a fast or slow speed. The speed where total drag is least is known as the minimum drag speed (V_{md}). It is a very important speed in performance. If flying faster or slower than V_{md}, drag increases.

THE EFFECT OF AEROPLANE WEIGHT ON DRAG

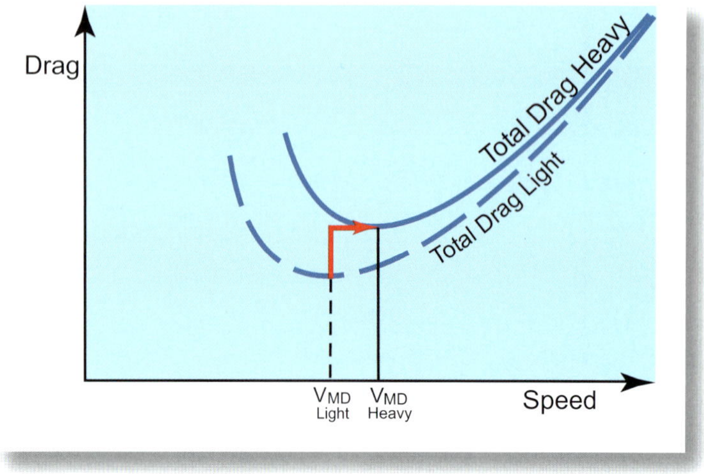

The above graph shows total drag with speed for two aeroplanes that are identical, except that one aeroplane is heavier than the other.

Note that the heavier aeroplane has:

(i) More drag at all speeds, and
(ii) V_{md} is at a faster speed.

This can be summarised by saying that the drag curve has moved up and to the right.

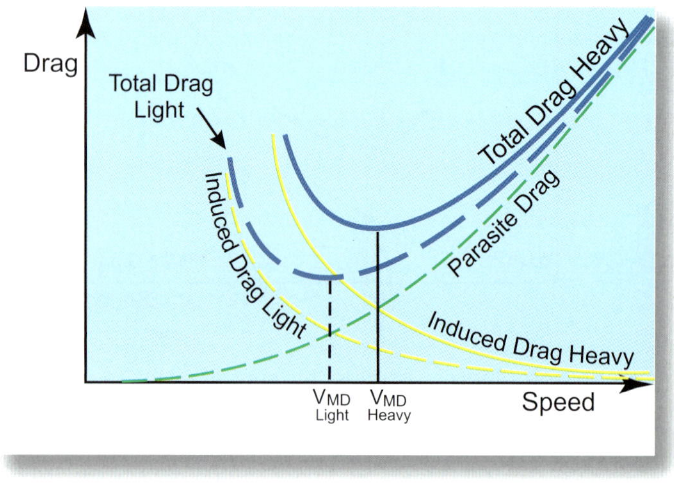

The above graph shows us why the drag curve moves up and to the right.

A dashed yellow line shows the original induced drag. Because a heavier aeroplane requires more lift at the same CAS, the angle of attack must have increased (and therefore C_L increases).

Because the C_L has increased, the induced drag increases ($C_{Di} = C_L^2$/Aspect Ratio). The continuous yellow line shows this increased induced drag for the heavier aeroplane. However, the increase in aeroplane weight has a negligible effect on the parasite drag, which is shown in green.

The dashed blue line shows the original total drag curve. The effect of the heavier aeroplane's increased induced drag is to push the total drag curve up and right. Conversely, the total drag curve for a lighter aeroplane would move down and to the left.

This has important implications in performance because as fuel is used during flight, an aeroplane becomes lighter. This means that as a flight progresses, drag decreases and V_{md} (as well as most other V speeds) is slower.

THE EFFECT OF FLAPS AND UNDERCARRIAGE ON DRAG

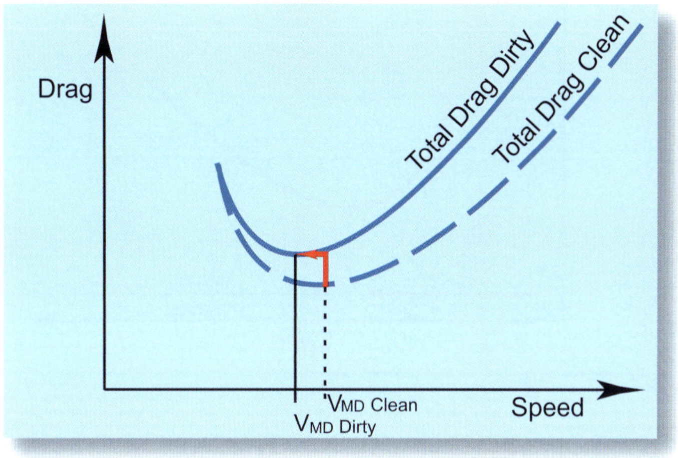

The above graph shows total drag with speed for two aeroplanes that are identical, except that one aeroplane is clean and the other aeroplane is dirty with flaps and undercarriage extended.

The dirty aeroplane has:

(i) More drag at all speeds, and
(ii) V_{md} is at a slower speed.

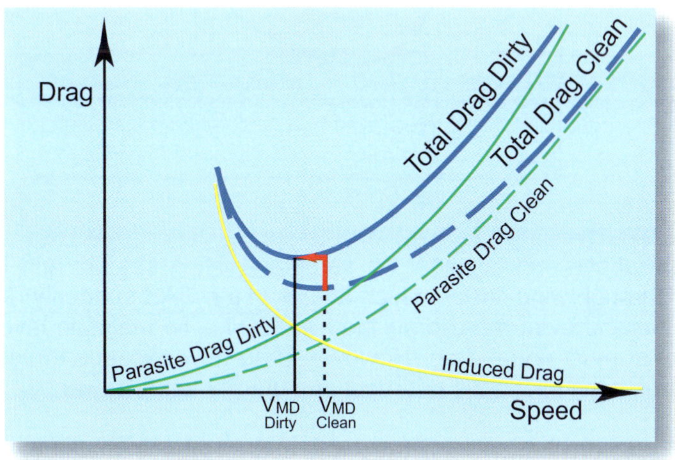

The above graph shows the original parasite drag as a dashed green line and the original induced drag as a yellow line. If the lift does not change, the extension of the flaps and undercarriage results in the parasite drag increasing (shown by the continuous green line). The graph shows that the new total drag, shown by the continuous blue line, has moved up and to the left.

This increase in drag is generally detrimental to performance. However, during the approach to land, both the increase in drag and reduction in V_{md} are beneficial. The increase in drag is useful because it allows a higher thrust setting in what is otherwise a very low thrust phase of flight. The reduction in V_{md} is useful because it reduces the speed instability on the "back" of the drag curve, which is discussed in the following paragraph.

THE "BACK" OF THE DRAG CURVE AND SPEED STABILITY

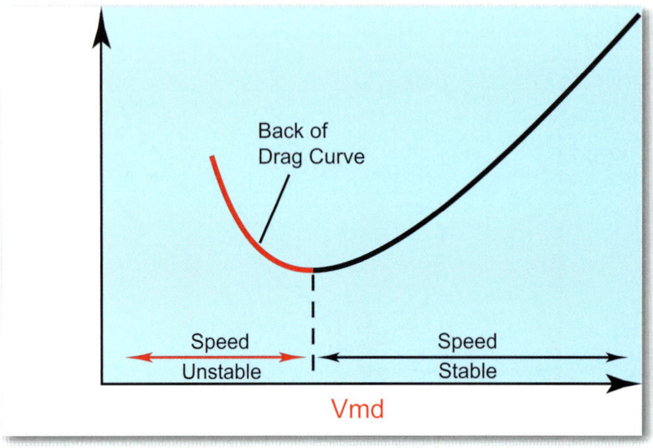

The above diagram shows the total drag curve or thrust required curve. The speeds slower than V_{md} are known as **on the back of the drag curve** or **the back of the thrust required curve**. The problem with flying at speeds slower than V_{md} is that the aeroplane is speed-unstable.

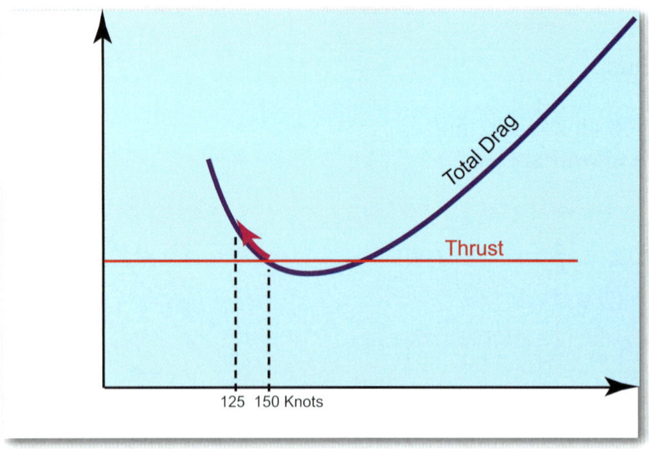

Refer to the diagram above and consider an aeroplane flying straight and level at 150 kt. The aeroplane now flies through wind shear, which results in the CAS suddenly reducing to 125 kt. At this slower speed, there is even more drag than at 150 kt. To maintain level flight at the same speed of 125 kt, thrust must equal drag. However, drag now exceeds thrust and the aeroplane slows further and stalls if the pilot does not react and quickly apply power.

Flying slower than V_{md}, on the back of the drag curve, means that the aeroplane is speed-unstable. If the aeroplane suddenly flies faster, it continues to accelerate, and if slower, it continues to slow down. When the aeroplane is speed unstable, such as on the approach to land, the pilot must react quickly in changes to CAS by adjusting the power. However, at speeds faster than V_{md}, the aeroplane is speed stable.

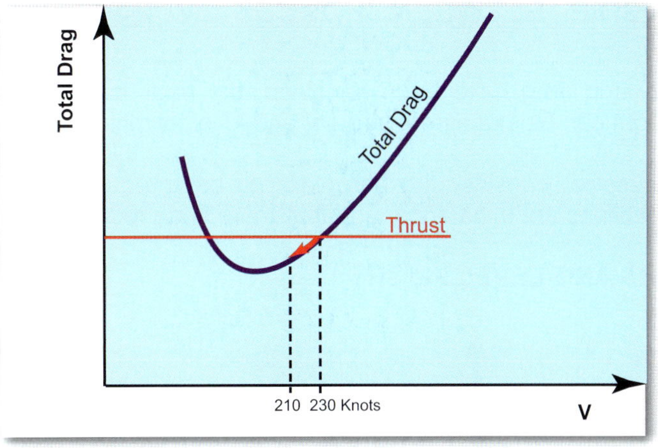

Consider flying straight and level at 230 kt and then entering wind shear, which results in the CAS reducing to 210 kt. The total drag has now decreased. There is more thrust than drag, so the aeroplane accelerates back to its original speed of 230 kt without the pilot changing the power setting.

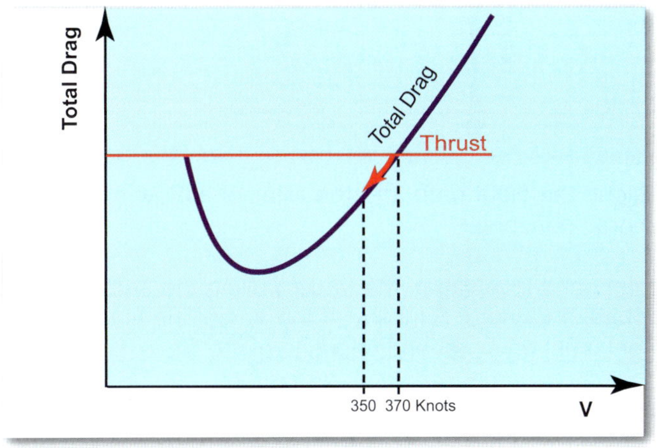

As speed increases above V_{md}, the gradient or steepness of the curve increases.

In the graph above, consider the aeroplane flying at 270 kt. The gradient or slope of the drag curve at this speed is much steeper than at slower speeds. This means that after flying through wind shear resulting in the same 20 kt drop in CAS, there is a much bigger reduction in drag. The aeroplane now accelerates back to its original speed of 270 kt much more quickly.

In summary, the faster the airspeed is above V_{md}, the greater the speed stability. Conversely, the slower the airspeed is below V_{md}, the greater the speed instability.

THE RELATIONSHIP BETWEEN FORCES IN DIFFERENT PHASES OF FLIGHT

Now that lift, weight, and drag have been reviewed, the relationship between these forces in different phases of flight can be examined: straight and level, climbing, descending, and gliding.

Throughout this discussion, consider the aeroplane to be in equilibrium. This means that the forces in opposite directions are in balance, and that there is no resulting turning moment.

STEADY, STRAIGHT-AND-LEVEL FLIGHT

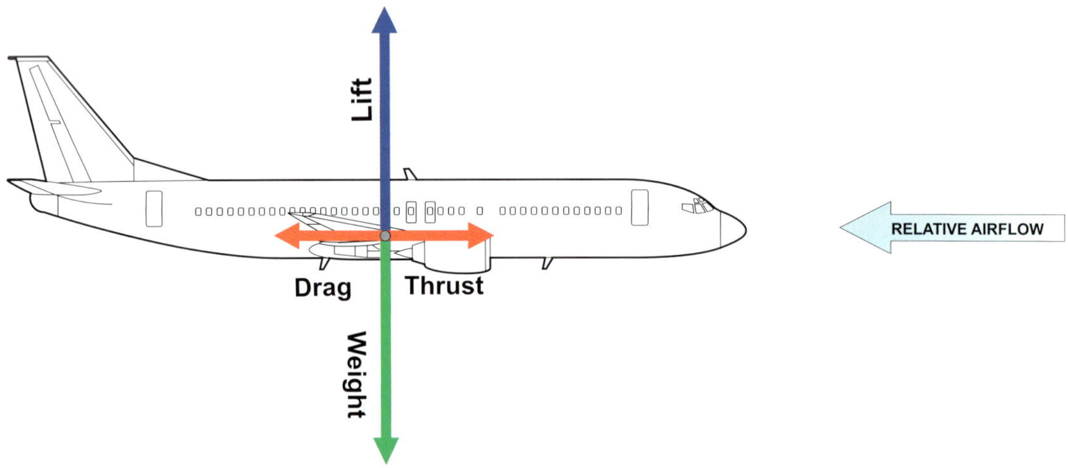

In straight-and-level flight, the flight path and the relative airflow are horizontal. This means that lift will be vertical and drag horizontal.

In unaccelerated, straight-and-level flight, the thrust pulling the aeroplane forward must equal the drag pulling the aeroplane backward. Similarly, if the aeroplane is to remain level and not enter a climb or descent, weight must be equal and opposite of the lift.

In steady, straight-and-level flight:

L = W, and
T = D

Note: During these notes and in the JAA examinations, it is normally assumed that thrust is parallel to the flight path. However, in situations of low-speed flight, this is actually not the case.

STEADY CLIMBING FLIGHT

In a straight climb at the same airspeed, the forces in any opposite direction must be equal.

Because it is simpler and more useful, the forces parallel to and at right angles to the flight path are discussed.

FORCES PARALLEL TO THE FLIGHT PATH

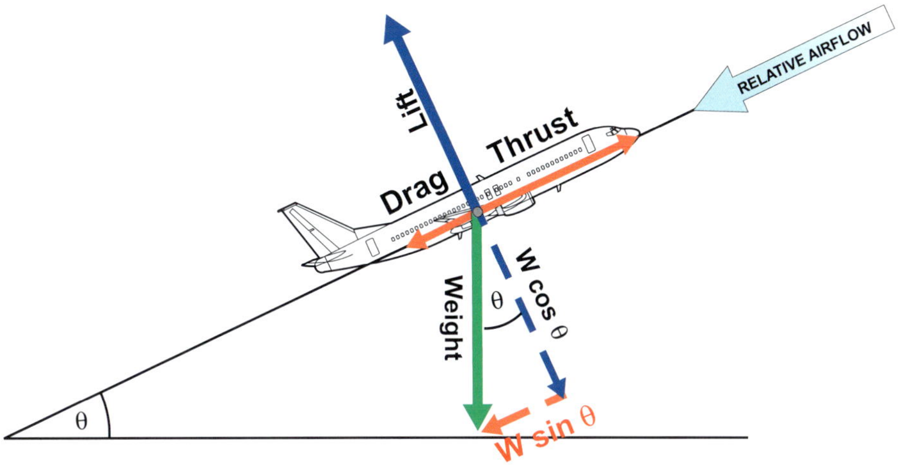

In the above diagram the forces parallel to the flight path are in red. The only force pulling forward up the flight path is thrust. If the aeroplane is to remain at the same velocity, a force and/or components of forces pulling backward must balance the thrust. These are drag plus a part of weight, W sin θ.

Therefore,

$$T = D + W \sin \theta$$

FORCES PERPENDICULAR TO THE FLIGHT PATH

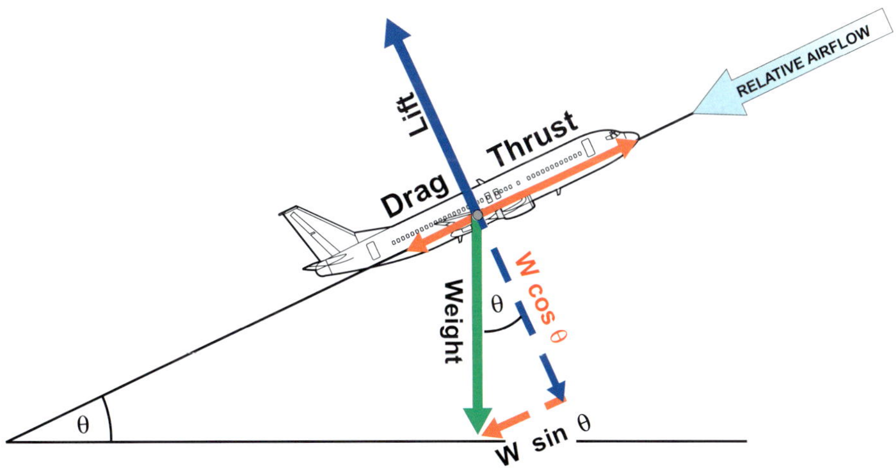

In the above diagram the forces perpendicular to the flight path are in blue. If the aeroplane is not to diverge from a straight climbing flight path, the forces perpendicular to the flight path must also be in balance. This means that lift must be equal and opposite to the part of weight at right angles to the flight path, W cos θ.

Therefore,

$$L = W \cos \theta$$

To summarise, in a steady climb:

L = W cos θ, and
T = D + W sin θ

This means that in a steady climb:

(i) Weight is greater than lift (W > L), and
(ii) Thrust is greater than drag (T > D).

Note: The first of these two statements, that weight exceeds lift, often upsets students. It may help to think of the forces acting vertically. Now weight is balanced by lift plus a part of thrust (W = L + sin T). Hence, weight must be greater than lift.

STEADY DESCENDING FLIGHT

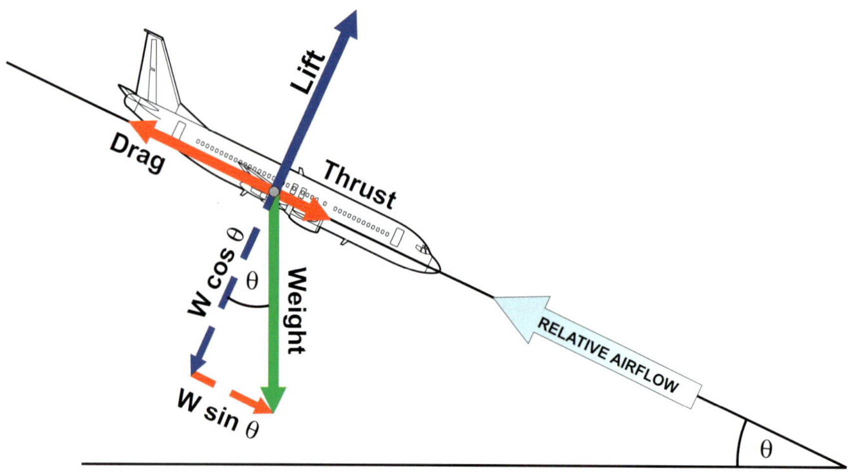

Looking again at the forces parallel and perpendicular to the flight path, to descend at a constant angle, lift must equal the component of weight, W cos θ (shown in blue).

From practical flying experience, you know that when lowering the aeroplane's nose to descend, thrust must be reduced, otherwise the aeroplane accelerates. The above diagram shows that this is because a component of weight (W sin θ) is now acting in the same direction as thrust. For these two forces to be balanced by drag, which is the only force pulling backward up the flight path, thrust must be much smaller than in straight-and-level flight. These forces, which are parallel to the flight path, are shown in red.

Therefore,

D = T + W sin θ, and
L = W cos θ

This means that weight is greater than lift (W >L) and drag is greater than thrust (D>T).
The terms **descent** and **descending flight** normally mean a powered descent. If the engines are producing no thrust, such as when they have failed, this is called a **glide**.

THE GLIDE

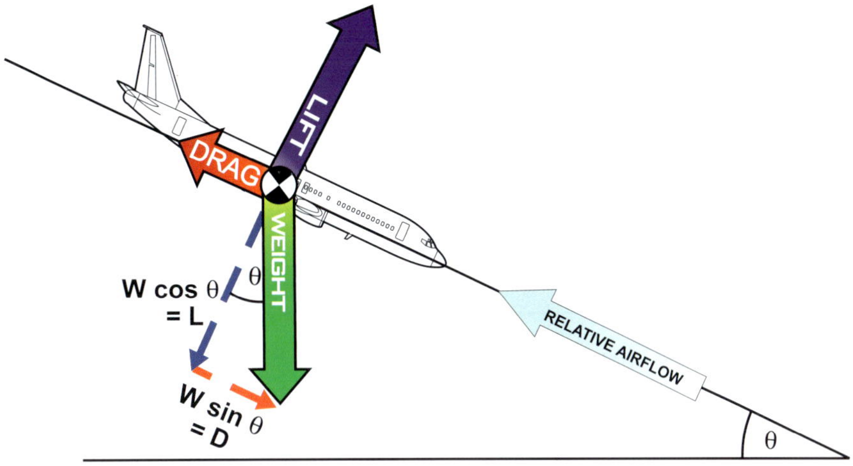

Because the term **glide** always means a descent with no thrust, there are only three forces acting on the aeroplane in a glide; namely lift, weight, and drag.

Looking at the above diagram, the balancing forces are now simplified with:

$D = W \sin \theta$, and
$L = W \cos \theta$

However, it is the fact that the two components of weight are equal to lift and drag that is most significant. This is shown in the diagram above.

There is a special relationship between the angle of descent, lift, and drag.

$$\text{Tan } \theta = \frac{D}{L}$$

This means that the angle of the glide path is steepest when the ratio of drag to lift is greatest. The glide path is shallowest and range maximum when the ratio of drag to lift is minimum (D/L min). This is the same as saying the ratio of lift to drag is maximum (L/D max). This means that only the lift to drag ratio determines glide range with respect to the air and not aeroplane weight.

For a typical training aeroplane, the L/D ratio is maximum at about 4 degrees angle of attack. This corresponds to the speed V_{md}; the speed where drag is minimum.

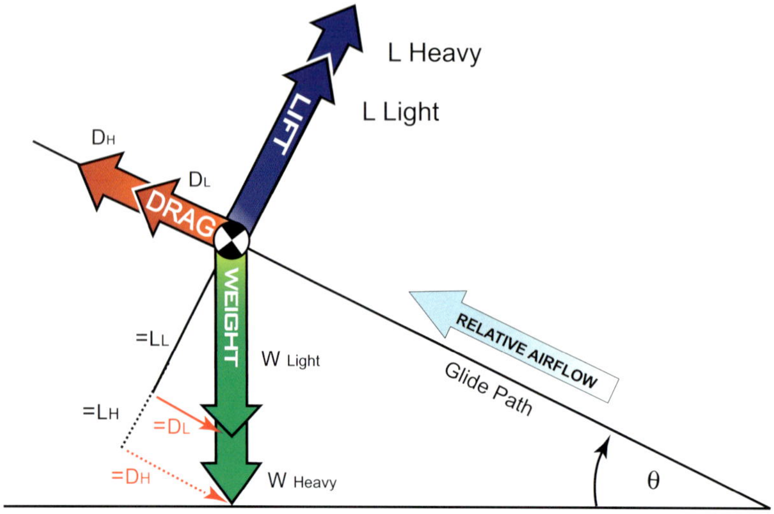

The above diagram shows that if the angle of attack (V_{md}) stays at 4 degrees, a heavier aeroplane increases its lift and drag in the same proportion and glides the same distance. This is a commonly misunderstood concept and is often examined in the JAA exam.

The basic theory of flight needed for performance has now been covered.

Chapter 3
Thrust and Power

INTRODUCTION

Aeroplane performance centres around two forces acting on an aeroplane. These forces, which act in opposite directions, are thrust and drag. Drag was introduced in the last chapter. In this chapter, engine thrust and its relationship to power are examined.

Thrust is a force exerted by an aeroplane because a large quantity of air, which has mass, is accelerated backward. A propeller generates thrust by producing a relatively small change in velocity to a large mass of air. Conversely, a turbojet utilises a smaller mass flow but imparts a much greater change in the air's velocity. Both types of aeroplane engine therefore produce thrust by a change in velocity of the air.

VARIATION OF JET THRUST WITH SPEED

The red line in the diagram below shows us that jet thrust does not vary significantly with airspeed. This is because thrust depends on mass flow multiplied by the velocity change imparted by the engine. As speed increases, the mass flow increases due to ram effect. However, the velocity change decreases due to intake momentum drag. The product of mass flow and velocity increases, therefore, thrust remains almost constant with speed.

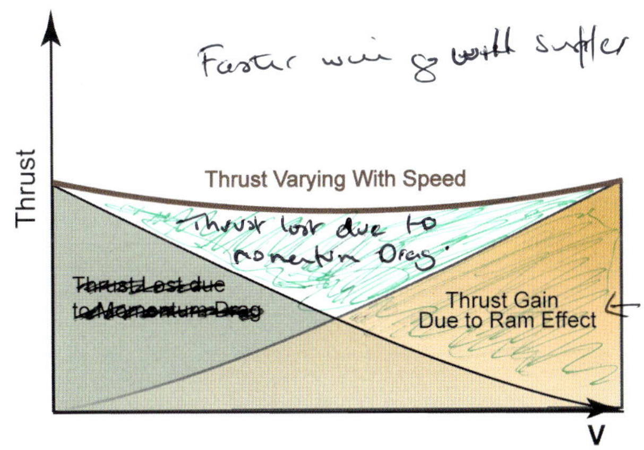

INTAKE MOMENTUM DRAG

As an aeroplane's forward speed increases, the additional velocity imparted by the engine reduces. This is because the velocity of the air entering the engine is increasing, while the exit speed remains constant. The velocity increase imparted by the engine reduces, resulting in a loss in thrust. This loss in thrust is known as intake momentum drag. The intake momentum drag at different speeds is shown by the green area in the above diagram.

RAM EFFECT

At higher speeds, there is an increase in the mass of air that is accelerated. This is due to the stagnation pressure increasing, which increases the air density and mass flow. The increase in mass flow, which results in thrust increasing, is known as ram effect. The area shaded orange in the previous diagram shows the increase in thrust due to ram effect as aeroplane speed increases.

The previous diagram shows us that at any given airspeed, the loss of thrust from intake momentum drag is approximately equal to the increase in thrust from ram effect. Hence, thrust remains approximately constant with speed.

HIGH AND LOW BYPASS RATIO ENGINES

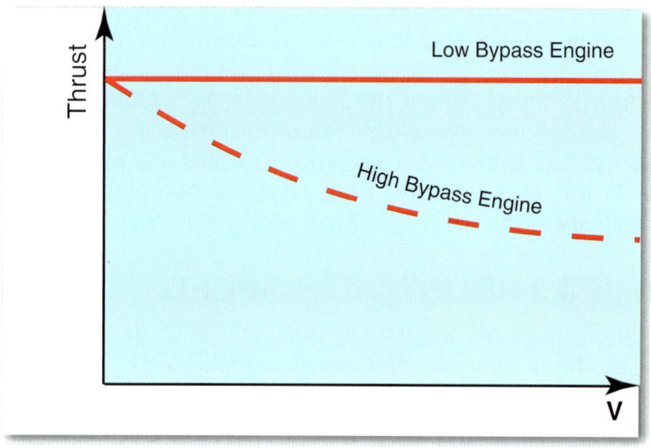

The statement that thrust is constant with speed is only true for low bypass ratio engines. In the above diagram, the continuous red line shown is for a low bypass ratio engine. However, the dashed red line shows that thrust reduces with forward speed for a modern, high bypass ratio engine. This is because the ram effect is now insufficient to compensate for the intake momentum drag.

These notes and the JAR performance exam only consider low bypass ratio engines. Therefore, assume that thrust is constant with speed.

VARIATION OF THRUST WITH ALTITUDE

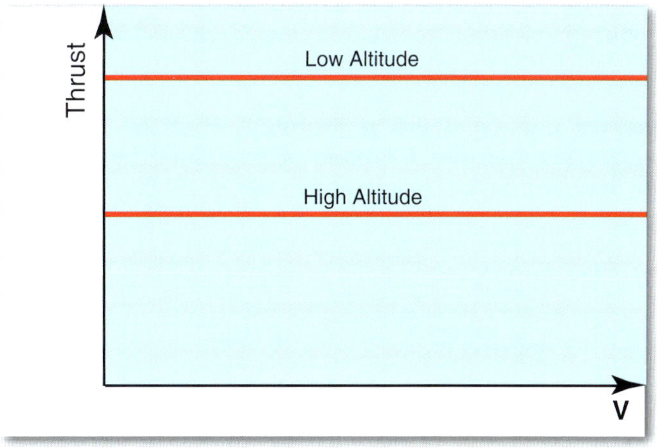

As altitude increases, thrust available reduces because the air density and, therefore, mass flow reduce. The above diagram shows the reduction in thrust available as altitude increases.

VARIATION OF THRUST WITH TEMPERATURE

Although an increase in temperature slightly reduces air density and, therefore, mass flow, in practice it is either the TGT limit or rpm limit that restricts the available thrust.

On hot days (above ISA + 15°C), the TGT limit is reached first. If the outside air temperature gets hotter, the TGT is reached at a slightly slower rpm, resulting in the mass flow and thrust available reducing. Conversely, the thrust available increases as the outside air temperature gets colder. This is because the rpm at which the TGT becomes limiting is faster, and, therefore, the mass flow is greater. Therefore, as temperature increases above ISA + 15°C, thrust reduces. The red line in the graph below shows this.

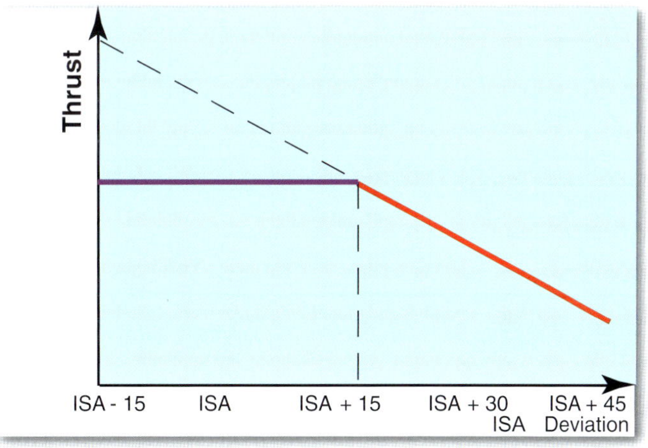

However, at outside air temperatures below ISA + 15°C, the rpm limit is reached first. Provided the thrust is regulated by the rpm limit, the thrust does not change with temperature. This is shown by the blue line in the above graph.

The rpm can be limited manually by a flight engineer, but is normally achieved today electronically by flat rating the engine below ISA + 15°C.

FLAT-RATED ENGINES

At all temperatures, an increase in pressure altitude reduces thrust available. This means that an aeroplane has more thrust available at an airfield at mean sea level than an airfield on a mountain. However, at a given pressure altitude, the thrust available may or may not vary with temperature change.

Thrust available does not change if the temperature changes between temperatures below ISA + 15°C, because the engines are flat-rated. Conversely, thrust would reduce at a given pressure altitude if the temperature increased above ISA + 15°C.

Figure 4.5

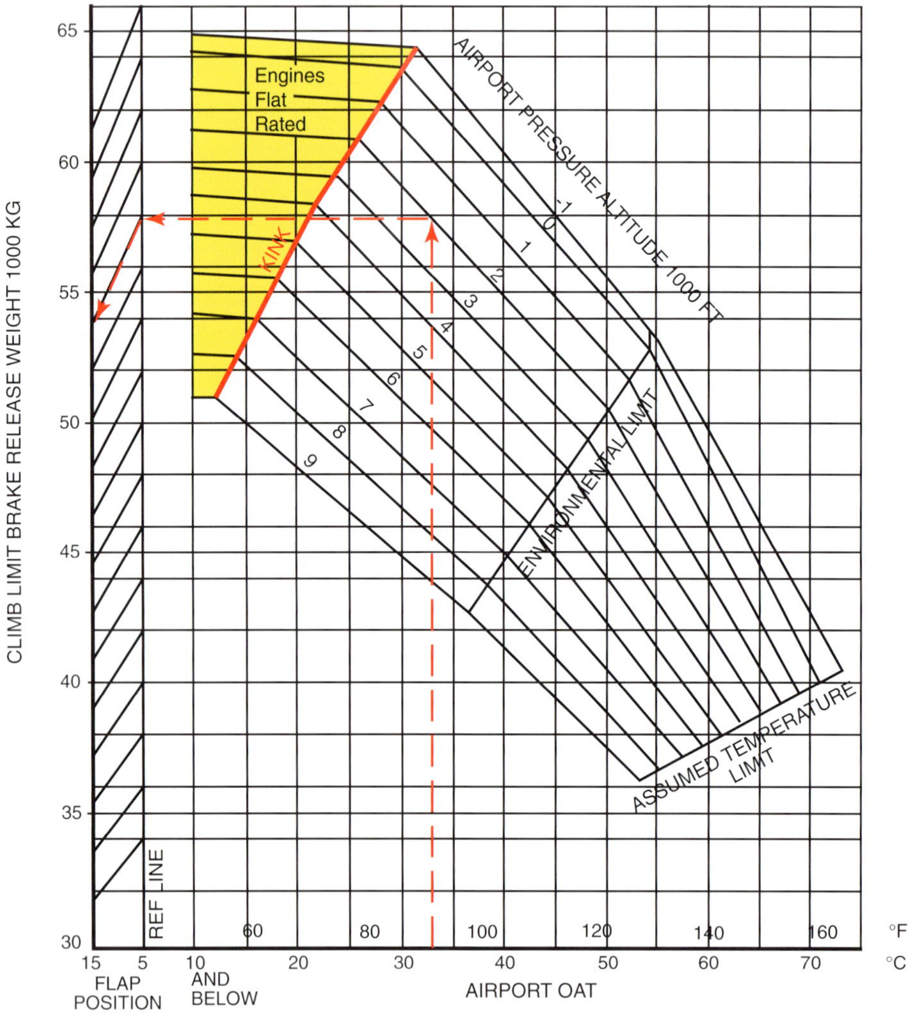

The above diagram is figure 4.5 in CAP 698. It is a graph which establishes the climb-limited take-off mass for a given airfield pressure altitude and temperature. The climb limited take-off mass is the heaviest mass at which the aeroplane just achieves the minimum climb gradient required after take-off. The greater the thrust available, the greater the climb mass for the same gradient.

At hot temperatures (above ISA + 15°C), the climb mass reduces as temperature increases. However, at temperatures below ISA + 15°C (shaded yellow), the pressure altitude lines are now almost horizontal, showing that air temperature does not affect the climb mass. This is because the engine is flat-rated below ISA + 15°C.

The **kink** referred to in JAR questions is shown in red and is at ISA + 15°C. A kink is also present in figures 4.4 and 4.29 in CAP 698. This kink represents the different temperatures at different altitudes, below which the engines are flat-rated.

POWER

Power is often spoken about as if it were the same as thrust. Although they are related, they are not the same. Thrust is a force that accelerates and decelerates an aeroplane if not balanced by other forces acting in the opposite direction. Power is force multiplied by speed.

Power is defined as the rate of doing work. Because work is a force times a distance, the following formula applies:

$$\text{Power} = \frac{\text{Work}}{\text{Time}} = \frac{\text{Force x Distance}}{\text{Time}} = \text{Force x Velocity}$$

In aviation, there are two types of power: power available and power required.

POWER AVAILABLE FOR A JET

Power available is thrust multiplied by TAS (Power Available = Thrust x V).

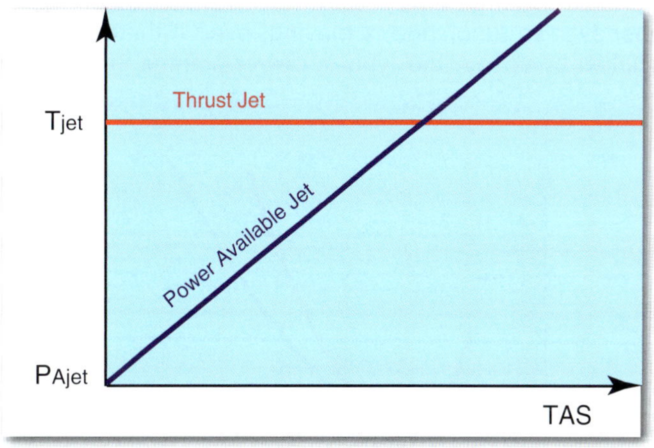

The red line in the above graph shows thrust for a jet against TAS. Thrust is approximately constant with forward speed.

The blue line in the graph shows power available for a jet against TAS. Power available increases as TAS increases. This is because thrust, which is constant, is multiplied by an increasing TAS.

Note that before brakes release on the take-off run, TAS is zero and, therefore, there is no power available although there is considerable thrust.

POWER AVAILABLE FOR A PROPELLER-DRIVEN AEROPLANE

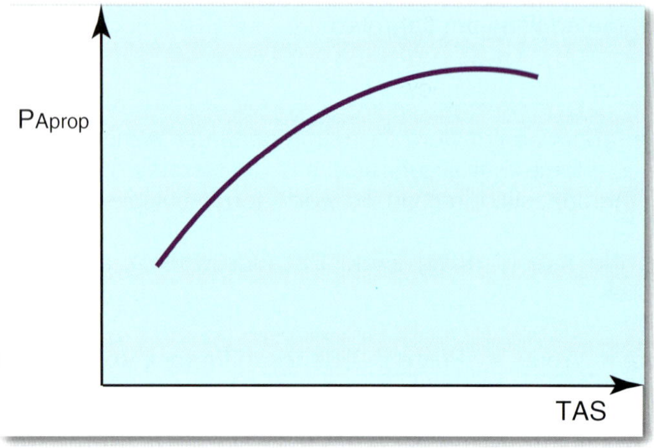

The blue line in the above graph shows power available for a propeller-driven aeroplane. Although power available generally increases with forward speed, at fast and slow forward speeds, power available drops because of reduced propeller efficiency.

POWER REQUIRED

Power required is the force of drag multiplied by TAS (Power Required = Drag x V). Therefore, power is required whenever an aeroplane is moving, even if there is no thrust. Because power required is drag multiplied by speed, the type of power plant is irrelevant to the power required curve.

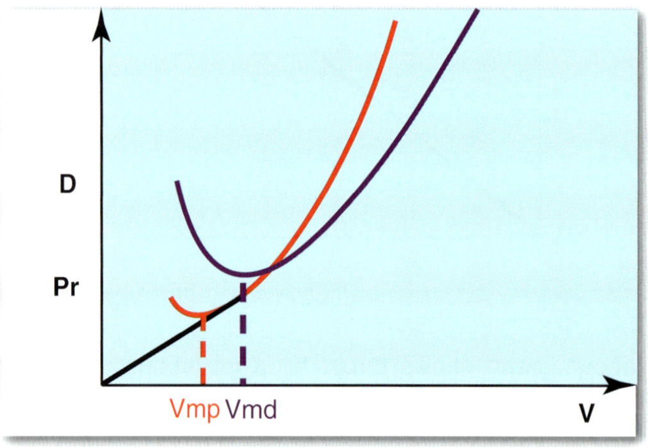

The total drag curve is in blue in the above graph. Superimposed on it is a red curve, which is the power required curve. The power required curve is determined for each speed by multiplying the drag at that speed by the TAS. The power-required curve looks very similar to the total drag curve and can be confused with it in the JAR exam if care is not taken.

The relationship between the drag curve and the power-required curve is very important in performance. There are two significant points to note before moving on.

First, the relationship between the bottom of the drag and power curves should be examined. The speed for minimum drag, V_{md}, is at the bottom of the blue drag curve. The bottom of the red power required curve is also an important speed, V_{mp}, the speed for minimum power.

Looking at the previous graph, V_{mp} is slower than V_{md}. V_{mp} is actually at 0.76 V_{md}, which is just over three quarters of the minimum drag speed. This means that if V_{md} were 100 kt, V_{mp} would be 76 kt.

Second, looking at the tangent to the power curve, this speed occurs at V_{md}. This is because the tangent gives the best ratio of speed to power required (TAS/power required), and as power required is itself drag multiplied by speed, the tangent to the power required curve (TAS/TAS x Drag) must be at the speed where drag is minimum.

Chapter 4 Regulations and Aerodromes

INTRODUCTION

Aircraft performance centres on providing a statistical level of safety. The first part of this chapter looks at the regulations and requirements that provide the safety margins. The second part of the chapter covers aerodrome descriptions and requirements.

DETERMINATION OF AEROPLANE PERFORMANCE

The purpose of planned performance is to determine the maximum take-off weight that ensures a pre-determined level of safety in all stages of flight. For this to be possible, numerical data is obtained, which establishes both the average and spread of distances used and gradients achieved.

Performance figures, such as take-off distance required, are described as **measured**, **gross**, or **net** performance. Although knowledge of measured performance is useful to understand how performance figures are obtained, the JAR exam mainly considers gross and net performance.

MEASURED PERFORMANCE

Before a new aircraft type can enter service, the manufacturer must measure the performance of pre-production aircraft. The measured data includes, for example, take-off and landing distances and flight path gradients in aircraft configurations of flap/slat/undercarriage and with all engines working and engine(s) out.

The averages of each set of data are known as measured performance. However, these figures were obtained in new aeroplanes flown by experienced and highly skilled test pilots. To establish the average for an operating fleet, the measured performance must be adjusted.

GROSS PERFORMANCE

Gross performance is the average performance that a fleet of aircraft can be expected to achieve when satisfactorily maintained and flown in accordance with the techniques described in the flight manual. It is a good reference for performance calculations but provides no safety margin.

Note: In some questions in the JAA exam, gross performance may be referred to as a **demonstrated** distance.

NET PERFORMANCE

Net performance is the gross performance diminished by a margin laid down by the appropriate authority.

Gross performance cannot be used for public transport in normal all-engine situations, because the fleet does not achieve these average figures all the time. An adequate safety margin must be applied which results in net performance. The greater the size of the safety margin for a particular phase of flight, the lower the risk of an accident. Equally, unlikely events require small or no safety margins. However, allowing for larger engine-out safety margins results in lighter take-off masses and, therefore, less revenue-earning load. Performance regulations provide a balance of safety to airline profitability when determining the size of the safety margin. The safety margin required for public transport is based on an incident probability of one in one million flights (10^{-6}), making an incident a ‘remote’ possibility.

COMPARING GROSS AND NET PERFORMANCE

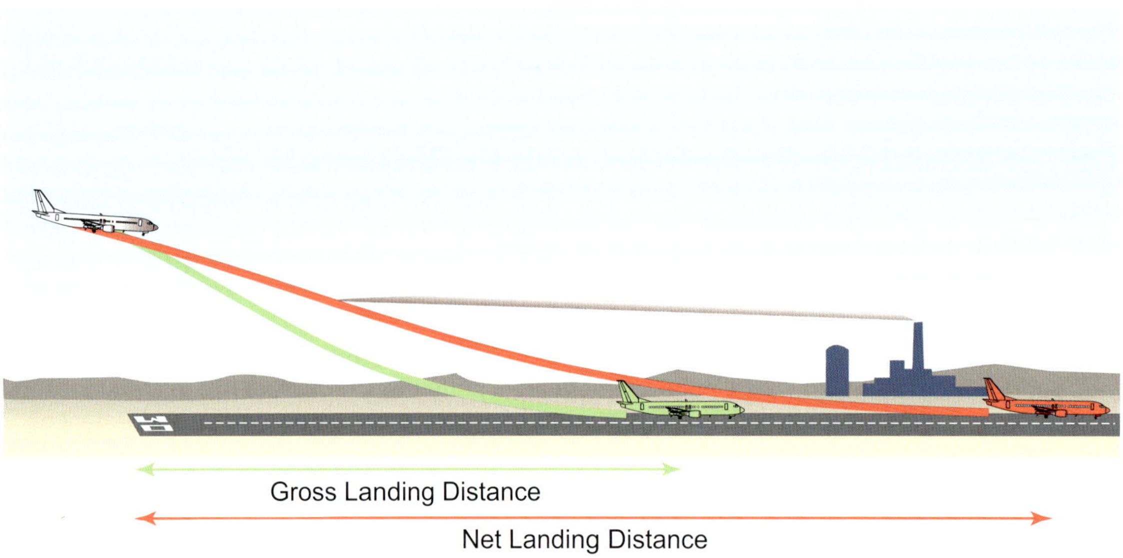

The above diagram shows an aeroplane landing. The green line shows where an aeroplane would stop on an average day. The red line shows where an identical aeroplane would stop on a one-in-one-million ‘bad’ day. Note that the net landing distance is longer than the gross landing distance. For public transport, always ensure that the runway distance and runway available are at least as long as the net landing distance required.

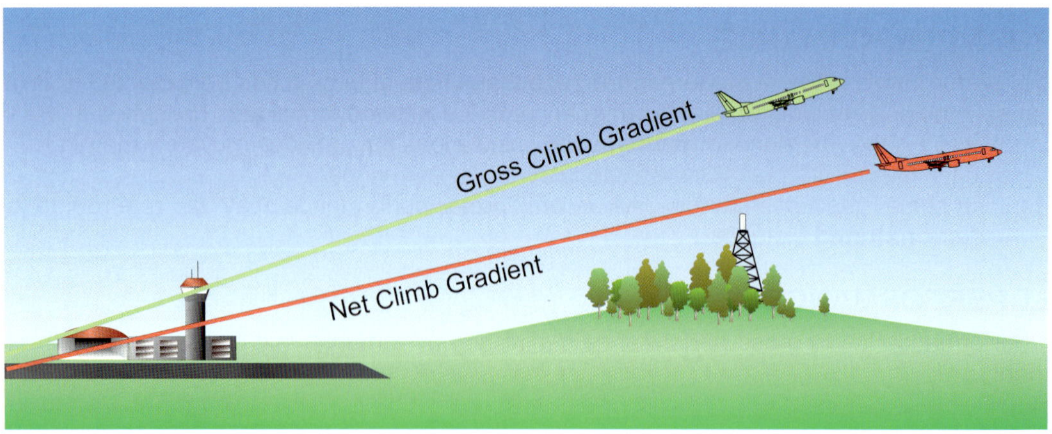

The preceding diagram shows an aeroplane climbing after take-off. On an average day, the aeroplane achieves the green gross climb gradient. However, on a one-in-one-million bad day, the aeroplane climbs at a shallower angle only achieving the red net climb gradient. For public transport, always check that net climb gradients achieve the required gradients and obstacle clearance margins.

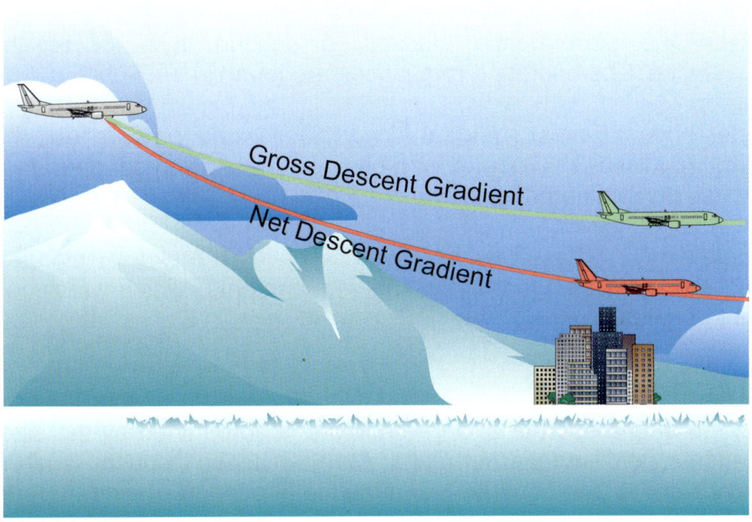

In the descent, the net descent gradient is steeper than the gross gradient to allow for the one-in-one-million bad day.

AEROPLANE PERFORMANCE CLASSES

Under JAR, aeroplanes are categorised into three classes: A, B, and C.

	Multi-Engine Jet Aeroplanes	Propeller Aeroplanes	
		Multi Turboprops	Piston
10 or more passenger seats or MTOM greater than 5700 kg	**A**	**A**	**C**
9 or less passenger seats and MTOM 5700 kg or less	**A**	**B**	**B**

CLASS A AEROPLANES

Class A includes all multi-engine jet aeroplanes and multi-engine turbo propeller aeroplanes with ten or more passenger seats **or** a maximum take-off mass (MTOM) exceeding 5700 kg.

Class A aeroplanes have the most stringent performance requirements, found in JAR 25.

CLASS B AEROPLANES

Class B includes all propeller-driven aeroplanes having nine or less passenger seats **and** a MTOM of 5700 kg or less. The class includes single and twin-engine aeroplanes, and the performance requirements, which are much less stringent than Class A, are found in JAR 23.

CLASS C AEROPLANES

Class C includes large piston-powered multi-engine aeroplanes. They must have either ten or more passenger seats **or** have a maximum take-off mass exceeding 5700 kg.

PERFORMANCE LEGISLATION

The airworthiness requirements legislated in JAR 23 and 25 state the appropriate minimum acceptable performance levels in each stage of flight. However, to ensure similar safety standards between the performance classes, a second layer of legislation, **operating regulations**, are needed. The operating regulations are found in JAR-OPS.

Class A aeroplanes have the most stringent airworthiness requirements and, therefore, the least stringent operating regulations. Class A aeroplanes are allowed to operate in poor weather conditions and to use contaminated runways.

Conversely, single-engine Class B aeroplanes have the least stringent airworthiness requirements and the most stringent operating requirements, which preclude public transport operations at night or in IMC.

AERODROMES

The type of aircraft that can operate at an aerodrome is determined by the size of manoeuvring areas, runway lengths, and surface strengths. Many of these aspects, such as knowledge of aerodrome reference codes, are covered in operational procedures. Aircraft performance focuses on the aerodrome characteristics that affect take-off and landing. A thorough understanding of runway lengths and take-off centreline areas is necessary. These lengths and areas are covered in the remaining part of this chapter.

TAKE-OFF RUN AVAILABLE (TORA)

Take-off run available (TORA) is the distance between the point on the surface of the aerodrome at which an aeroplane can commence its take-off run to the nearest point, in the direction of take-off, at which the surface of the aerodrome is incapable of bearing the weight of the aeroplane under normal operating conditions.

The TORA normally corresponds to the physical length of the runway pavement.

CLEARWAY

The clearway is an area that may be provided at the end of the TORA, in the direction of take-off, which is free of obstacles that could cause a hazard to aeroplanes in flight.

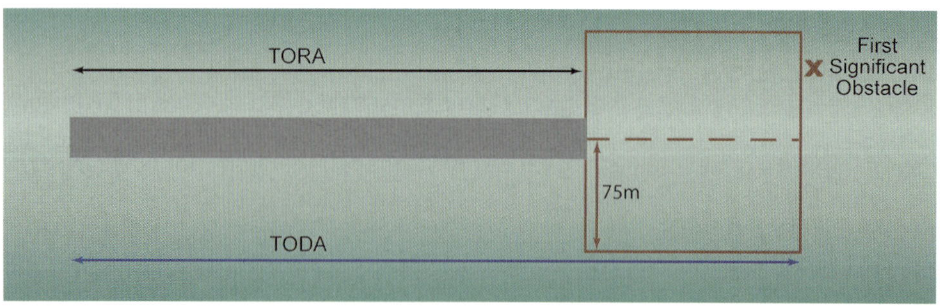

The above diagram shows the dimensions of the clearway. Sideways, the clearway extends 75 m either side of the extended runway centerline. Lengthwise, the clearway extends to the first non-frangible obstacle to a maximum of 50% of the TORA in situations where an excessively long clearway exists.

Because a clearway is only used for safe overflight, it may be ground or water (provided it is under the control of the appropriate authority). The clearway exists beneath a surface that starts at ground level at the end of TORA and then slopes upward at a gradient of 1.25% away from the runway. To be included in the clearway, no part of the ground or any objects (exceeding 0.9 m) may protrude through this surface.

TAKE-OFF DISTANCE AVAILABLE (TODA)

The above diagram shows that the take-off distance available is the runway plus clearway. However, the clearway cannot exceed 50% of the runway it supports. TODA is the lesser of:

(i) TORA plus clearway, or
(ii) 1.5 times TORA

STOPWAY

A stopway is a defined obstacle-free rectangular area on the ground at the end of TORA at least the same width as the associated runway prepared as a suitable area in which an aeroplane can be stopped in the case of an abandoned take-off. The area is prepared so that the aeroplane can roll without hazard to occupants or structural damage.

The stopway must be no narrower than the runway with which it is associated and must be centred around the runway's centreline. The stopway does not need to be as well maintained or as strong as the associated runway and, in some cases, may actually have been runway in the past.

ACCELERATION STOP DISTANCE AVAILABLE (ASDA)

Acceleration stop distance available (ASDA) is the distance from the point on the surface of the aerodrome at which an aeroplane commences its take-off roll to the nearest point in the direction of take-off at which the aeroplane cannot roll over the surface of the aerodrome and be brought to rest in an emergency without risk of accident.

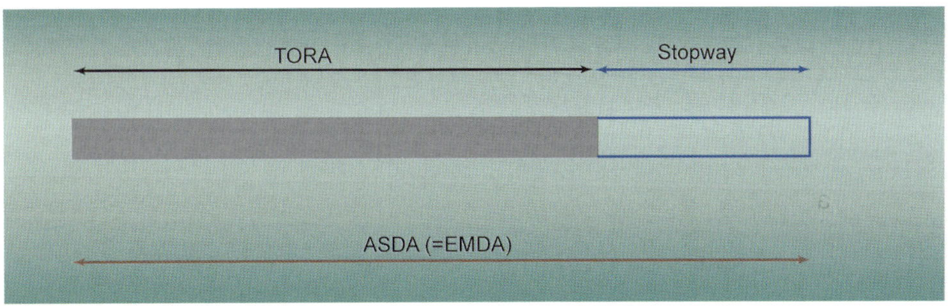

The above diagram shows that ASDA equals TORA plus stopway. ASDA used to be known as emergency distance available (EMDA), a term still used occasionally in the JAA exams and in aviation.

BALANCED FIELD

Balanced field refers to a take-off area where TODA equals ASDA. This means that any clearway equals stopway. It is useful because it simplifies performance calculations for maximum field length take-off mass.

PAVEMENT AND AIRCRAFT CLASSIFICATION NUMBERS

Finally, consider if the surface of the runway and other manoeuvring areas are strong enough for the operation of particular aeroplanes.

The ACN/PCN method has been developed by ICAO as the international method of reporting the bearing strength of pavements. Aircraft classification numbers (ACN) give a relative load rating of the aircraft on pavements for certain specified sub-grade strengths. ACN values for most aeroplanes have been calculated by ICAO and are published in aeronautical information publications.

The pavement classification number (PCN) represents the load bearing strength of the pavement in terms of the highest ACN that can be accepted on the pavement for unrestricted use.

A PCN is reported in a five-part format. Apart from the numerical value, notification is also required of the pavement type (rigid or flexible) and the sub-grade support category. Additionally, provision is made for the aerodrome authority to limit the maximum allowable tyre pressure. A final indication is whether the assessment has been made by a technical evaluation or from past experience of aircraft using the pavement.

Example: PCN80/R/B/W/T

The PCN is 80. The pavement is rigid of medium strength and there is no tyre pressure limitation. It was assessed by technical evaluation. It is the numerical value of the PCN that is compared to the ACN.

ACN/PCN AND OVERLOAD OPERATIONS

An individual aerodrome is allowed to permit overload operations as long as the pavement remains safe for use by an aeroplane. PCN has a safety factor allowed for, which means that an aeroplane with an ACN 10% greater than PCN would be acceptable as long as the pavement is in good condition.

Chapter 5
Take-Off

INTRODUCTION

This chapter looks at take-off in general and the variables that affect the take-off distance required. Take-off with reference to the different performance classes is discussed in later chapters.

THE TAKE-OFF

The take-off commences when the aeroplane starts to accelerate along the runway and ends when the aeroplane climbs through a specified height, called the screen height. The screen is an imaginary ‘sheet of paper’ 35 ft high (50 ft for Class B aeroplanes) which must be cleared by the lowest part of the airplane (either gear or tail). The take-off consists of two sections, a ground roll and an airborne section. The ground roll is the take-off run required (TORR). The total distance from brake release to the screen is the take-off distance required (TODR).

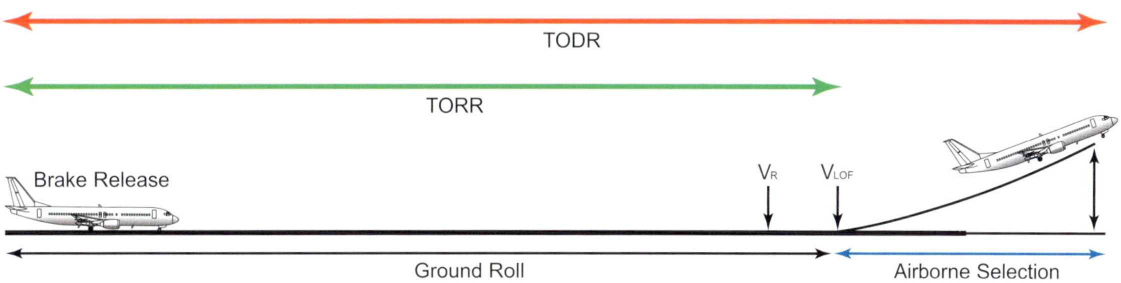

In addition to showing TORR and TODR, the above diagram shows two speeds important during take-off. The V speeds are indicated airspeeds (IAS) or calibrated airspeeds (CAS) depending on whether the aeroplane has an air data computer that removes instrument and position errors in the former. This is significant because changes in air density result in the aeroplane achieving the same IAS or CAS at different true airspeeds (TAS) and ground speeds (GS). On hot days at high elevation aerodromes, the TORR and TODR are longer for identical aeroplanes.

V_R, the rotation speed, is the V speed at which the pilot starts to apply back pressure to initiate rotation. At V_R, the pilot starts to raise the nose and the nose wheel leaves the ground, but the main wheels (and aeroplane) do not leave the ground until the lift-off speed (V_{LOF}). The aeroplane now climbs and accelerates with a steadily increasing pitch angle until the desired climb attitude is achieved.

FORCES ACTING ON THE AEROPLANE DURING THE TAKE-OFF RUN

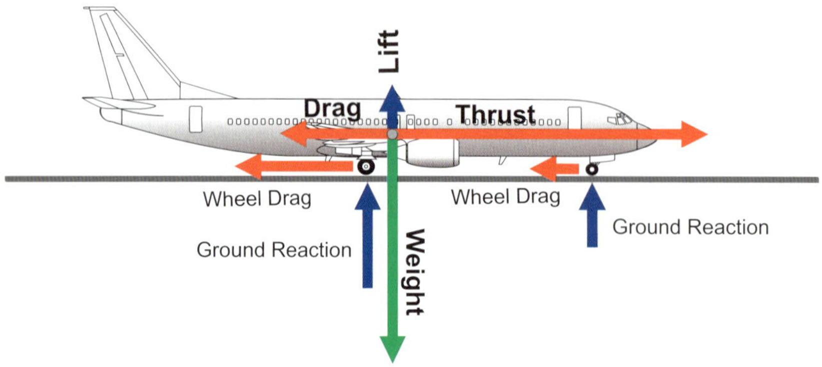

During the take-off run, the majority of the aeroplane's weight is balanced by the reaction of the runway. However, as speed increases, and particularly as the angle of attack increases following rotation, an increasing proportion of the aeroplane's weight is balanced by lift. This results in the weight on the wheels decreasing and, therefore, the wheel drag reducing.

However, the total drag on the aeroplane increases during take-off. This is due to the parasite drag increasing as the airspeed increases and a large increase in induced drag following rotation.

It is at these slow speeds just after take-off that induced drag attains its greatest value for the entire flight. To create sufficient lift at these very slow speeds requires large values for the coefficient of lift. This is achieved by extending flaps and slats and flying at high angles of attack. Due to the early separation and reduced coefficient of lift caused by a rough aerofoil surface, it is critical that de-icing is carried out prior to take-off, when it has its deadliest effect.

For acceleration to occur during take-off, thrust must exceed drag. Chapter 3 explained that although jet thrust is approximately constant over the aeroplane's entire speed range, thrust decreases slightly as speed increases at these lower speeds. This is because the reduction of thrust due to intake momentum drag is not completely offset by ram effect. Propeller-driven aeroplanes suffer a greater loss of thrust as forward speed increases. Therefore, during the take-off run, the thrust reduces for all aeroplane types.

ACCELERATION DURING TAKE-OFF

Newton's second law of motion is summarised by the equation:

Force = mass multiplied by acceleration, or
F = ma, and rearranging,
a = F/m

During take-off, the horizontal acceleration depends on the sum of the horizontal forces divided by the aeroplane mass.

$$\text{Acceleration} = \frac{\text{Thrust - Drag}}{\text{Mass}} = \frac{\text{Excess Thrust}}{\text{Mass}}$$

Having discovered that thrust decreases while drag increases during take-off, it is clear that acceleration during take-off is not constant and actually decreases. This is shown in the diagram below of the horizontal forces against speed. Note that the red shaded area between the thrust and aeroplane drag is the excess thrust. As speed increases, the excess thrust and, hence, acceleration, reduces.

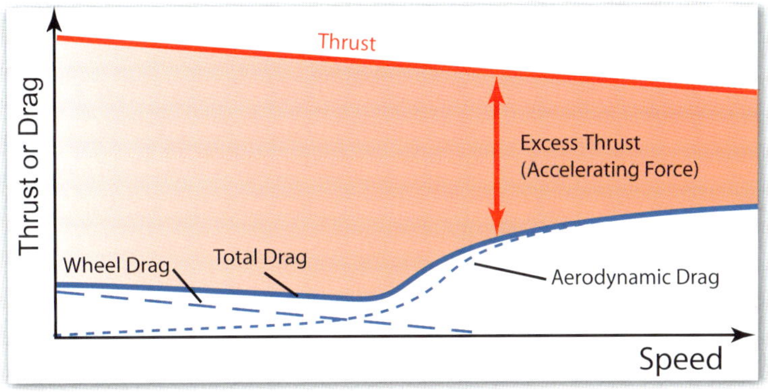

THE EFFECT OF ACCELERATION ON TAKE-OFF SPEED AND DISTANCE

The greater the acceleration, the more rapidly V_R is achieved, and the shorter the take-off distance. However, if the take-off speed increases by 10%, this increases the take-off distance by approximately 20%. This is because at constant acceleration, the distance is proportional to V^2. (For small percentage increases, the effect of squaring looks like doubling, see mathematics chapter for further explanation).

However, land availability and the cost of constructing and maintaining long runways restricts runway distances available. It is necessary to keep take-off (and landing) speeds as slow as possible by using lift augmentation devices. As aeroplane mass increases (due to increased revenue earning payload), the increased take-off speed results in longer take-off distances. The field length limited take-off mass is the heaviest an aeroplane can be in a given configuration and aerodrome conditions on a given length runway.

FACTORS AFFECTING TAKE-OFF DISTANCE REQUIRED

As already stated, the take-off distance required (TODR) varies with aerodrome conditions, aeroplane mass, and aeroplane configuration.

AEROPLANE MASS

A heavier aeroplane accelerates more slowly and needs to achieve a faster take-off speed. This results in a longer take-off distance required. When the TODR equals the take-off distance available (TODA), the aeroplane is at its **field limited take-off mass (FLTOM)** for the given flap setting.

AERODROME PRESSURE ALTITUDE

The higher an aerodrome's pressure altitude, the longer the TODR. This is because the air is less dense, which affects both the engine thrust and actual speed at rotation. The reduction in air density reduces the engine mass flow and, therefore, thrust, which results in slower acceleration. Second, the reduced air density results in a faster TAS for the same calibrated airspeed V_R.

TEMPERATURE

Hotter temperatures result in lower air density. Again, this reduces the thrust and, therefore, acceleration of the aeroplane and necessitates a faster TAS for the same V_R.

WIND

The head or tailwind component along the runway affects the ground speed of the aeroplane for the same rotate speed, V_R, which is a CAS. A reducing headwind or increasing tailwind increases the actual ground speed, which equates to the same V_R. Acceleration to a faster actual ground speed results in a longer take-off run and distance.

RUNWAY SLOPE

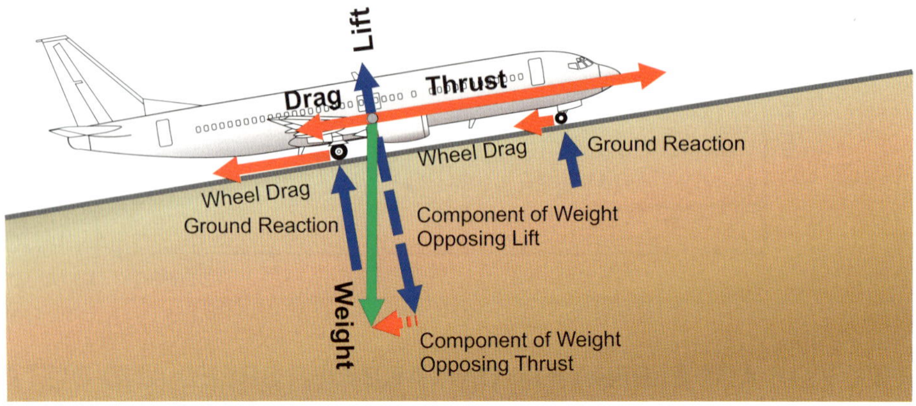

An aeroplane taking off from on an upsloping runway has to overcome a component of weight in addition to drag. This results in slower acceleration and a longer take-off distance. Conversely, a downslope decreases take-off distance, because a component of weight is now acting in the same direction as thrust.

RUNWAY SURFACE

The greater the rolling friction or the presence of extra drag due to water, slush, or wet snow on the runway, the less the acceleration and the longer the take-off distance. Class B aeroplanes taking off from grass, compared to hard runways, have a much greater take-off distance. Water, slush, and wet snow that are thrown up onto the aeroplane cause considerable impingement drag.

AEROPLANE FLAP SETTING

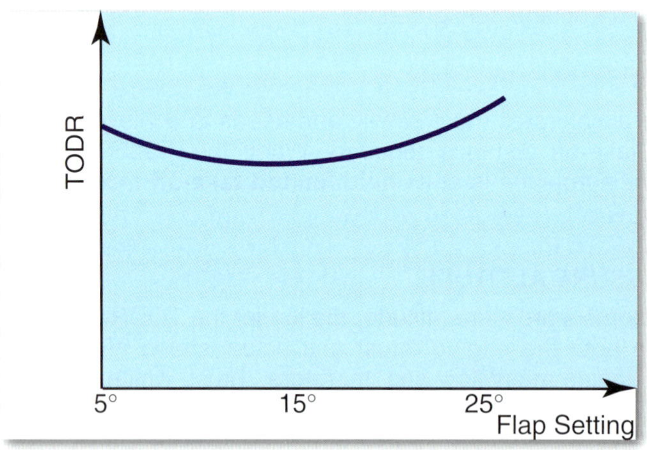

The above graph shows that the take-off distance required decreases as flaps increase to an optimum value (normally about 15°) and then increases again. Flaps increase the camber and coefficient of lift of the wing. This reduces the take-off speed for a particular aeroplane mass and the distance needed to accelerate to that slower speed. The flaps, however, also increase parasite drag. At settings greater than the optimum, the increase in drag reduces the acceleration so much that it takes a longer distance to reach the slower take-off speed.

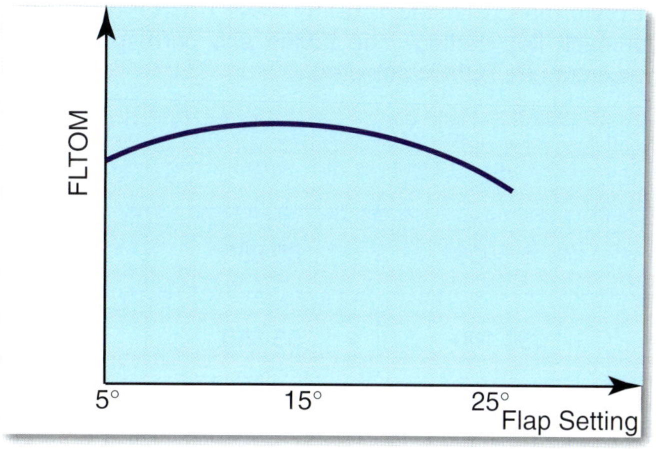

However, the field length available is fixed, so a more practical graph is of maximum take-off mass at different flap settings. This maximum take-off mass for a particular runway length is known as a **field length limited take-off mass (FLTOM)**. Up to the optimum flap setting, an increase in flaps increases the FLTOM. However, increasing flaps beyond the optimum setting would be detrimental, with the FLTOM decreasing.

DETERMINING THE MAXIMUM TAKE-OFF MASS AND CORRESPONDING FLAP SETTING

Looking at the above graph, some might think that to maximise revenue-earning payload, take-off should always be at the field length optimum flap setting of about 15°. However, the aeroplane's take-off mass also has to be light enough for the aeroplane to climb at a minimum gradient once in the air.

Climb gradient depends on excess thrust and aeroplane weight.

$$\% \text{ Gradient} = \frac{T - D}{W} \times 100$$

Any increase in flap setting increases drag. The increase in drag reduces the excess thrust (T - D) available for climbing. Therefore, to achieve the same minimum required climb gradient with increased flaps, the climb-limited take-off mass must reduce. Although increasing flap setting increases the FLTOM, it reduces the climb limited TOM.

The actual maximum performance limited take-off mass (PLTOM) depends on the FLTOM and climb limited TOM for each flap setting. The tables and corresponding graph below show an example of how the maximum PLTOM is selected.

Flap setting	5°	10°	15°	20°
FLTOM kg	55 000	55 850	56 100	55 400
Climb limited TOM kg	58 100	55 850	53 600	51 350

The graph below shows the FLTOM (in red) and climb-limited TOM (in blue) against flap settings for the figures in the above table. The maximum PLTOM occurs where the two lines cross at approximately 55 850 kg and a flap setting of 10°.

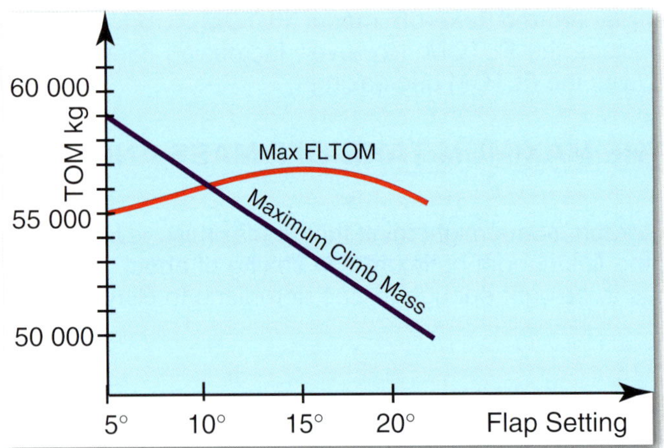

Alternately, the maximum PLTOM could have been found directly from the table.

First, find the lowest of the field length and climb limiting masses for each flap setting. These are the masses underlined in the amended table below. It is the heaviest allowable TOM at each given flap setting.

Flap setting	5°	10°	15°	20°
FLTOM kg	<u>55 000</u>	**<u>55 850</u>**	56 100	55 400
Climb limited TOM kg	58 100	**<u>55 850</u>**	<u>53 600</u>	<u>51 350</u>

Then select the greatest of the underlined values (shown in bold), which is 55 850 kg at flap 10°. The PLTOM is therefore 55 850 kg and requires the flaps to be at 10°.

Chapter 6
Climbing

INTRODUCTION

The basic principles of flight from chapter 3 are now applied to discover the effect of speed and other variables on climbing.

ANGLE OF CLIMB

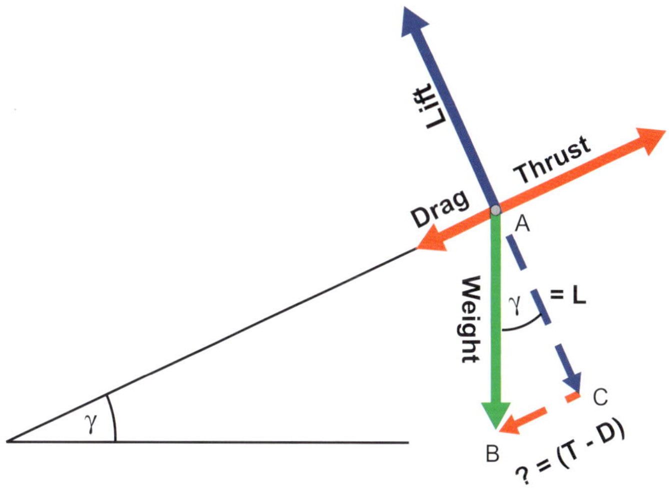

In chapter 3, the forces acting on an aeroplane in the steady climb were discussed. The above diagram shows the forces of lift, drag, weight, and thrust, and that:

Thrust is greater than drag, $T > D$
Weight is greater than lift, $W > L$
Load factor (Lift divided by Weight) is less than 1, or $LF < 1$

Looking again in the above diagram at triangle ABC, it is clear that:

The angle of climb **γ** (GAMMA) equals angle BAC,
The hypotenuse of the triangle (AB) is W,
The adjacent side of the triangle (AC) equals L, and
The opposite side of the triangle (BC) is labelled with a question mark.

BC is fundamental to climb angle. In chapter 3, trigonometry was used to find that BC equalled W sin γ. In performance, however, a much simpler and very important relationship is used. Side BC must equal thrust minus drag (T – D). This is because the forces pulling up the flight path must equal the forces pulling down the flight path if the aeroplane is to continue at the same speed. The only force pulling up the flight path is thrust, while the forces pulling down the flight path are drag and the unknown component of weight.

Therefore,

T = D + ?, rearranging
? = T - D

Note: By convention, the angle of the climb is normally known as **γ** (GAMMA). This is usually the case in the JAR questions. However, some questions use θ (THETA) as the angle of climb. To increase your familiarity with this alternative symbol, θ is used in chapter 3.

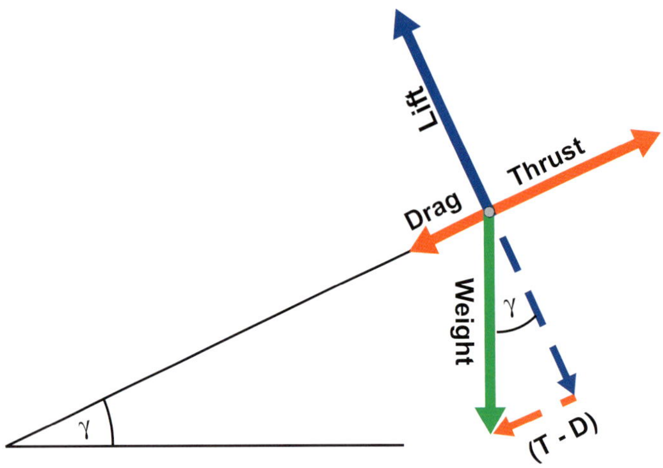

The above diagram of an aeroplane in a steady climb shows the component of weight parallel to the flight path as T – D. Using trigonometry, it becomes clear that:

$$\text{(sin) Angle of Climb} = \frac{T - D}{W} = \frac{\text{Excess Thrust}}{W}$$

This means that if thrust increases or drag decreases, excess thrust and the angle of climb increase. As weight increases, the angle of climb reduces.

In addition, provided that the angle of climb is small,

$$\text{Gradient of Climb} = \frac{T - D}{W} = \frac{\text{Excess Thrust}}{W}$$

It is excess thrust, the difference between thrust and drag, that are now examined further to see how speed, altitude, weight, configuration, and other variables affect the angle and gradient of climb.

V_X — BEST ANGLE OF CLIMB

V_X is the speed at which an aeroplane achieves its maximum angle or gradient of climb. Since angle of climb depends on excess thrust, V_X is the speed at which the difference between thrust available and drag is greatest. Because thrust available against speed is different for turbojet and propeller aeroplanes, it must be established at what speed V_X is for both types of aeroplanes.

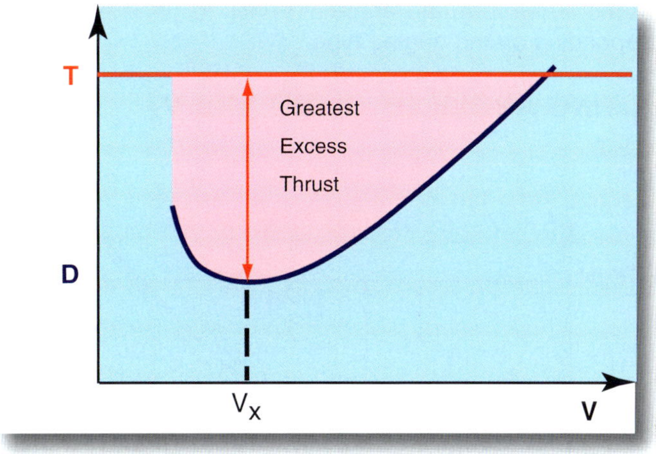

V_X FOR A TURBOJET AEROPLANE

In the above graph, a red line shows thrust against speed for a jet and a blue line shows total drag against speed. The graph shows us important information about both the angle of climb and the speed for the best angle of climb, Vx. When an aeroplane is flying at a speed where there is excess thrust (shown by the pink shaded area), the aeroplane can climb while maintaining the same speed.

The speed at which the excess thrust is greatest results in the maximum angle of climb. This speed is Vx.

For a turbojet aeroplane, V_X is at Vmd.

V_X FOR A PROPELLER AEROPLANE

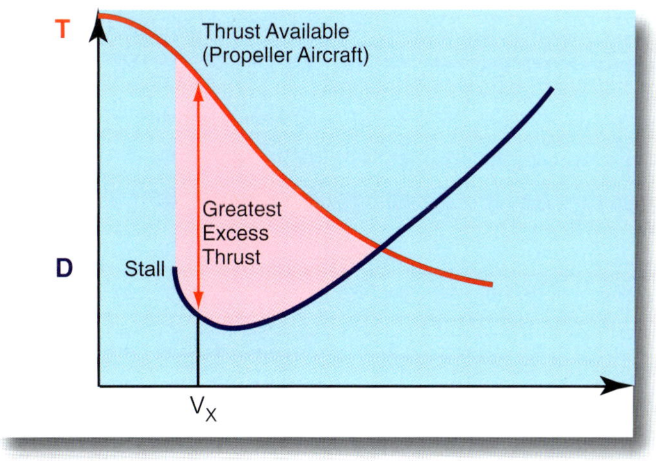

The above diagram shows drag and thrust for a propeller aeroplane against speed. The pink area again shows the excess thrust. V_X is again the speed at which angle and gradient of climb is greatest, because excess thrust is greatest.

However, it is important to note that V_X for a propeller aeroplane is much slower than Vmd and is slower than Vmp.

V_X AND ANGLE OF ATTACK

In the JAR exams, Vmd is considered to correspond with an angle of attack of 4°. This means that a jet aeroplane climbing at V_X is at 4° angle of attack. However, V_X for a propeller aeroplane is much slower than Vmd. Therefore, the angle of attack for V_X is much greater than 4° and can be close to the stall depending on the engine type.

FACTORS AFFECTING ANGLE OF CLIMB AND V_X

AEROPLANE WEIGHT

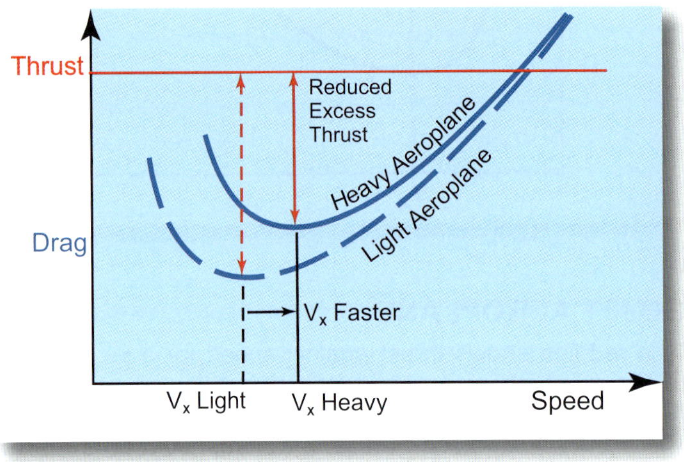

As shown in chapter 3, the total drag curve for a heavier aeroplane moves up and to the right. This was because the induced drag had increased.

The above graph shows the original total drag as a dashed blue line, and the total drag for a heavier aeroplane as a continuous blue line. The red line shows the thrust available for a turbojet.

An increased aeroplane weight has reduced the excess thrust and the angle of climb. V_X, the speed at which the best angle of climb is achieved, is therefore faster for the heavier aeroplane.

AEROPLANE CONFIGURATION

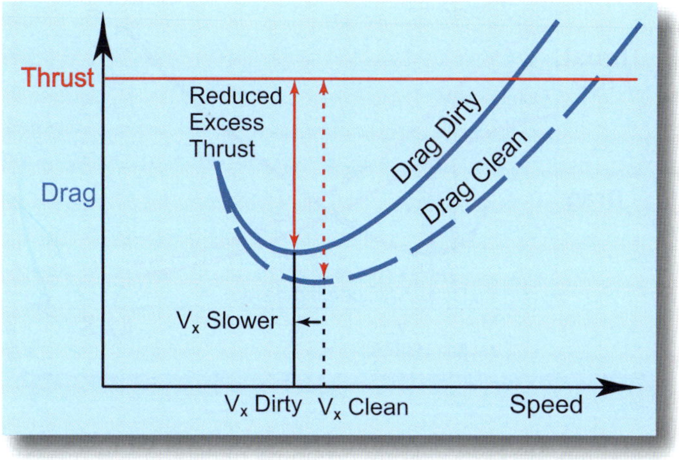

Making an aeroplane dirty by lowering the flaps or undercarriage moves the total drag curve. This time it moves up and to the left. This is because the parasite drag has increased. The above graph shows the total drag curve (in blue) and thrust available for a turbojet (in red). The movement of the total drag curve due to the lowering of flaps and undercarriage results in:

- The angle of climb reducing, because the excess thrust has reduced
- V_X, the speed for the best angle of climb, is slower

ALTITUDE

Considering V_X as a CAS, the total drag curve does not move as altitude increases because the TAS increases to compensate for the reduction in air density. However, the thrust does reduce as altitude increases.

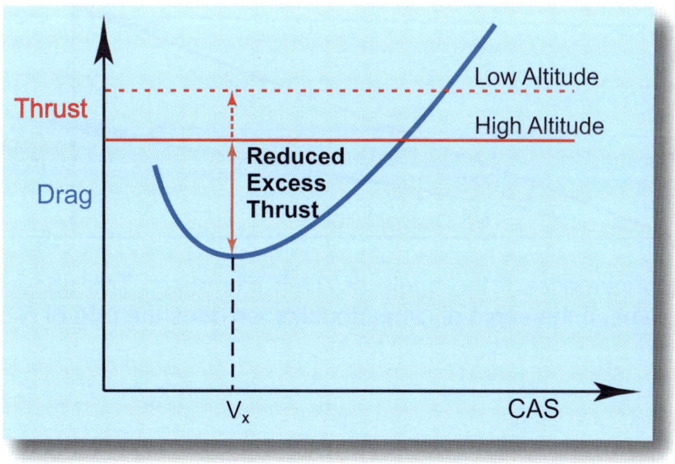

The graph on the previous page for a turbojet shows us that as altitude increases:

- The angle of climb reduces, but
- V_X (as an IAS) remains constant.

However, if V_X is considered as a TAS, V_X increases. (In the JAR exams, V_X is usually a CAS, but it is occasionally considered as a TAS.)

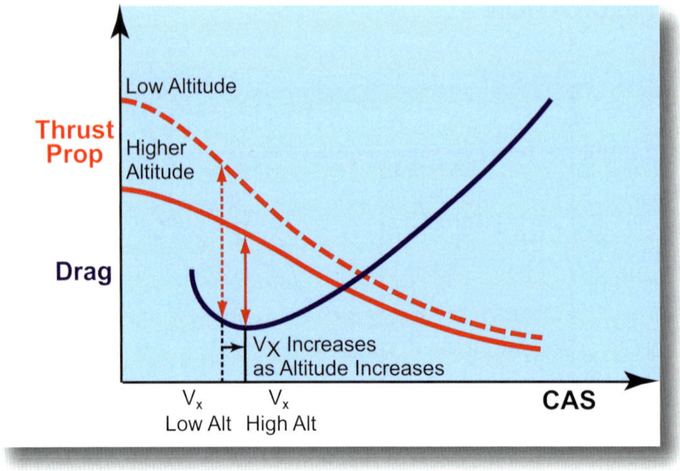

The above graph looks at the effect of altitude on angle of climb for a propeller aeroplane. Again, the angle of climb reduces as the altitude increases. In this case, V_X (CAS) reduces as altitude increases. This is rarely asked about in the JAR exams.

ACCELERATING OR TURNING

If an aeroplane accelerates, excess thrust is used to increase the airspeed and, therefore, less excess thrust is available for climbing. Similarly, if an aeroplane turns, the lift must increase, resulting in the drag increasing. The excess thrust again reduces. Therefore, if an aeroplane either accelerates or turns while climbing, the angle of climb reduces.

RATE OF CLIMB

Rate of climb is purely a vertical speed. In aviation, it is normally given in feet per minute and is read on the vertical speed indicator (VSI).

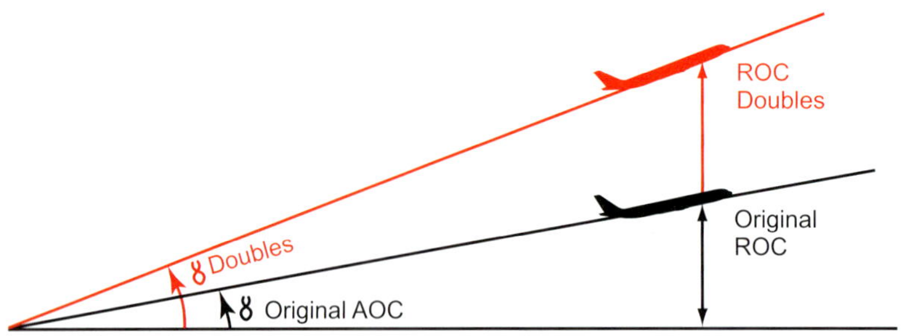

The rate of climb increases if the angle of climb increases. The above diagram shows that at small angles of climb, if the angle of climb doubles, so does the rate of climb.

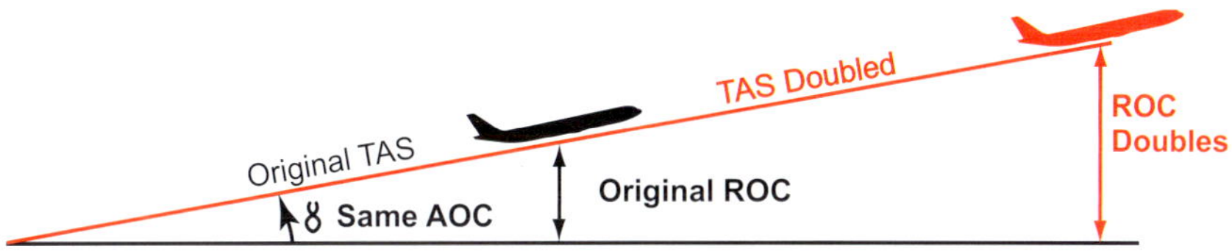

However, the rate of climb also increases if the TAS of the aeroplane along the flight path increases. The above diagram shows that if the TAS doubles, the rate of climb (ROC) doubles. Rate of climb, therefore, depends on both the angle of climb and the TAS as shown in the following equation:

Rate of climb = Angle of climb x TAS

And since angle of climb equals thrust minus drag divided by weight,

$$\text{Rate of Climb} = \frac{T - D}{W} \times \text{TAS}$$

Thus:

$$\text{Rate of Climb} = \frac{T \times \text{TAS} - D \times \text{TAS}}{W}$$

So,

$$\text{Rate of Climb} = \frac{\text{Power Available} - \text{Power Required}}{W}$$

Note that rate of climb depends on weight and excess power.

V_Y — BEST RATE OF CLIMB

V_Y is the speed at which an aeroplane achieves its maximum rate of climb. Since rate of climb depends on excess power, V_Y is the speed at which the difference between power available and power required is greatest. Because power available is thrust available times TAS, power available again differs for turbojet and propeller aeroplanes and must be considered separately.

V_Y FOR A TURBOJET AEROPLANE

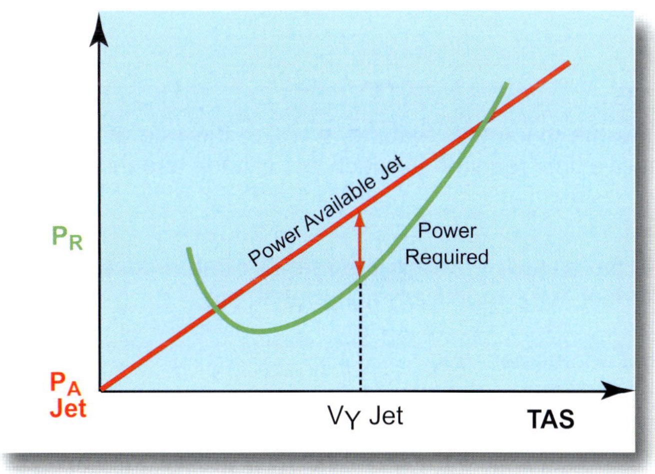

The above diagram shows power available for a turbojet (red line) and power required (green line). The speed at which the excess power is greatest, and, therefore, the rate of climb is greatest, is at V_Y. V_Y for a turbojet is much faster than Vmp (the speed for minimum power). It is also faster than Vmd (the speed for minimum drag).

Therefore, V_Y is always faster than V_X unless at the theoretical absolute ceiling referred to below, when $V_X = V_Y$.

V_Y FOR A PROPELLER AEROPLANE

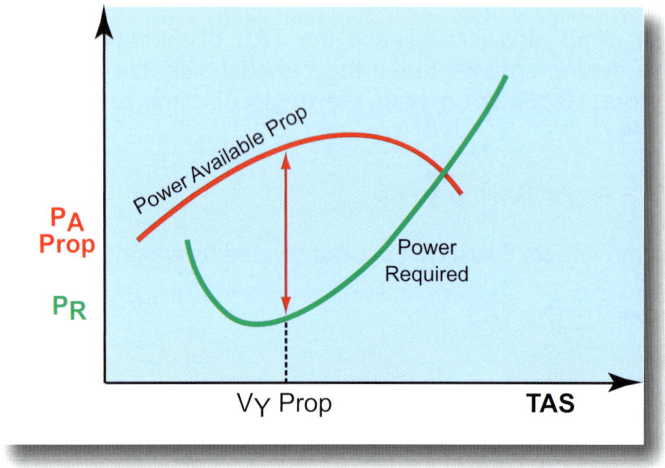

The above graph shows power available (red line) and power required (green line) for a propeller-driven aeroplane.

V_Y, the speed where there is greatest excess power, is close to Vmd, but will reduce with an increase in altitude. However, V_X for a propeller-driven aeroplane is normally close to Vmp and the stall.

For a propeller-driven aeroplane, V_Y is slower than Vmd. V_Y is again faster than V_X (unless at the absolute ceiling).

V_Y AND ANGLE OF ATTACK

For a turbojet aeroplane, V_Y is faster than Vmd and, therefore, the angle of attack is less than 4°. However, V_Y for a propeller-driven aeroplane is close to Vmd and requires an angle of attack of approximately 4°.

ABSOLUTE CEILING

The absolute ceiling is the theoretical altitude at which the rate of climb is zero. It is theoretical because of the excessive time required to reach this altitude and the need to stay at exactly V_Y.

SERVICE CEILING

The service ceiling is the altitude at which the rate of climb reduces to a specified value. These values, which are intended to be practically achievable, are:

> 500 fpm for jet aeroplanes, and
> 100 fpm for propeller aeroplanes

FACTORS AFFECTING RATE OF CLIMB AND V_Y

AEROPLANE WEIGHT

As the total drag curve moves up and to the right for a heavier aeroplane, the power required curve also moves up and to the right.

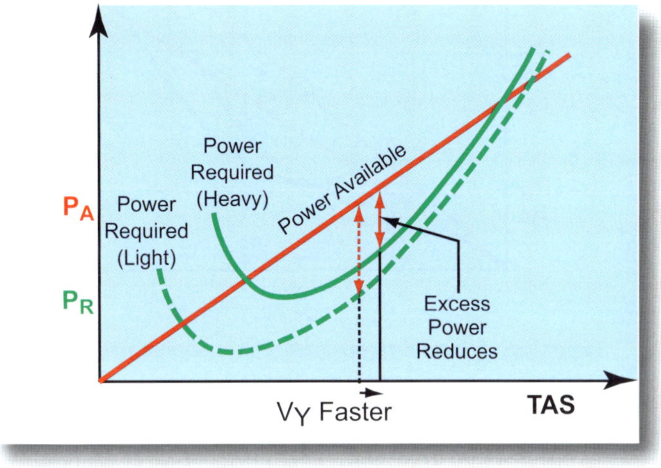

The above graph shows the original power required as a dashed green line and the power required for a heavier aeroplane as a continuous green line. The red line shows the power available for a turbojet. Therefore, as weight increases, the excess power reduces and the rate of climb reduces. Note that V_Y, the speed for maximum rate of climb, is faster for the heavier aeroplane.

AEROPLANE CONFIGURATION

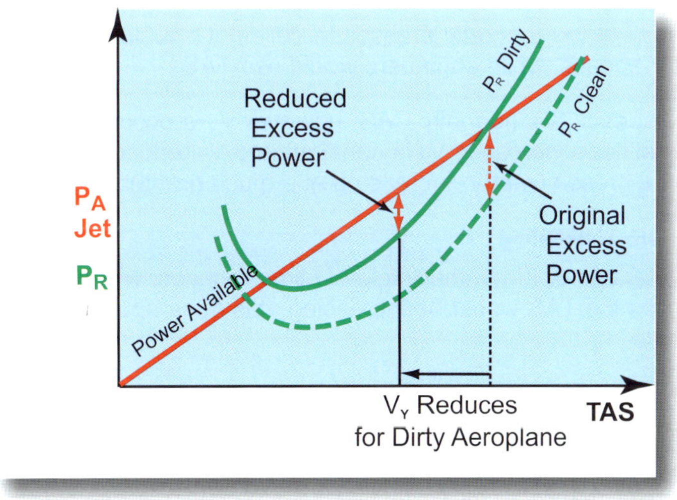

As the total drag curve moves up and left when the flaps or undercarriage is lowered, so does the power required curve. The above graph shows us that this movement of the power required curve (in green) in relation to the power available for a turbojet (in red) results in:

- The rate of climb reducing, because the excess power has reduced, and
- The speed, V_Y, for the maximum rate of climb is slower.

ALTITUDE

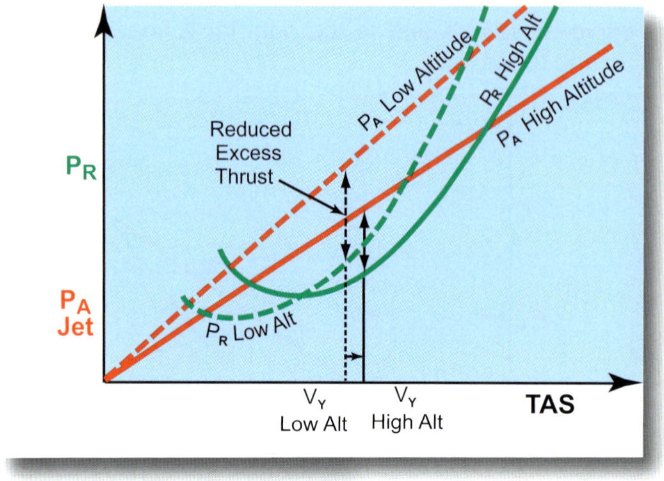

Power required is drag times TAS. Although the total drag curve as a CAS does not move as altitude increases, it moves to the right if drawn against TAS. This is because for the same CAS, the TAS increases as the air density reduces. The above graph of power available and power required plotted against TAS shows us that as altitude increases:

- The excess power and rate of climb reduce
- V_Y (TAS) increases to a slightly faster speed

However, pilots normally think of V_Y and V_X as calibrated airspeeds. As altitude increases:

- The excess power and rate of climb reduces
- V_Y (CAS) reduces

V_Y (CAS) reduces until at the theoretical absolute ceiling it equals V_X. By convention, pilots use calibrated airspeed V speeds, while engineers would use TAS.

In the JAR exam, V speeds are normally CAS, however V_Y is occasionally considered as a TAS. In terms of CAS, as altitude increases V_X is constant and V_Y reduces. In terms of TAS as altitude increases, V_X and V_Y increase (with V_X increasing at a much greater rate than V_Y).

ACCELERATING OR TURNING

If an aeroplane accelerates or turns, the angle of climb reduces, which reduces the rate of climb. Although in both cases the TAS would be increasing, this does not overcome the dominant effect of reduced climb angle.

CLIMBING SUMMARY

- Angle and gradient of climb depend on excess thrust divided by weight.
- V_X is the speed at which the maximum angle or gradient of climb is achieved.
- For a turbojet, V_X is at Vmd, and the required angle of attack is 4°.
- For a propeller aeroplane, V_X is at approximately Vmp with an angle of attack close to $C_{L\ max}$.
- Rate of climb depends on excess power divided by weight.
- V_Y is the speed at which the maximum rate of climb is achieved.
- V_Y is faster than V_X for all aeroplanes types, except theoretically at the absolute ceiling when V_Y would equal V_X. ($V_Y \geq V_X$).
- For a turbojet, V_Y is faster than Vmd, and the required angle of attack is less than 4°.
- For a propeller aeroplane, V_Y is approximately Vmd with an angle of attack of approximately 4°.

Chapter 7 Descending and Gliding

INTRODUCTION

In this chapter, you will apply your knowledge of descending from chapter 3 to look at how different variables affect the angle and rate of descent, the glide, and glide range and endurance.

DESCENT

FORCES IN THE DESCENT

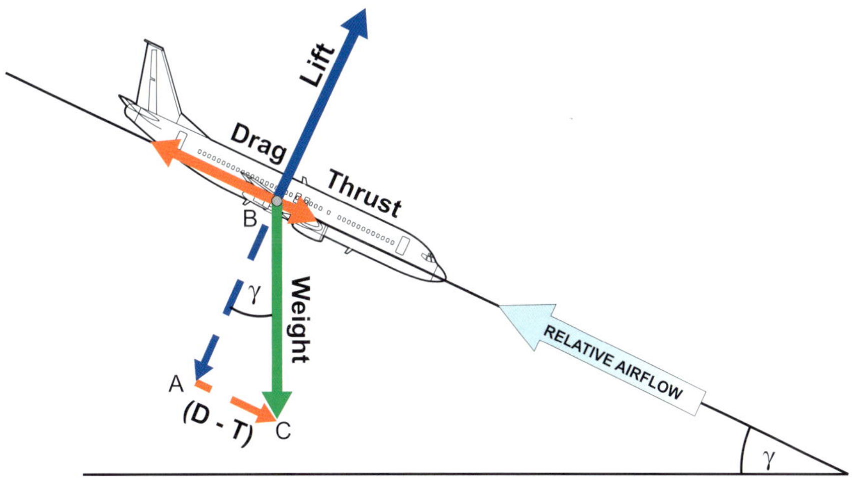

The above diagram shows the forces acting on an aeroplane in a steady, straight descent. Because the forces in opposite directions must be equal, it is apparent that:

- The component of weight opposite to lift must equal lift
- The component of weight parallel to the flight path must equal D–T

The angle of descent GAMMA (γ) is also the angle in the triangle ABC. Therefore,

$$\text{Sin}\ \gamma = \frac{AC}{BC} = \frac{D - T}{W}$$

Therefore, the greater the drag compared to the thrust, the steeper the angle of descent.

SPEED FOR MINIMUM ANGLE OF DESCENT

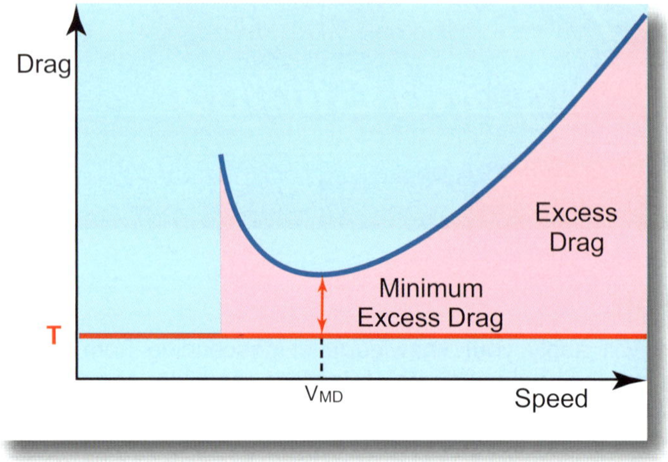

Because the angle of descent depends on D-T/W, the angle of descent is shallowest when drag exceeds thrust by the smallest amount. The amount that drag exceeds the thrust available is also known as excess drag. In the previous graph of thrust and drag for a jet, the excess drag is shaded pink. The speed at which the excess drag is minimum is at V_{md}. Therefore, both maximum angle of climb and minimum angle of descent are at V_{md} for a jet.

SPEED FOR MAXIMUM ANGLE OF DESCENT

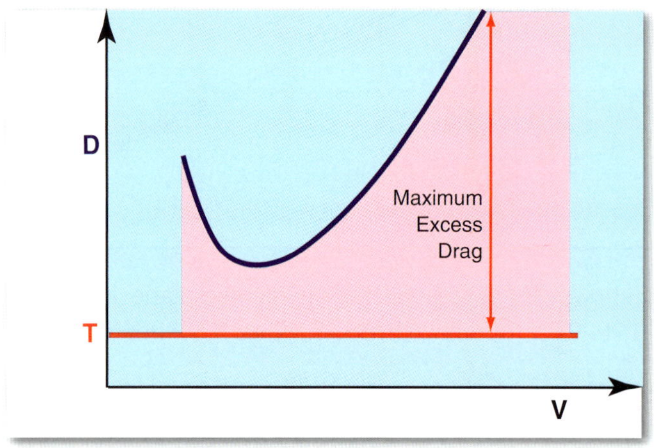

The above graph shows that there is greater excess drag at high speed than at low speeds. The steepest angle of descent is achieved by staying fast. The angle of descent would increase further by deploying speed brakes, which can usually be extended at high speeds. The benefit of the increased drag of flaps and undercarriage is usually offset by the large reduction in parasite drag at the much slower limiting speeds V_{FE} and V_{LO}. The speed and configuration for maximum angle of descent are type specific.

SPEED FOR MINIMUM RATE OF DESCENT

Rate of descent depends on both the angle of descent and the speed down the flight path. Rate of descent is not minimum at V_{md}, where the angle of descent is minimum, because the speed is moderately fast. Rate of descent is actually minimum at V_{mp} (the velocity for minimum power). This means that maximum endurance (maximum time in the air) is achieved at V_{mp}.

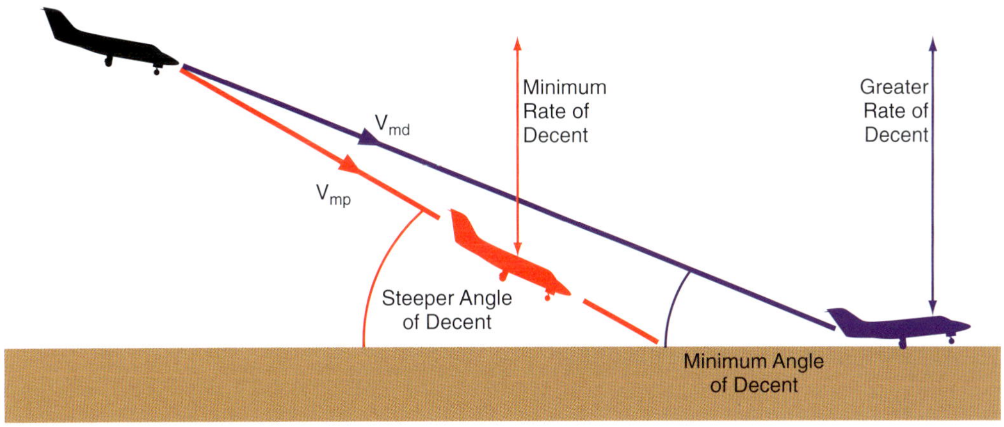

The above diagram shows two aeroplanes descending, one at V_{md} and the other at V_{mp}. Although the aeroplane descending at V_{mp} has a slightly steeper angle of descent, the much slower speed (76% of the speed at V_{md}) results in a lower (minimum) rate of descent.

SPEED FOR MAXIMUM RATE OF DESCENT

To achieve a maximum rate of descent, both the angle of descent and the speed down the flight path should be as large as possible. This is at a fast speed, but the limiting speed of drag devices may result in this being at or below M_{mo}/V_{mo}.

GLIDING

The term gliding refers to unpowered flight. The aeroplane may have engines, but they are no longer producing thrust.

FORCES IN THE GLIDE

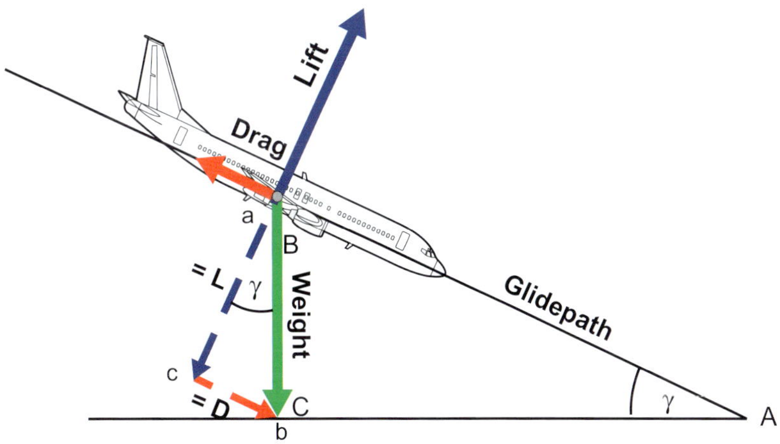

The above diagram shows that the forces in the steady glide are simplified because of the absence of thrust. Because forces in opposite directions must be equal, it should be clear that:

- The component of the weight in the direction of the glide path must equal drag, and
- The component of the weight normal to the glide path must equal lift.

The gradient of descent depends on the ratio of height loss (BC in the large triangle ABC) to horizontal distance travelled (AC). Because triangle abc is similar to triangle ABC:

$$\text{Gradient} = \frac{BC}{AC} = \frac{bc}{ac} = \frac{D}{L}$$

Therefore, the gradient (and angle) of descent is smallest when D/L is smallest. Since D/L is smallest when L/D is greatest, many important points about gliding become obvious.

To glide at the shallowest glide angle, giving maximum still-air range:

- The L/D ratio must be maximum
- The aircraft must fly at V_{md}
- The aircraft must fly at 4° angle of attack

FACTORS AFFECTING THE GLIDE ANGLE

AEROPLANE WEIGHT

If it remains at V_{md}, a heavier aeroplane has the same lift/drag ratio and same glide angle and range. This is because the lift and drag have increased in the same proportion. However, the actual speed of V_{md} alters. A heavier aeroplane has to glide at a faster speed to be at V_{md} because the drag curve has moved up and to the right (see page 3.6).

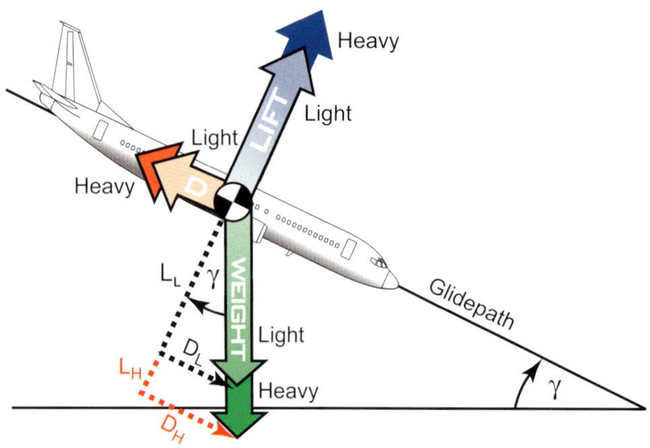

FLAPS AND UNDERCARRIAGE

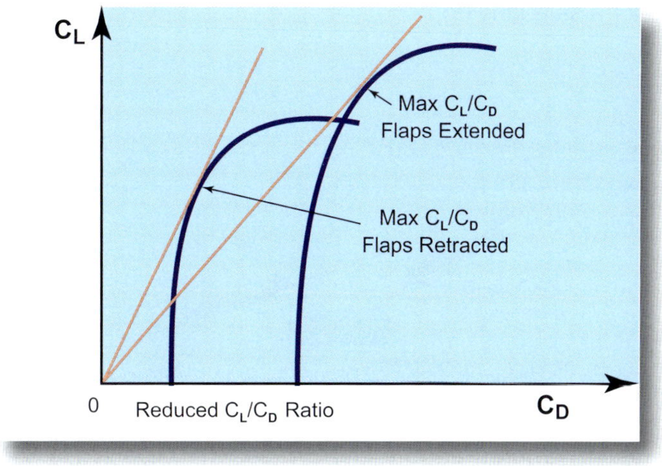

The above drag polar (C_L against C_D) shows that flaps reduce the lift/drag ratio, which will steepen the glide path.

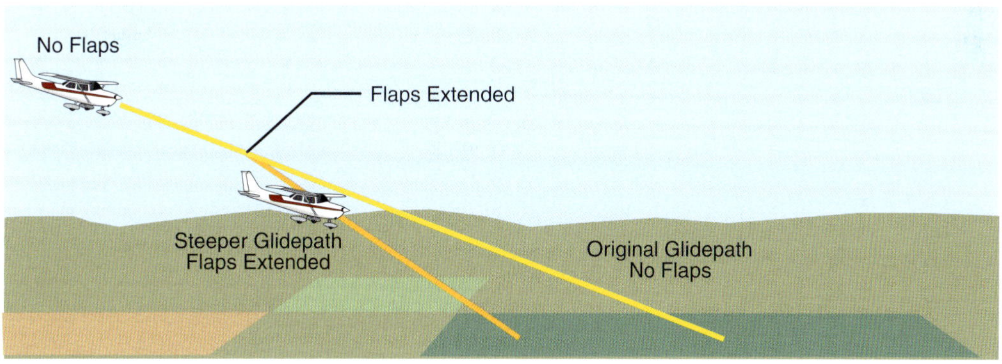

Be particularly aware of this when practising forced landings in light aeroplanes. Do not extend flaps until a landing well into the chosen landing area is assured. This is because of the much steeper resulting glide path, which brings the aiming point back toward you.

Flaps increase the angle of descent and reduce the range.

WIND

It is conventional to use ground range and glide path angles with respect to the ground when considering the glide for a safe landing.

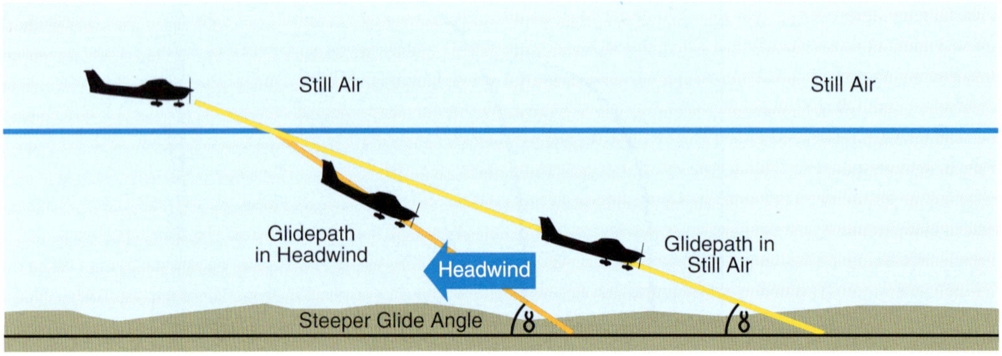

A headwind decreases the ground range and increases the glide angle. However, flying slightly faster than V_{md} reduces the time in the headwind and results in the best possible ground range in the headwind. A tailwind increases ground range and reduces the glide angle with respect to the ground.

Chapter 8
The Cruise

INTRODUCTION

Public transport aeroplanes spend the majority of their airborne time in the cruise. Although the relationship between the forces in the cruise is simple at first glance, there are subtleties together with economic and engine considerations that must be explored.

FORCES IN LEVEL FLIGHT

In any steady flight condition, the forces on the aeroplane must be in balance. In straight-and-level flight, when the relative airflow is horizontal, the relationship between these forces is at its simplest. The diagram below of an aeroplane in steady, straight-and-level flight shows that:

Lift must balance weight	L = W, and
Thrust must balance drag	T = D.

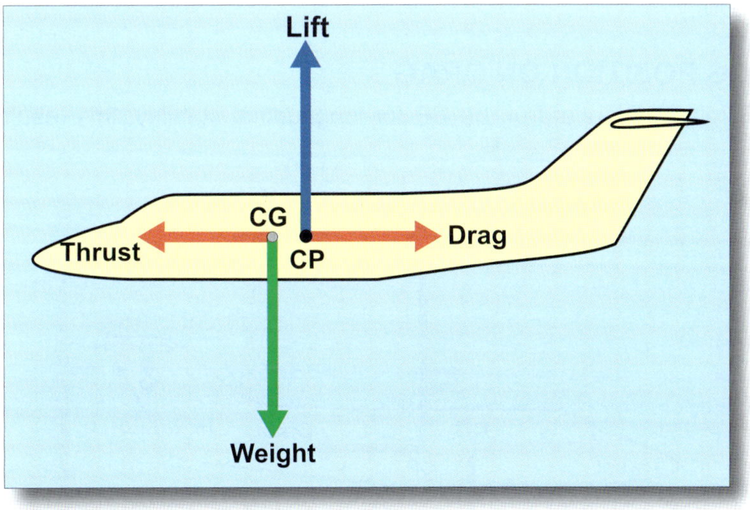

Not only must the forces be in balance for steady flight, but also the turning moments of those forces. Look more closely at the above diagram to see that the centre of gravity (CG) of the aeroplane is forward of the centre of pressure (CP). This is the normal situation because of the need for longitudinal stability.

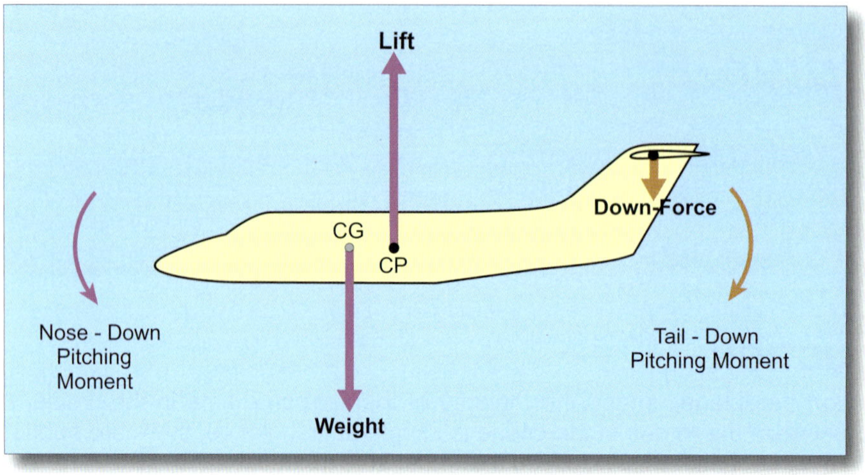

However, because the CG is in front of the CP, the lift-weight couple causes a nose-down pitch moment. The above diagram shows that for equilibrium, an equal tail-down/nose-up pitch moment is required. This is achieved by the tailplane providing a downward lift force, which acts about the aeroplane's centre of gravity.

Therefore, for straight-and-level flight:

- Lift = Weight + Tailplane downward lift force
- Thrust = Drag

EFFECT OF CG POSITION ON DRAG

Although the CG must be forward of the CP for longitudinal stability, this results in a penalty of extra drag.

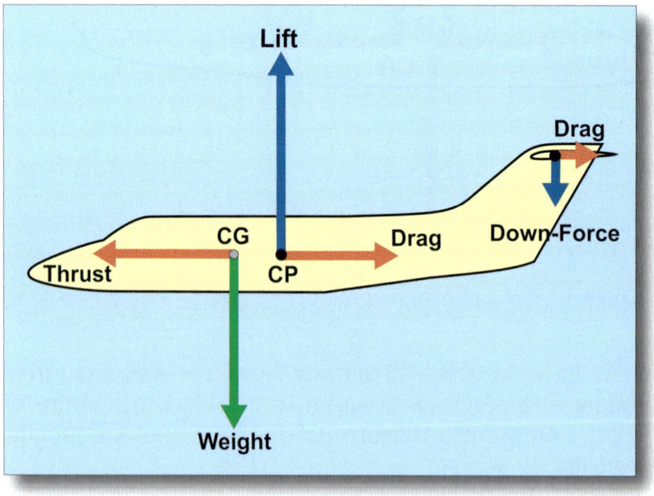

The above diagram shows that the two downward forces must be balanced by the wing's upward lift force. This means that wing lift must increase. Whenever lift is generated, so is drag. The increased drag from the wing plus the drag from the tailplane results in increased drag, which must be balanced by an increase in thrust if the aeroplane is to remain at a constant speed.

Therefore, as CG position moves forward, drag increases. This causes the fuel flow to increase and range and endurance to decrease.

MAXIMUM STRAIGHT-AND-LEVEL FLIGHT SPEED

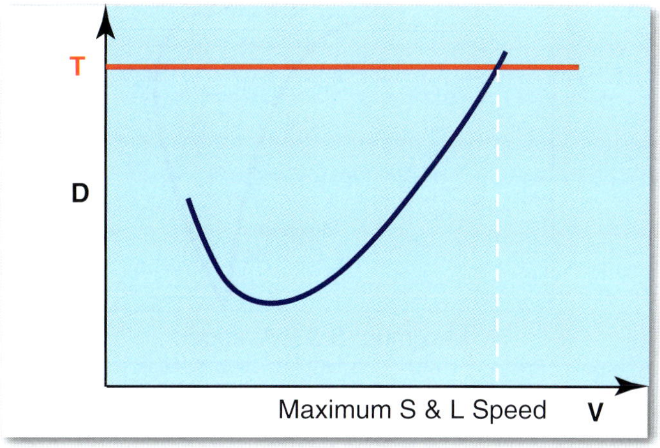

To be at the maximum straight-and-level speed, drag must equal the thrust available. In the above graph, this must occur at the intersection of the thrust available and drag curves. Since maximum continuous thrust is maximum thrust available, to equal it, drag must also be maximum (for the straight-and-level flight condition). This is an idea that is sometimes difficult to grasp. It is common for exam candidates to state that at the maximum achievable straight-and-level speed, thrust is maximum (at maximum continuous) but that drag is minimum. This would actually occur at the speed for maximum acceleration, because at V_{md}, where the drag is minimum, the excess thrust is the greatest.

THE EFFECT OF ALTITUDE ON MAXIMUM STRAIGHT-AND-LEVEL SPEED

In Chapter 2, it was seen that altitude had no effect on the total drag curve plotted against CAS. However, an increase in altitude does reduce the thrust available and has an effect on the maximum straight-and-level speed.

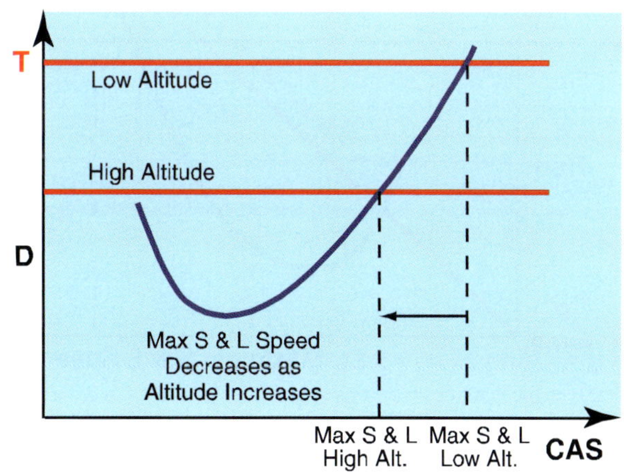

The above graph shows that at low altitude, when the greatest thrust is available, the maximum achievable straight-and-level speed is fastest. However, at higher altitudes, the thrust available progressively reduces. In the above graph, the intersection of the thrust available and drag curves moves progressively to slower calibrated airspeeds as the altitude increases.

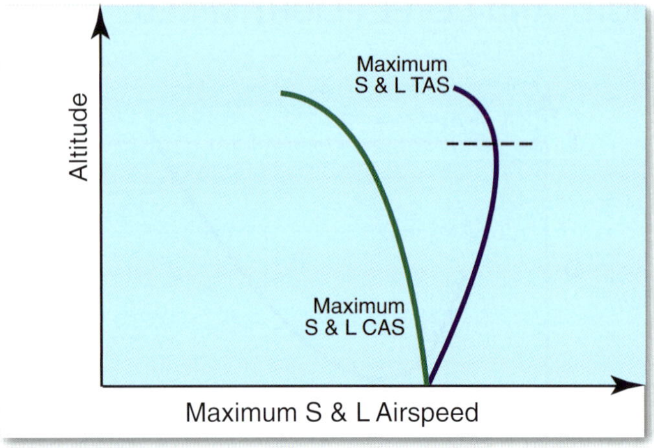

The above graph shows the maximum straight-and-level airspeed against altitude. The green line on the above graph shows that the maximum straight-and-level CAS decreases as altitude increases. However, looking at the blue line, the maximum straight-and-level TAS increases as altitude increases before decreasing at high altitude.

The above discussion on maximum achievable speed is based on the turbojet, which is the norm for ATPL exam questions. However, the altitude at which the maximum achievable TAS is attained for propeller-driven aeroplanes depends on engine type. For piston-engine aeroplanes, the maximum achievable TAS is fastest at low altitude. Turbo-propeller aeroplanes achieve their maximum TAS at a medium altitude. Note that the maximum achievable CAS reduces with altitude for all engine types.

MAXIMUM STRAIGHT-AND-LEVEL SPEED IN TERMS OF POWER

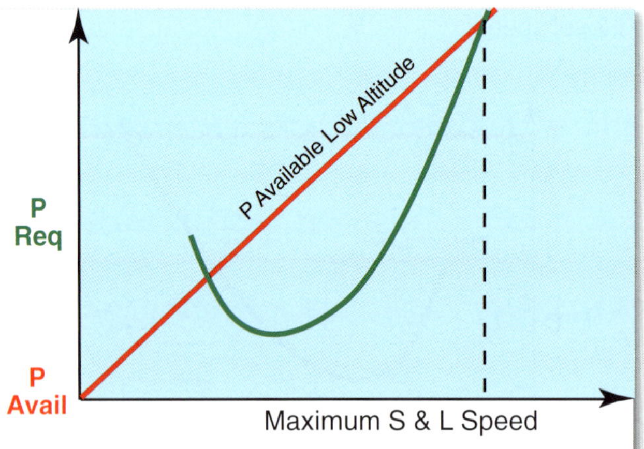

The above graph shows power required (green line) and power available (red line). The maximum achievable speed is also at the intersection of the power curves, where power required equals power available.

RANGE

Range can be described as the distance that can be flown on the fuel available. An aeroplane with full fuel tanks has a greater range than one with fuel tanks only half full. However, a number of other factors also affect range. Before looking at these, the term **specific range** is discussed.

SPECIFIC RANGE

There are two types of specific range, specific air range (SAR) and specific ground range (SGR). Specific air range is the range through the air, while SGR is the ground range. The difference is due to wind strength and direction. In the exam, and throughout the notes, consider specific range to be SAR. However, when wind is to be considered, specific range is assumed to mean SGR.

Specific range is the distance flown per unit of fuel. Using the aviation units nautical miles and kilograms:

$$\text{Specific range} = \frac{\text{nm}}{\text{kg}}$$

Dividing by time:

$$\text{Specific range} = \frac{\text{TAS}}{\text{Fuel Flow}}$$

To enable further understanding of range, the fuel flow for different types of aeroplanes must be considered.

FUEL FLOW

In a turbojet, the fuel flow is proportional to thrust. Therefore, as thrust increases, fuel flow increases. For aeroplanes driven by a propeller regardless of engine type, fuel flow is proportional to power. To enable the use of more effective terms of thrust and power, specific fuel consumption must be introduced.

SPECIFIC FUEL CONSUMPTION

Specific fuel consumption (SFC) in a jet is the fuel flow per unit of thrust, while SFC for a propeller is the fuel flow per unit of power. The SFC is only an engine consideration and is not affected by drag, which is an airframe consideration. In a turbojet engine, SFC is lowest when the air temperature is low and the engine is running at its design rpm of approximately 90 to 95% rpm. This means that SFC is proportional to temperature. It also means that the engine is most efficient at high altitude where the thrust required to overcome drag is approximately 90 to 95% of the thrust available.

SPECIFIC RANGE FOR A TURBOJET AEROPLANE

Because fuel flow in a turbojet is SFC multiplied by thrust required, the specific range equation can be written as:

$$\text{Specific Range} = \frac{\text{TAS}}{\text{SFC x Thrust Required}}$$

In steady, straight-and-level flight, thrust required equals drag and therefore:

$$\text{Specific Range} = \frac{\text{TAS}}{\text{SFC x Drag}}$$

This equation is much more useful because the aerodynamic and engine considerations can be looked at separately. The effect of the engine on aircraft performance is determined by the SFC, which is affected by altitude. Airframe considerations are determined by the relationship between TAS and drag.

SPEED FOR MAXIMUM RANGE IN A TURBOJET

The speed to fly a turbojet for maximum range depends on the aerodynamic considerations; TAS divided by drag. Since range is maximum when the ratio of TAS to drag is maximum, flying relatively fast but with as little drag as possible is ideal.

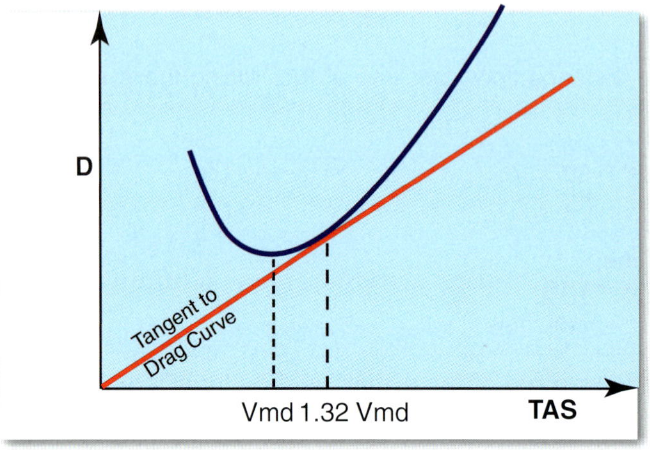

The above graph shows that although drag is minimum at V_{md}, the forward speed is only moderate. The ratio of TAS to drag is actually greatest at the tangent to the drag curve, which is at 1.32 times the speed for minimum drag. At this speed, a considerably greater TAS is achieved for only a small increase in drag. Having discovered that a turbojet should be flown at the tangent to the drag curve, which can also be described as 1.32 V_{md}, the effect of altitude on range must be considered.

OPTIMUM ALTITUDE FOR MAXIMUM RANGE IN A TURBOJET

Turbojet range is greatest at high altitude. This is due to both engine and aerodynamic considerations. The aerodynamic consideration is that as altitude increases, the TAS increases for the same CAS. However, it is the engine consideration, SFC, which results in the optimum altitude being at high altitude, although not as high as possible. This is because the SFC starts to increase again at very high altitude when the engine rpm exceeds its design rpm of between 90 to 95%.

SPECIFIC RANGE FOR A PROPELLER-DRIVEN AEROPLANE

Since fuel flow for a propeller-driven aeroplane (in straight-and-level flight) is power required multiplied by specific fuel consumption (SFC),

$$\text{Specific range propeller aeroplane} = \frac{\text{TAS}}{\text{SFC x Power Required}}$$

Now the aerodynamic and engine considerations can be looked at separately. The engine performance is determined by the SFC, while the airframe consideration is determined by the relationship between TAS and power required.

SPEED FOR MAXIMUM RANGE IN A PROPELLER-DRIVEN AEROPLANE

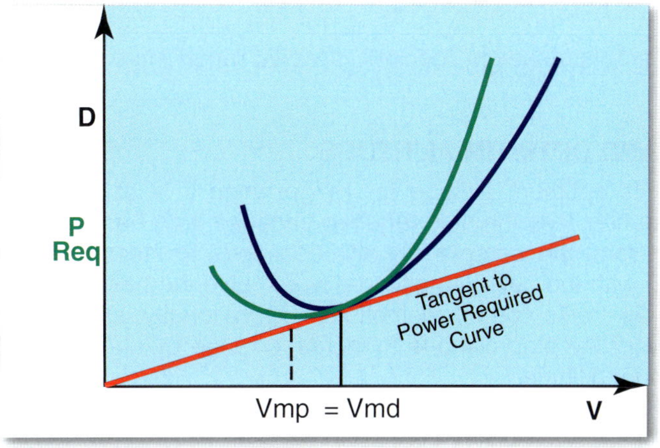

Range for a propeller-driven aeroplane is maximum at the speed where the ratio of TAS to power required is maximum. This is at the tangent to the power required curve. However, it is important to remember that the tangent to the power required curve is also the speed for minimum drag (V_{md}). The above graph of power required (in green) superimposed by the drag curve (in blue) shows this.

FACTORS AFFECTING RANGE

AEROPLANE MASS

Because of fuel burn, aeroplane weight reduces as a flight progresses. This affects specific range and the speed for maximum specific range.

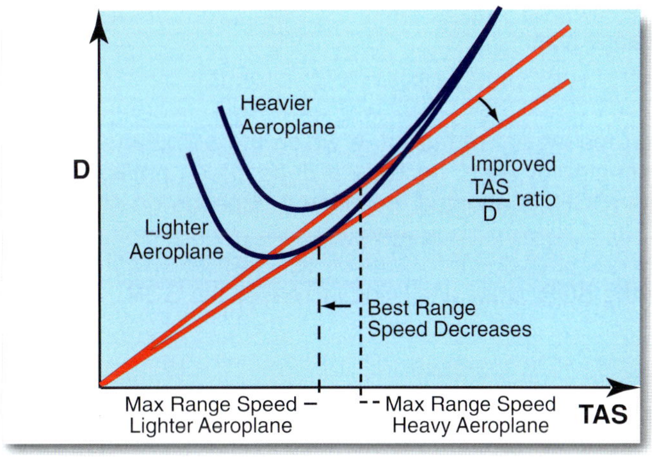

The above graph shows total drag against speed for a heavier and lighter aeroplane. The reduction in induced drag for the lighter aeroplane results in the drag curve moving down and to the left.

As a flight progresses, the specific range increases due to an increase in the ratio of TAS to drag. The ratio of the TAS to the drag is shown on the graph by the gradient of the tangent. The shallower the gradient, the greater the ratio of TAS to drag, and the greater the specific range.

As fuel is burnt, the speed for best range also decreases. The reason for this is seen in the above diagram, where the movement of the drag curve to the left has resulted in the tangent to the drag curve moving to a slower speed.

To summarise, as aeroplane weight reduces, specific range increases, and the optimum speed for range is slower.

REDUCED MASS AND OPTIMUM ALTITUDE

An aeroplane is at its optimum altitude for range when it is at its design rpm. However, as aeroplane weight reduces, less thrust is required because drag has decreased. For the engine to remain at its design rpm, the aeroplane's altitude needs to steadily increase. A steady cruise climb, which drifts up with the optimum altitude, would give the best range. However, this is often not possible due to air traffic control restrictions. Operationally, step climbs are normally used. The primary purpose of the step climb is to increase range by staying as close as operationally possible to the optimum altitude.

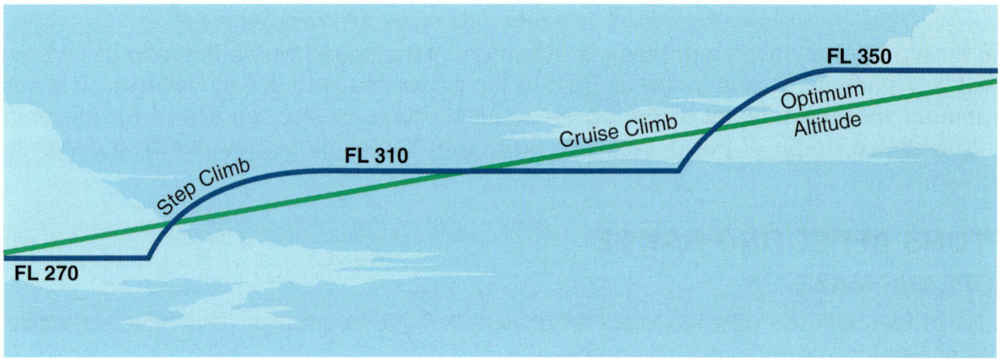

The above diagram shows both the cruise climb, which is at the optimum altitude, and the step climb. When a cruise climb is not permitted, a step climb should be centred about optimum altitude to minimise range loss.

WIND

Wind is the horizontal movement of the air in which the aeroplane is operating. The specific air range (SAR) is not affected by wind, because it depends on nm/kg of fuel or TAS/fuel flow. The specific ground range (SGR) is affected, because it depends on nm/kg fuel or groundspeed/fuel flow.

A headwind reduces the SGR, while a tailwind increases the SGR.

WIND AND TURBOJET SGR

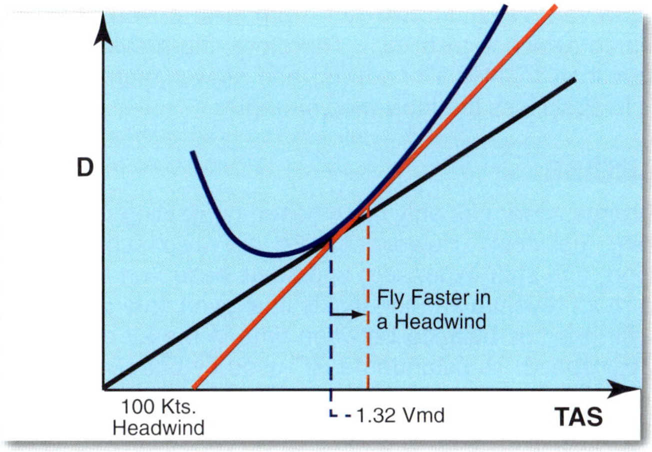

Maximum range for a jet is achieved at 1.32 V_{md}. However, the above graph shows that the best possible SGR does not occur at 1.32 V_{md} if there is a head or tailwind component. The tangent to the drag curve starts at the graph origin only for still air.

However, considering SGR with a headwind, the tangent starts to the right of the graph origin by the amount of the wind strength. The example above is for a 100 kt headwind. However, the tangent to the drag curve now occurs at a speed faster than 1.32 V_{md}, but the speed increment is less than the wind strength.

By flying at this slightly faster speed, the SGR is maximum for the given headwind conditions, although still less (worse) than in still air. This occurs because for every minute the aeroplane is in a headwind, the wind is pushing it backward. Therefore, the shorter the time exposed to the wind, the shorter the distance it is pushed back.

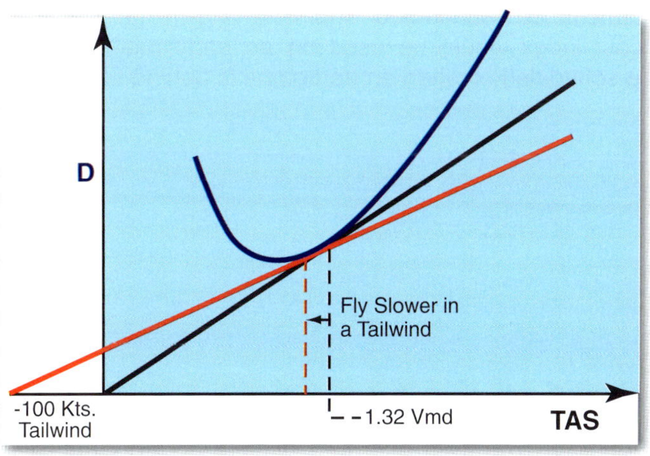

The speed for maximum SGR with a tailwind is found by the tangent to the drag curve, which starts to the left of the graph origin by the magnitude of the tailwind. A greater SGR is achieved at a speed slower than 1.32 V_{md} (the speed for maximum SAR). This is because a tailwind carries the aeroplane across the ground for free. The longer the aeroplane is exposed to a tailwind, the greater the distance carried without fuel burn.

The effect of wind on SGR can be summarised by the adage to get out of a headwind and stay in a tailwind.

WIND AND PROPELLER AEROPLANE SGR

As for the turbojet, it is beneficial to fly faster than the optimum SAR into a headwind and to slow down in a tailwind. However, maximum SAR for a propeller-driven aeroplane is at the tangent to the power required curve (which is also V_{md}). Therefore, the previous graph shows that the best possible SGR is faster than V_{md} for a headwind and slower than V_{md} in a tailwind. The speed increment/decrement is again less than the wind strength.

LONG-RANGE CRUISE

The consideration of range so far has only been based on gaining the maximum distance per unit of fuel (i.e. minimising fuel cost). However, there are also substantial fixed costs (such as aeroplane lease, airport, and staff expenses) and costs based on flying hours. Flying faster than range speed enables more revenue earning flights in a given time period and results in the airline making a greater profit. It is this balance between time in the air and fuel costs that results in a long-range cruise (LRC) speed. The standard LRC used by both Boeing and Airbus results in an airspeed (and corresponding Mach number) which is 4% faster. This reduces the range by 1%, which means that at LRC speed, the aeroplane covers 99% of the SAR. It is important to remember that LRC speed is faster than 1.32 V_{md}.

RANGE AND THE FMS

LRC is one of the profiles that can be selected through the aeroplane's flight management system (FMS). Another profile is ECON (economy), which provides a varying speed increase above range speed depending on the cost index. Cost index (the ratio of operating costs to fuel costs) is entered into the FMS initialisation pages. Because a route's earning potential is greater at different times of the day, an aeroplane can make more money by flying more high revenue sectors in these windows. To do this, the aeroplane flies at a faster TAS (and corresponding Mach number) within these high earning periods and flies closer to the SGR speed during lower revenue periods.

Cost indices range from 0 to 200; the higher the cost index, the faster the TAS above 1.32 V_{md} (and corresponding Mach number). A cost index of 0 means that the aeroplane flies at 1.32 V_{md}. This minimises fuel costs when the aeroplane is not required immediately for a further revenue earning sector or maintenance. Scheduled flights arriving in the late evening may use a cost index of 0. A high cost index would be used on an early morning sector when further high revenue flights can be scheduled or when an aeroplane is behind schedule.

PAYLOAD RANGE DIAGRAM

The payload range diagram is a planning tool for assessing payload on a particular sector. The greater the sector distance, the greater the fuel load required. At some point, the increase in required fuel affects the amount of revenue earning payload that can be loaded.

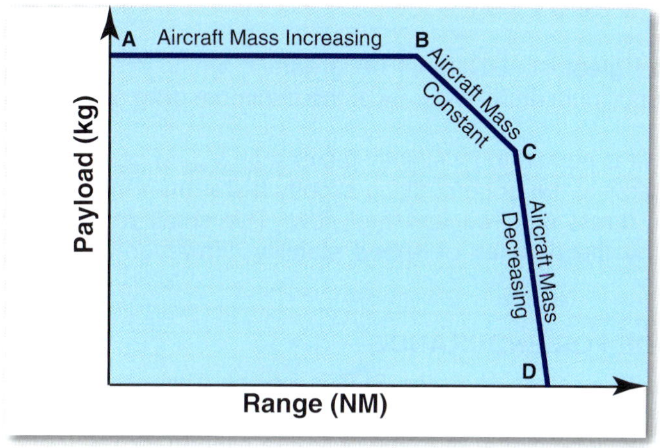

A payload range diagram is shown above. It is critical to understand that the vertical axis is payload and not aeroplane mass. The horizontal axis is aeroplane range.

The maximum payload that can be loaded without fuel is normally limited by the maximum zero fuel mass, although it could be limited by volume for a low-density payload. Therefore, A represents maximum payload, but the aeroplane has no range because it has no fuel. Range can only be achieved by loading fuel.

From A to B, the payload remains the same, but the range can increase if the fuel load is increased. The greater the fuel added to the constant payload, the greater the aeroplane mass.

At B; the aeroplane mass reaches the maximum take-off mass (MTOM). The only way to increase aeroplane range is to increase the fuel load by reducing the payload, since each kilogram of payload removed is replaced by one kilogram of fuel.

At C, the fuel tanks are full. The only way that range can be increased further is by reducing the payload. Aeroplane weight decreases between C and D.

The payload range diagram also highlights that payload is sometimes limited by the range required.

ENDURANCE

ENDURANCE FOR A TURBOJET

To fly straight and level for the longest possible time, fuel flow needs to be minimum. This is known as flying for endurance, and is used operationally for holding and when flying in a search area.

$$\text{Endurance} \propto \frac{1}{\text{Fuel Flow}} = \frac{1}{\text{SFC x Thrust}}$$

SPEED FOR MAXIMUM ENDURANCE IN A TURBOJET

Because thrust must equal drag in steady, straight-and-level flight, the above equation is rewritten to read:

$$\text{Endurance} \propto \frac{1}{\text{SFC} \times \text{drag}}$$

For endurance to be greatest, L/D must be greatest, which means drag must be minimum. Therefore, to fly for maximum endurance, fly at the minimum drag speed, V_{md}.

Practically, however, it is normal to fly slightly faster than V_{md} to gain speed stability. Because the drag curve is so shallow at the bottom, flying slightly faster than V_{md} results in only slightly more drag and, therefore, thrust required and fuel flow. The small reduction in endurance is then operationally offset by the benefits of speed stability. However, turbojet endurance is always maximum at V_{md}.

OPTIMUM ALTITUDE FOR ENDURANCE

In theory, endurance is greatest when the SFC is lowest. This occurs at high altitude. Since the drag and, hence, thrust required is less at V_{md} than at 1.32 V_{md}, the optimum altitude for endurance would actually be higher than the optimum altitude for range. Operationally, however, it is rare to be able to choose and maintain the optimum endurance altitude. This is because air traffic flow requirements necessitate aeroplanes moving down through a low altitude holding stack close to destination airports.

ENDURANCE FOR A PROPELLER-DRIVEN AEROPLANE

As for a turbojet, a propeller-driven aeroplane has maximum endurance when the fuel flow is minimum.

SPEED FOR MAXIMUM ENDURANCE

Fuel flow for a propeller-driven aeroplane in straight-and-level flight depends on SFC x power required, therefore:

$$\text{Endurance} \propto \frac{1}{\text{Fuel Flow}} = \frac{1}{\text{SFC x Power Required}}$$

For maximum endurance, 1/power required must be maximum. To achieve maximum endurance, fly at the minimum power required speed V_{mp} (which is 0.76 V_{md}).

However, because the aeroplane is speed unstable at V_{mp}, a propeller aeroplane normally holds at a speed faster than its best endurance speed.

OPTIMUM ALTITUDE FOR RANGE AND ENDURANCE IN A PROPELLER-DRIVEN AEROPLANE

The optimum altitude for range and endurance in a propeller-driven aeroplane varies depending on the engine type. Piston-engine aeroplanes generally have low optimum altitudes, while turboprops generally have medium optimum altitudes. This is because the propeller is more efficient at low altitude, but the jet engine is more efficient at high altitude.

FACTORS AFFECTING ENDURANCE

AEROPLANE MASS

A lighter aeroplane has less drag, less thrust required, and a reduced fuel flow. Therefore, a lighter aeroplane has greater endurance than a heavy aeroplane.

WIND

Wind does not affect endurance because the horizontal position of the aeroplane is irrelevant for endurance. In summary, a headwind reduces specific ground range (distance over the ground) but does not affect specific air range (distance through the air).

INTRODUCTION

The landing distance required is from the threshold to the point where the aeroplane comes to a complete stop. Like the take-off distance required, the landing distance required has an airborne section and a ground run section. This means that the aeroplane does not touch down at the threshold, but at a distance down the runway.

SPEED AND LANDING DISTANCE REQUIRED

The landing distance varies with factors such as airfield conditions, aeroplane weight, reverse thrust, and braking. These are discussed later in the chapter. This section looks at the speed at the threshold and the effect this has on landing distance.

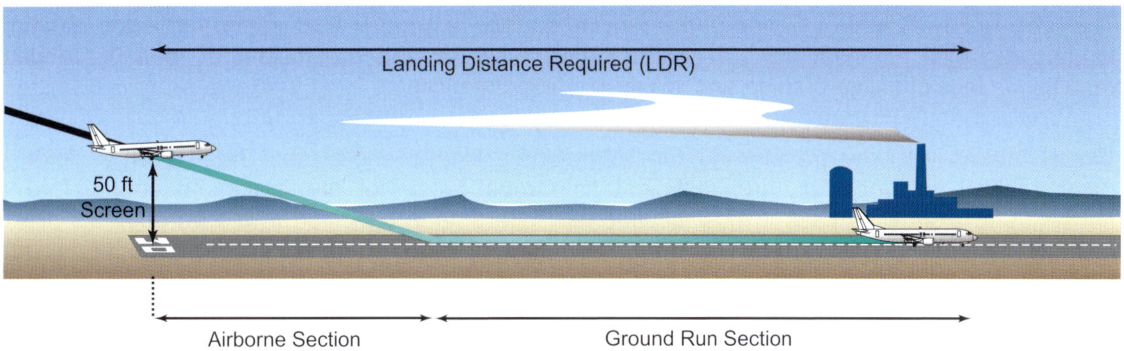

At the threshold, the lowest part of the aeroplane should just clear a screen 50 feet high. At this point, the aeroplane should be at the landing reference speed, which is V_{REF}. It is this combination of height and speed that results in large variations in landing distance required (LDR).

In the take-off chapter, it was noted that take-off distance was proportional to the square of the take-off speed. This means that a 10% increase in take-off speed increases the take-off distance by 20%. Similarly, a 10% increase in the speed at the screen results in a 20% increase in the landing distance. It is important to fly accurately on the final approach if large increases in landing distances are to be avoided.

The use of lift augmentation devices to allow slower approach speeds is, therefore, commercially vital if profitable landing weights are to be maintained on a given length runway. However, the approach must not be slower than V_{REF}, because it also provides a safety margin above the stall and the minimum control speed. V_{REF} must not be slower than the greater of minimum control speed in the landing configuration, V_{mcl}, and 1.3 times the stall speed in the landing configuration (V_{S0}). For class A aeroplanes with a stall reference speed in the landing configuration (V_{SR0}), V_{REF} must not be slower than the greater of V_{mcl} and 1.23 V_{SRO}.

A pilot must fly accurately on approach because speeds above V_{REF} and threshold heights in excess of the screen result in longer landing distances. Flying slower than V_{REF} gives insufficient margin above the stall.

FORCES DURING THE GROUND RUN

During the landing ground roll, the forces decelerating the aeroplane are braking, aerodynamic drag, and potentially reverse thrust.

BRAKE DRAG

It is actually the brakes which provide the majority of the deceleration on the landing run. It is essential that the brakes are as effective as possible. For this, it is important that the aeroplane's weight is fully on the wheels, rather than being partly balanced by lift, as early as possible on the ground run. This is achieved by using lift dumpers once the aeroplane has touched down.

Antiskid systems are very important for effective braking, particularly on damp to contaminated runways. It is recommended that a positive touchdown is made and braking is commenced immediately to ensure that landing distances do not become excessive. Provided the antiskid is operating, braking can commence above the hydroplaning speed, V_p, if the runway is contaminated. Normally, however, the pilot does not apply the brakes themselves but uses one of the three auto-brake settings (soft, medium, or hard). The auto brake system commences braking immediately as soon as there is weight on the wheels.

The braking co-efficient of friction of the runway surface is another very important factor affecting landing distance. On wet, icy, or contaminated runways, the co-efficient of friction reduces, resulting in less effective braking and longer landing distances.

Wheel brakes work by transferring the aeroplane's kinetic energy into heat energy. After a landing, they are very hot, and sufficient time must lapse for the brakes to cool before a subsequent take-off, in case it must be aborted. The time is specified in the aeroplane's brake cooling schedule and is varied with aeroplane weight, landing speed, airfield conditions, and whether reverse thrust is used.

REVERSE THRUST

Reverse thrust is the second most important retarding force during the landing run. It is much more effective on turbo-propeller aeroplanes than jet aeroplanes, when it typically only provides a 10% reduction in landing distance. Reverse thrust is most effective at high speeds and must be cancelled at low speeds to prevent debris ingestion. Many jet operators do not use reverse thrust on landing, which increases engine costs, preferring instead to increase brake wear. Reverse thrust, however, is especially important on icy or contaminated runways, where braking is less effective because of the runway's low coefficient of friction.

AERODYNAMIC DRAG

While airborne at slow speeds, the induced drag is high. Once the nose wheel touches, the induced drag becomes very small. It is parasite drag that dominates aerodynamic drag during the landing run. Flaps, slats, and undercarriage essential for the landing are also beneficial, providing more parasite drag at all speeds. However, because parasite drag is proportional to V^2, it provides less deceleration as the aeroplane's speed slows. Overall, aerodynamic drag is the least significant retarding force on the landing run because of the aeroplane's slow speed.

FACTORS AFFECTING THE LANDING DISTANCE

AEROPLANE MASS

Landing distance increases as aeroplane mass increases. This is because the aeroplane touches down faster and has slower deceleration.

The landing speed is faster because the speed at the threshold, V_{REF}, must have a safety margin above the stall speed. Since a heavier aeroplane has a faster stall speed, the speed at which the aeroplane first touches increases. The above section stated that a 10% increase in landing speed results in a 20% increase in landing distance. However, once landed, the heavier aeroplane has a smaller deceleration because of its larger mass. Newton's second law of motion, F = ma, states that the deceleration depends on the decelerating force divided by the mass. The deceleration must be less as the decelerating force is constant and the mass has increased.

Alternatively, consider the amount of kinetic energy of the aeroplane at touchdown. Since kinetic energy is $\frac{1}{2}mV^2$, the increase in mass has a twofold effect on the kinetic energy; directly on the mass and indirectly on the speed (V) at touchdown.

AIR DENSITY

Air density affects the actual TAS for the same CAS. V_{REF} is a calibrated airspeed that is related to dynamic pressure. If the air density reduces, such as at hot or high altitude airfields, the same CAS is actually achieved at a faster TAS. The real speed of the aeroplane at touchdown is faster and the landing distance required is longer.

It is worth noting that air density has a greater effect on take-off distance required than on landing distance required. This is because of the need for much higher take-off thrust settings. Low air density reduces the thrust available, which compounds the need to reach a faster TAS for the same calibrated rotate speed.

WIND

For the same calibrated touchdown speed, the actual groundspeed that an aeroplane touches down at is affected by wind.

A tailwind increases the touchdown groundspeed and increases the landing distance required. A headwind reduces the groundspeed and landing distance required. However, because wind is never constant, all wind components must be factored to allow for a lull in a headwind and gust in a tailwind.

Regulations require that only 50% of a headwind component is used and 150% of a tailwind component. There is no allowance made for the change in wind direction and a cross wind has no safety margin.

RUNWAY SURFACE

Brake effectiveness depends on the braking co-efficient of friction. Operating from wet runways is very common. Allow for its effect on landing distance. JAR-Ops requires that 115% of dry landing distance required be used for the wet landing distance if the operating manual does not include an allowance for a wet runway.

SLOPE

On a sloping runway, weight has a component parallel to the landing direction. A downslope increases landing distance required, while an upslope reduces landing distance required. However, because the effect of slope is small, JAR 25 requires that slopes less than 2% to be ignored for landing distance required calculation. However, allow for the detrimental effect of downslope in Class B landing distance calculations.

SAFETY FACTORS FOR PUBLIC TRANSPORT

Due to the wide variation in landing distances for the same conditions, public transport flights are required to apply safety factors to the gross landing distance required. These safety factors are also recommended for private flights.

The gross landing distance required for jet aeroplanes must not exceed 60% of the landing distance available. This means that the gross or **demonstrated** landing distance required must be multiplied by 1/0.6 = 1.67. This means that on average, you should complete your landing with almost half (40%) of the runway ahead of you. If you find this is not the case, you should reassess your landing technique!

The safety factor for Class A turboprops and Class B aeroplanes is slightly smaller. The gross landing distance required for propeller aeroplanes must not exceed 70% of the landing distance available. This means that the gross or demonstrated landing distance required must be multiplied by 1/0.7 = 1.43.

These public transport safety factors are in addition and cumulative to others such as for a wet runway. Therefore, if the demonstrated or gross landing distance required for a jet on a dry runway is 2000 m, the minimum landing distance that must be available is:

2000 m x 1.67 x 1.15 = 2000 m x 1.92 = 3840 m

Conversely, for a propeller aeroplane on a dry runway, if the LDA is 1800 m, the gross LDR would be:

1800 m x 0.7 = 1260 m

These landing factors are often examined in the JAR Performance paper.

Chapter 10
Class A Take-Off

INTRODUCTION

Not all performance classes allow for an engine failure during the take-off run. Class B aeroplanes do not have the power to continue and climb away after suffering an engine failure on the runway or having just left the ground. Class A aeroplanes, however, must have safe provision to either reject the take-off or continue with one engine failed at any speed on the take-off run. This ability to either safely stop or go at any point during take-off underpins this chapter.

CLASS A TAKE-OFF

ASDA AND V_{STOP}

If rejecting a take-off on the take-off run, the aeroplane must be able to come to a stop within the acceleration stop distance available (ASDA). The length of the runway plus stopway influences the fastest speed from which it is possible to stop, which is known as V_{STOP}.

V_{STOP} is faster when the ASDA is longer, but for a given ASDA, the issue is how heavy can the aeroplane be? A very light aeroplane accelerates more quickly and achieves faster speeds within the same distance. A very light aeroplane is also able to decelerate more rapidly after a decision to reject a take-off. V_{STOP} is faster for a light aeroplane than a heavier aeroplane.

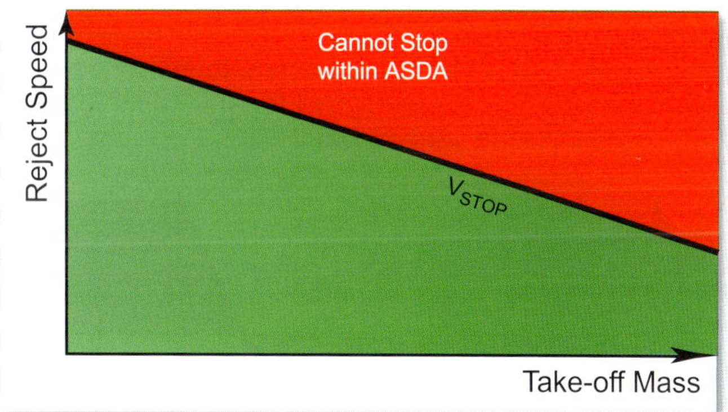

The graph shows V_{STOP} against take-off mass. At light take-off masses, V_{STOP} is fast, but at heavier take-off masses, V_{STOP} is slower. To be able to stop safely within the ASDA, reject the take-off at V_{STOP} or at a speed slower than V_{STOP}. This is shown by the green shaded area. Remember V_{STOP} is the fastest speed from which a take-off can be safely rejected. The slower the speed at which the decision is made to reject a take-off, the greater amount of ASDA ahead that will not have to be used.

The area shaded red shows speeds for particular take-off masses, from which it would not be possible to stop within the ASDA, a situation not allowed for Class A public transport operations.

TODA AND V_{GO}

V_{GO} is the slowest speed from which a take-off can be continued having just suffered an engine failure. For a given take-off distance available (TODA), V_{GO} varies with aeroplane mass.

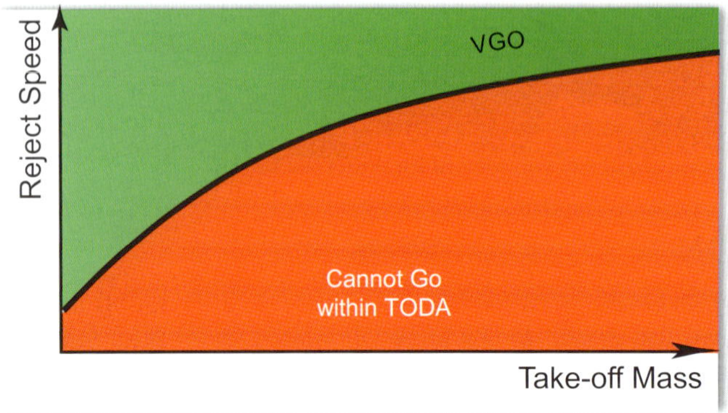

Looking at the graph above, the slowest speed from which the take-off can be safely continued, V_{GO}, increases as aeroplane mass increases. The faster above V_{GO} the aeroplane is when an engine fails, the greater the unused TODA. The take-off should be safe if the engine fails at V_{GO} or faster and the take-off is continued. This is shown by the area shaded green in the graph. However, if the aeroplane suffered an engine failure and the pilot decided to continue at speeds slower than V_{GO}, shown by the red shaded area, sufficient TODA would not be available.

DECISION SPEED — V_1

V_1 is the speed from which an aeroplane can both:

- Safely stop within the acceleration stop distance available, and
- Safely go within the take-off distance available.

At first glance, V_1 looks like the best speed for an engine to fail, since there is the ability to both stop and go. However, V_1 is actually the worst speed for an engine to fail. Although it is possible to both stop and go at V_1, the aeroplane uses all the distance available in either case.

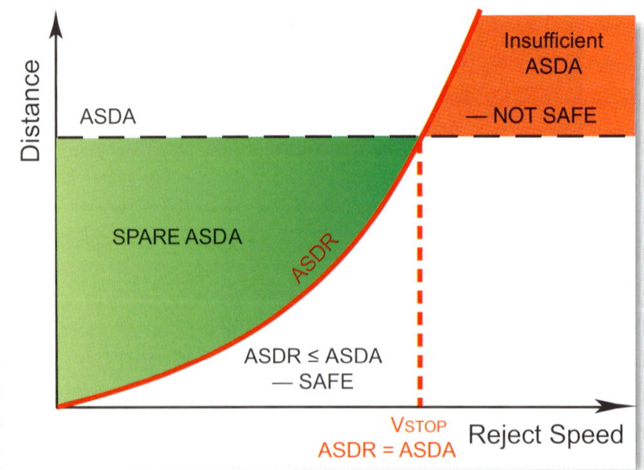

The above graph shows the effect of the actual reject speed on the acceleration stop distance required for a given aeroplane mass. The faster the speed on the take-off run at which the engine or other significant system fails, the longer the ASDR.

V_1 is the speed at which the ASDR equals the ASDA and is the fastest speed from which the aeroplane can abort the take-off within the acceleration stop distance available on an average day.

It is now possible to see that the slower the engine failure below V_1, the shorter the ASDR and the greater the spare distance ahead.

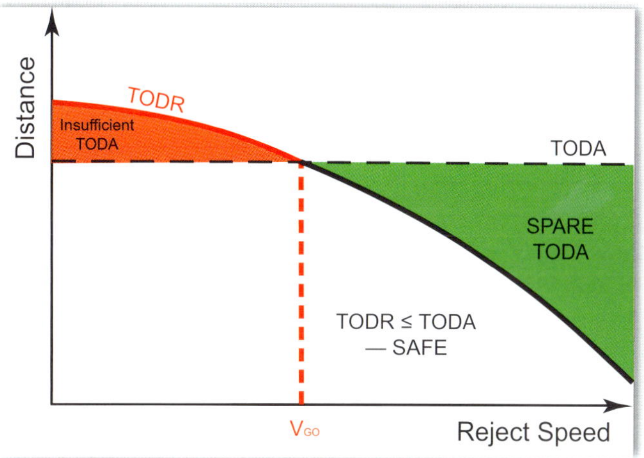

The above graph shows the go situation following an engine failure. The slower the actual speed at which the engine fails, the greater the time accelerating with one less engine and the longer the TODR is. At engine failure speeds slower than V_1, the TODR would be longer than the TODA, which is normally not acceptable.

At V_1, the TODR equals the TODA, and there is no spare distance available. However, as the speed of engine failure increases above V_1, the TODR reduces, and there is more spare distance available. This is because the aeroplane accelerates on all engines for a longer time.

THE GO OR STOP DECISION

A pilot may reject a take-off due to an engine or other major system failure. It is the engine failure situation that affects the ability to go due to the large reduction in excess thrust. However, both the engine failure and all engine operating (with other major system failure) situations must be allowed for in the stop case.

If an engine fails on the take-off run before V_1, the take-off must be rejected. An engine failure recognised after V_1 means that take-off must be continued. Obviously, a pilot does not fly an aeroplane with a major problem to its original destination. Instead, the pilot climbs and positions for an approach at the same airport, jettisoning fuel if practical and necessary.

The **decision** occurs if the pilot recognises the failure at V_1. It is only at this speed that the pilot can decide to continue or abort, and the decision must be made rapidly.

THE FIELD LENGTH LIMITED TAKE-OFF MASS

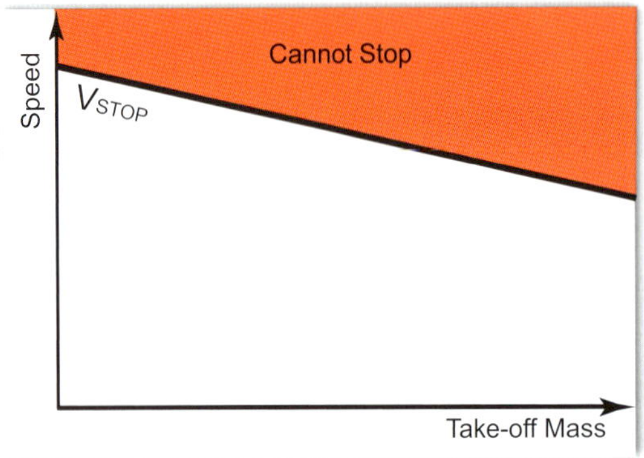

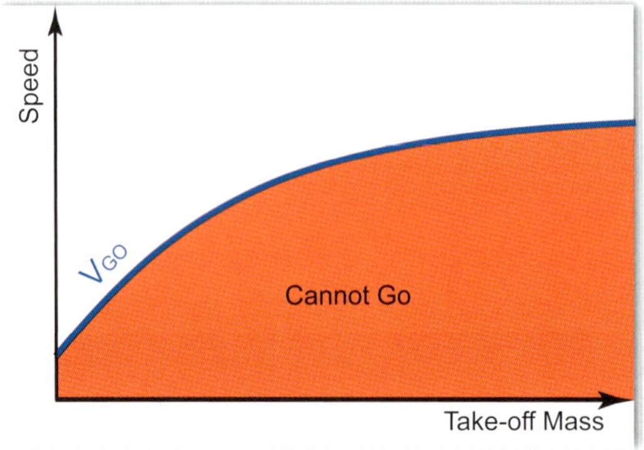

The above graphs show that V_{STOP} and V_{GO} vary with take-off mass for a given length runway. The graph below combines the above two graphs.

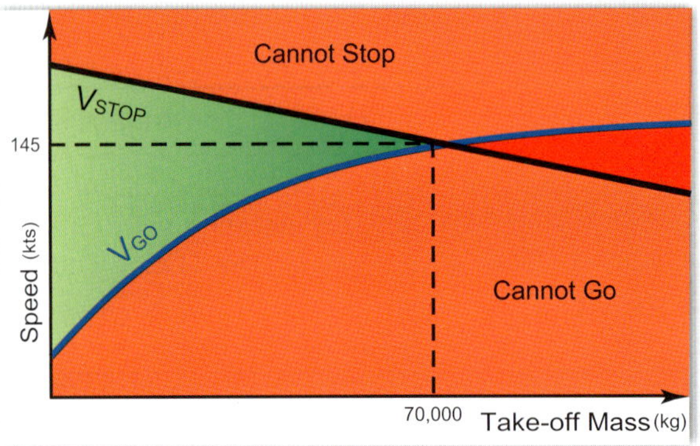

Looking at the graph, the V_{STOP} and V_{GO} lines intersect at a take-off mass of 70 000 kg. On this runway, under these conditions, and at this mass, V_{STOP} and V_{GO} equal V_1. If the failure is recognised at the V_1 of 145 kt, there would be no spare distance available whether the decision was to go or stop. The aeroplane is field length limited, and 70 000 kg is the **field length limiting take-off mass (FLTOM)**.

RANGE OF V_1

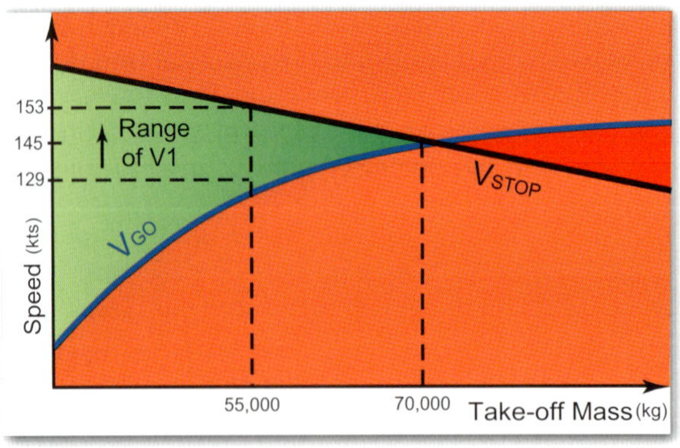

At take-off masses lighter than the FLTOM of 70 000 kg, a range of speeds is opening up at which the aeroplane could either stop or go.

At a take-off mass of 55 000 kg, the take-off could continue from a speed of 129 kt and stop from any speed up to and including 153 kt. There is a range of speeds (129 to 153 kt) from which it would be safe to both go and stop.

However, if a failure did occur between V_{GO} and V_{STOP}, it is not the place or time for a debate whether to continue or reject the take-off. A V_1, which is between V_{GO} and V_{STOP}, is specified before the take-off. The pilot rejects the take-off if a significant failure occurs before this V_1 speed and continues thereafter.

In summary, whenever an aeroplane commences a take-off which is not field length limited, a V_1 is used which is within a range of possible V_1s. The pilot is normally not aware of the actual V_{GO} and V_{STOP} speeds, although usually aware that a range exists.

RESTRICTION OF V_1

The following pages look at what can restrict V_1, particularly when the aeroplane is not field length limited, and there is a large speed range between V_{GO} and V_{STOP}.

V_1 AND V_R

For a take-off mass which is not field length limited, the most common limitation on a V_1 is V_R, the speed at which rotation is initiated.

At V_R, the pilot has made the decision to go and has commenced rotation; a stop decision is now invalid. When V_{STOP} is faster than V_R, the chosen V_1 cannot exceed V_R. In this case, it is normal that the chosen V_1 is equal or slightly slower than V_R.

V_1 cannot exceed V_R, or $V_1 \leq V_R$

V_1 AND V_{MBE}

V_{MBE} is the maximum brake energy speed. It is the fastest speed at which the brakes can convert all of the aeroplane's kinetic energy into heat and not fade. An aeroplane's kinetic energy depends on its mass and groundspeed at V_1. The heavier the aeroplane, the slower V_{MBE} is. However, for a given mass, the maximum groundspeed is also at different calibrated V_{MBE} speeds as the air density and wind change. V_{MBE} is slowest and most likely to limit V_1 when the aeroplane is heavy, the aerodrome is at high pressure altitude and hot, and there is a tailwind component. Since the aeroplane must be able to stop from V_1:

V_1 must not exceed V_{MBE}, or $V_1 \leq V_{MBE}$

V_1 AND V_{MCG}

At the slow end of a V_1 range is the requirement that the pilot must have directional control to continue accelerating along the runway and take-off.

After an engine failure in a multi-engine aeroplane, there is asymmetric thrust from the remaining working engines. The size of the thrust from the working engines and, therefore, yawing tendency vary with the air density. In cold, low airfield conditions, the thrust is greatest and, therefore, the yawing moment is greatest.

To stop the yaw, the pilot uses rudder, which must produce a sideways aerodynamic force of sufficient magnitude. With the rudder at full deflection, the size of this rudder lift force varies only with CAS. The slowest CAS at which a sufficient sideways force is created is V_{MCG}. At speeds slower than V_{MCG}, the rudder is not able to stop the yaw. The throttles must be closed and the take-off rejected. This means that to be able to go from V_1:

V_1 must be faster than V_{MCG}, or $V_{MCG} \leq V_1$

SAFE PREFERENCE FOR V_1

The speed of V_1 determines the speed up to which the take-off is rejected. It is generally preferable to delay the "must go" situation for as long as possible by using a fast V_1. This is because a rejected take-off, ending with the aeroplane safely on the ground, is normally the safest option.

When an aeroplane is not field length limited, a range of V_1s exist. Because remaining on the ground is normally safest, it is typical to see a fast chosen V_1, which is often equal to V_R. This is definitely the case when take-off mass is limited by a climb or obstacle requirement, making the "go" situation definitely more hazardous than the "abort".

However, the potential problem with rejecting take-off at high speeds is that the aeroplane may veer off the runway or perform badly using more than the planned average acceleration stop distance. At most aerodromes, this is not a major problem, since the area to the sides and end of the runways is not hazardous. However, there are runways that extend into water, where a high-speed abort is not the preferred option. On these runways, a V_1 at the slow end of an available range is safest. This commits the pilot to taking off following an engine failure at a slower speed rather than risking a higher speed abort.

V SPEEDS DURING TAKE-OFF

During the take-off run and initial climb, there are a number of important calibrated V speeds. The non-flying pilot calls some of them, while others specify the speed of an event, which may or may not have safety margins relating to other speeds.

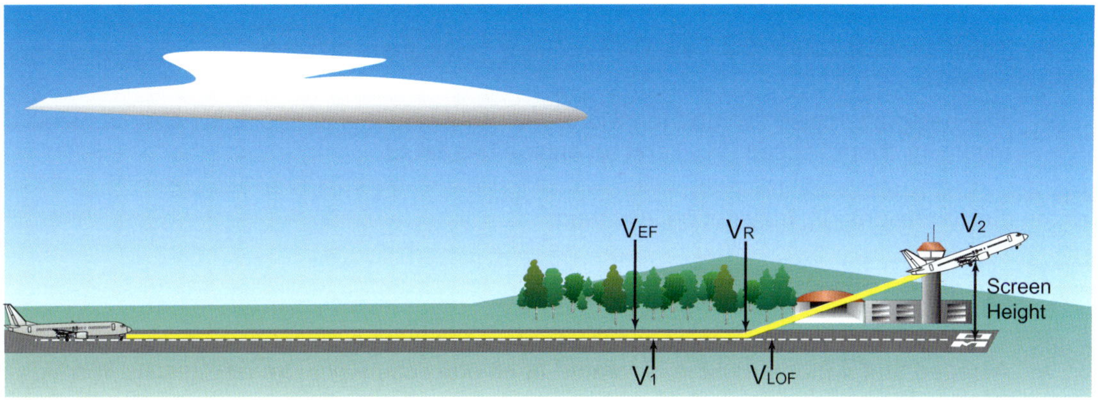

The above diagram shows the important speeds during take-off. The slowest speed is the speed at which the pilot transfers from tiller steering to aerodynamic controls. Although this speed is well below V_{MCG}, the pilot has directional control because all engines are operating, giving symmetrical thrust. It could be, for example, 60 kt.

The next called speed is V_1. Once V_1 has been called, the pilots know that they will continue the take-off should an engine fail or not. However, should the stop/go decision need to be made at exactly V_1, the corresponding actual speed of the engine failure (V_{EF}) must be just before V_1. This means that V_1 is always faster that V_{EF}.

It is important to note that V_{EF} is not any speed at which an engine or other major problem could occur. It is the speed at which an engine or other major problem would have to occur to be recognised at V_1. V_{EF} is, therefore, always just a little slower than V_1. It is normal to talk about "an engine failing at V_1", rather than the completely correct and longer statement "an engine fails at the V_{EF} corresponding to V_1".

The final called speed is V_R, the rotate speed. However, because the nose is raised progressively, the aeroplane does not leave the ground until a higher speed, V_{LOF} (the speed at which the aeroplane lifts off). If the aeroplane is not field length limited, it is possible that the V_1 and V_R speeds are the same.

When the aeroplane just clears the screen height (normally 35 ft for Class A aeroplanes), the take-off is considered complete. At this point, the aeroplane should be no slower than V_2, having suffered an engine failure at V_1.

In summary, the important speeds during take-off, in ascending order are:

$$V_{EF} < V_1 \leq V_R < V_{LOF} < V_2$$

V_R RESTRICTIONS (JAR 25.107)

It has already been stated that V_R cannot be slower than V_1. Having initiated rotation at V_R, the pilot cannot decide to reject the take-off. In addition, V_R is the speed at which the aeroplane begins the process of becoming airborne. If an aeroplane's CAS reduced just after take-off, this could be fatal, because:

- The aeroplane could stall if the CAS reduces below the stall speed, or

- The aeroplane could fly into the ground with no directional control if the CAS is below the minimum control speed (V_{MC}) and an engine has failed.

For the above reasons, V_R may not be less than:

- V_1
- 105% of V_{MC}
- The speed that allows V_2 to be reached before reaching a height of 35 ft, or
- A speed that if the aeroplane is rotated at its practical maximum rate results in a V_{LOF} of not less than:
    - 110% of V_{MU} (a stall speed) with all engines working and 105% of V_{MU} with one engine inoperative, or
    - 108% of V_{MU} with all engines working and 104% of V_{MU} with one engine inoperative.

This gives V_R a safety margin of at least 5% above V_{MC} and approaching 10% above the stall. However, before continuing further, understand V_{MC} and V_{MU}.

MINIMUM CONTROL SPEED — V_{MC}

V_{MC} is the lowest CAS at which, when the critical engine is suddenly made inoperative, it is possible to maintain directional control and straight flight with an angle of bank of not more than 5°.

The operating engine(s) cause the asymmetric thrust and the directional control (yawing) problem. The size of the yawing moment varies with engine thrust and air density. The engine thrust and, therefore, the yawing moment, are greatest when the air is dense. The pilot prevents the yaw by applying rudder. Once full rudder has been applied, the sideways lift force from the rudder can only be increased by increasing the CAS. The minimum CAS at which directional control can be maintained is V_{MC}.

Because asymmetrical thrust from the remaining engine(s) causes the yaw, the yawing moment is greatest at cold, low-altitude airports. V_{MC} is fastest at low, cold airports and decreases with decreasing air density.

MINIMUM UNSTICK SPEED — V_{MU}

V_{MU} is the lowest CAS at which an aeroplane can safely lift off the ground and continue the take-off climb without undue hazard. Therefore, V_{MU} is related to the stall speed out of ground effect. However, it differs from other stall speeds because V_{MU} does vary with air density. This is because at high angles of attack, the vertical component of thrust is significant and reduces the lift required from the wings. In high density situations (low, cold aerodromes), thrust and the vertical component of thrust increase, which means that reduced required lift can be achieved at a slower CAS. Therefore, V_{MU} reduces as air density increases.

V_R AND AIR DENSITY

V_R is a CAS and should not vary with changes in air density. However, because V_R may not be less than the specified percentages above V_{MC} and V_{MU}, it is affected by air density.

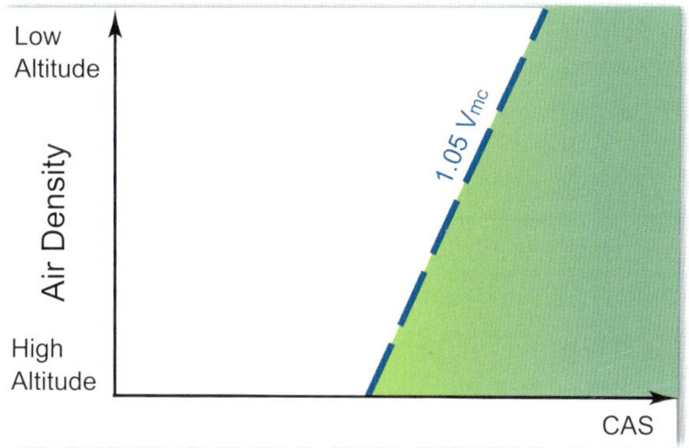

The graph above shows the minimum value of V_R with air density. The dashed blue line is 1.05 $V_{MC,}$ which increases as air density increases. To be safely above the minimum control speed, the CAS must be on this dashed blue line or to the right of it in the green area.

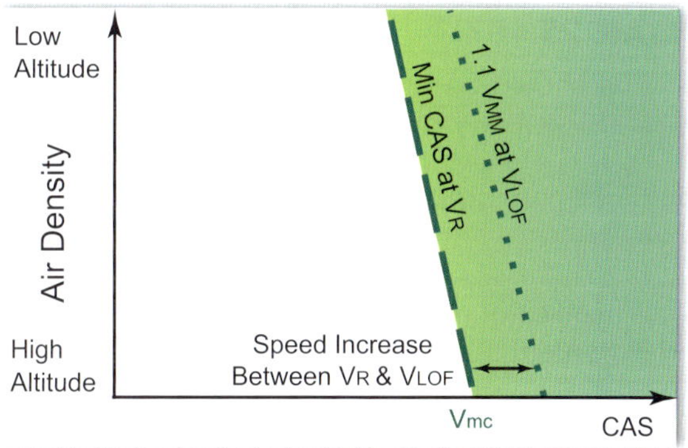

This graph shows a dotted line which is 1.1 V_{MU} (the all engine requirement), but at V_{LOF} not V_R. Assuming the maximum practical rate of rotation, which gives the smallest speed increment between V_R and V_{LOF}, the dashed line shows the minimum speed at V_R, which results in 1.1 V_{MU} at V_{LOF}. To be sufficiently above the stall, the aeroplane must be on the dashed line or in the green area to the right of the line.

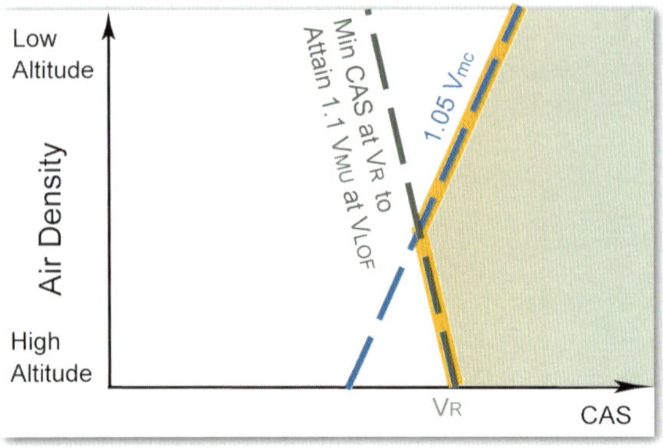

The above graph combines the previous two graphs to show the effect of air density on V_R. To be sufficiently above both V_{MC} and the stall, V_R must be on the highlighted line or to its right in the tinted area.

Summarising this graph in words:

- At cold, low altitude (high air density) airports, V_{MC} limits V_R, while
- At hot, high altitude (low air density) airports, V_{MU} limits V_R.

V_2 RESTRICTIONS (JAR 25.107)

V_2 is the minimum speed that should be achieved at a height of 35 ft, having suffered a critical engine failure at V_1.

V_2 must provide a specified minimum gradient of climb with an engine having failed at V_1 and may not be less than:

- V_{2MIN} (which allows a sufficient margin above V_{MC} and the stall), and
- V_R plus the speed increment attained between V_{LOF} and 35 ft.

However, even with the critical engine out, the acceleration is normally large enough that V_2 is faster than V_{2MIN}.

V_{2MIN}

V_{2MIN} may not be less than:

- 1.1 V_{MC}, and
- 1.13 V_{SR} (except for 4-engine turbo-propeller aeroplanes and some jets where the margin is reduced to 1.08 V_{SR}).

This gives V_{2MIN} a safety margin of at least 10% above V_{MC} and approaching 13% above the reference stall speed.

V_{2MIN} AND AIR DENSITY

Like V_R, V_{2MIN} varies with air density. This time, however, the stall speed V_{SR} is not affected by air density, although V_{MC} is affected.

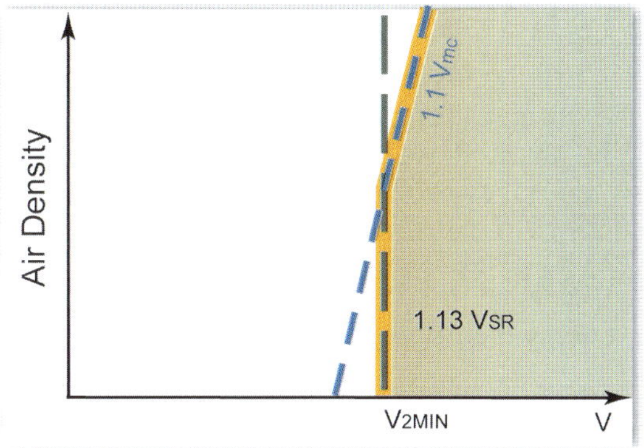

The dashed blue line on the above graph is 1.1 V_{MC}. To be at least 10% above the minimum control speed, the airspeed must be on this line or to its right.

The dashed green line is 1.13 V_{SR}. This line is vertical because the CAS stall speed does not vary with air density. To be at least 13% above the stall reference speed, the airspeed must be on this green line or to its right.

To be sufficiently above both the minimum control speed and the stall reference speed, V_{2MIN} must be on the highlighted line or to the right.

As for V_R, V_{2MIN} is likely to be limited by:

- V_{MC} in high air density conditions (cold, low altitude airports)
- V_{SR} in low air density conditions (hot, high altitude airports)

EFFECT OF FLAPS AND AEROPLANE WEIGHT ON V_R AND V_{2MIN}

Extending flaps or reducing aeroplane weight decreases the stall reference speed. The effect of this is shown in the graph below for V_{2MIN}.

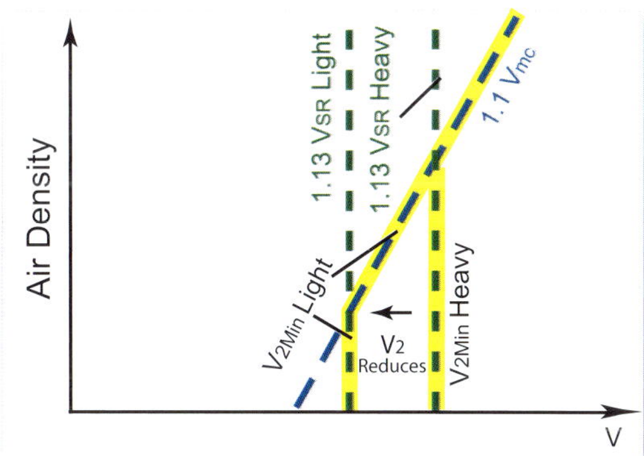

The reduction in V_{SR} results in:

- V_{2MIN} reducing at aerodromes with lower air density
- V_{MC} determining V_{2MIN} in more situations

To summarise, both V_R and V_{2MIN} are more likely to be limited by V_{MC} when:

- The ambient temperature is cold
- The aerodrome is at low pressure altitude
- The flaps are at a higher setting
- The aeroplane is lighter

AERODROME DISTANCES

An operator makes money from carrying payload. The greater the payload and, therefore, aeroplane take-off mass, the greater the profit. However, structural or performance requirements may limit take-off mass. The take-off weight must be restricted to ensure that the distances required, as defined by JAR, do not exceed the distances available.

TAKE-OFF DISTANCE (JAR 25.113)

Take-off distance on a dry runway is the greater of:

- 115% of the horizontal distance along the take-off path with all engines operating from the start of the take-off to the point at which the aeroplane is 35 ft above the take-off surface (shown in green in the diagram below).

- The horizontal distance along the take-off path from the start of the take-off to the point at which the aeroplane is 35 ft above the take-off surface for a dry runway, assuming the critical aeroplane fails at V_{EF} (shown in red in the diagram below), or

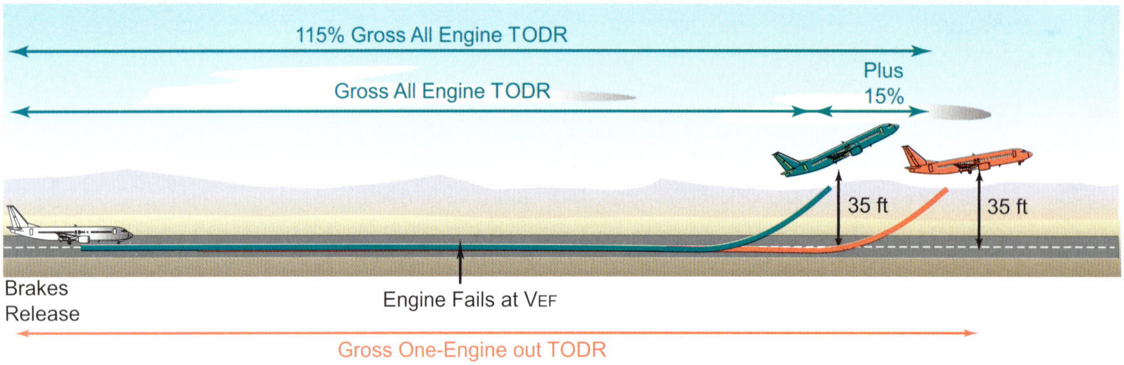

This means that there is a safety factor of only 15% for the all engine take-off distance requirement. There is no safety factor for the engine failing at the worst possible time, which is V_{EF} corresponding to V_1. This is because the probability of engine failure during the take-off run is already below the minimum statistical level of safety required.

The minimum TODA is the greater of:

- 1.15 times the all engine TODR, and
- The gross one engine out TODR.

In the above diagram, the minimum TODA would have needed to equal the gross one engine out TODR. In the JAR exam, this is often examined practically.

Example: If the all engine TODR is 3000 m and the one engine out TODR is 3400 m, what is the minimum take-off distance that must be available?

The answer is the greater of:

1.15 x 3000 m = 3450 m and 3400 m, which is 3450 m

It is worth noting, however, that if the one engine out case had been 3600 m, this would have been the minimum take-off distance available. However, because the take-off distance required is slightly longer on a wet runway, there is a separate JAR requirement for TODA on a wet runway.

Take-off distance on a wet runway is the greater of:

- 115% of the horizontal distance along the take-off path with all engines operating from the start of the take-off to the point at which the aeroplane is 35 ft above the take-off surface (shown in green in the diagram below).

- The horizontal distance along the take-off path from the start of the take-off to the point at which the aeroplane is 15 ft above the take-off surface for a wet runway, assuming the critical engine fails at V_{EF} (shown in red in the diagram below) or

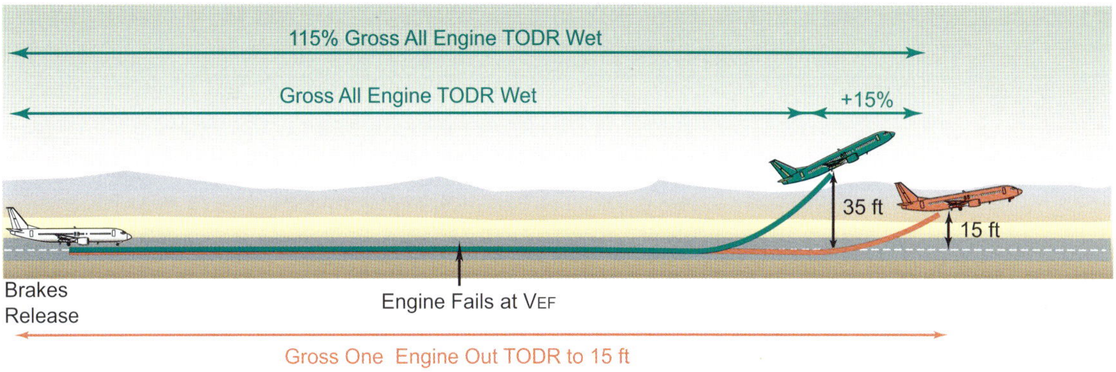

Compared to the dry runway requirement, the wet runway safety margin remains for the frequently-occurring all engine situation but degraded in the one engine out case. It is significant to note that V_{1wet} is a slower speed than V_1. The reduction to V_{1wet} from V_1 allows for the degraded braking performance on the wet runway in the rejected take-off case. However, if an engine fails at V_1, and the decision is to go, the aeroplane is only at a height of 15 ft by the end of TODA. This would be an inadvisable situation if the take-off were obstacle limited, because the minimum obstacle clearance is now reduced from 35 ft to 15 ft.

TAKE-OFF RUN (JAR 25.113)

The take-off run on a dry runway is the greater of:

- 115% of the horizontal distance along the take-off path from the start of the take-off to the point equidistant between V_{LOF} and where the aeroplane is 35 ft above the take-off surface with all engines operating (shown in green in the diagram below).

- The horizontal distance along the take-off path from the start of the take-off to the point equidistant between V_{LOF} and where the aeroplane is 35 ft above the take-off surface with an engine having failed at V_{EF} (shown in red in the diagram below) or

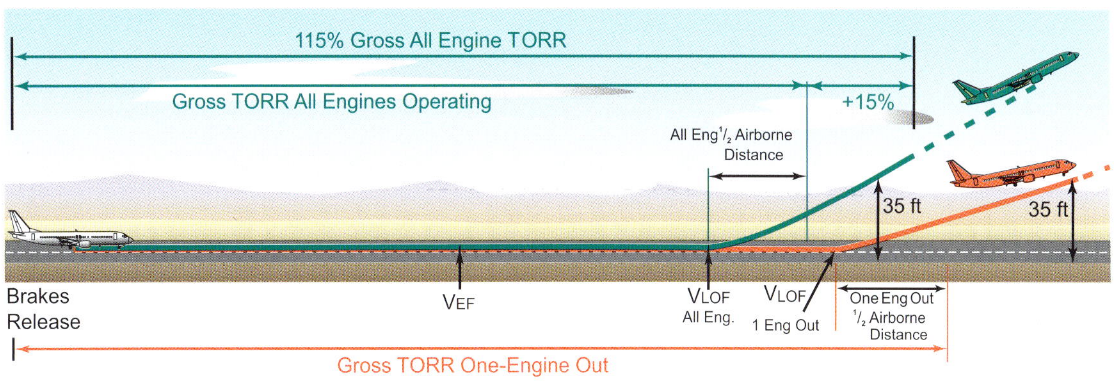

The take-off run on a wet runway is the greater of:

- 115% of the horizontal distance along the take-off path with all engines operating from the start of the take-off to a point equidistant between the point at which V_{LOF} is reached and the point at which the aeroplane is 35 ft above the take-off surface (shown in green in the diagram below).

- The horizontal distance along the take-off path from the start of the take-off to the point at which the aeroplane lifts off, with the critical engine failing at V_{EF} (shown in red in the diagram below), or

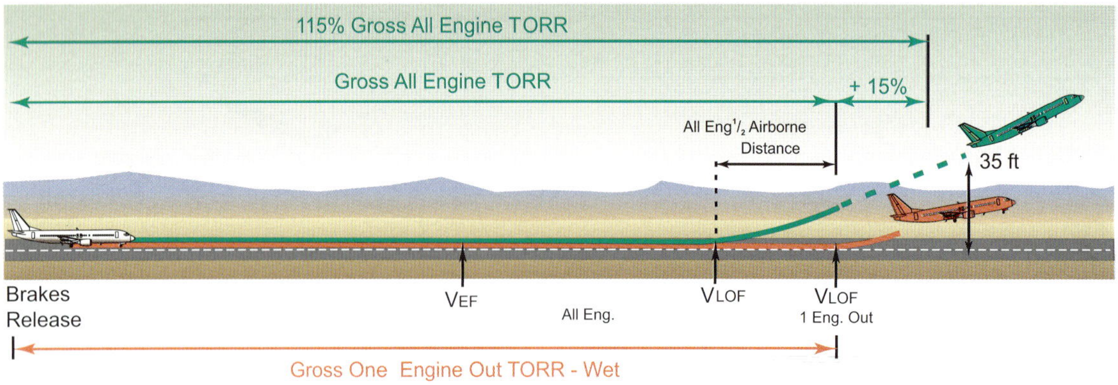

As in the take-off distance requirements, there is a gross to net safety margin of 15% for the all engine case but no safety margin for the extremely remote engine out case. The JAR exam again has calculation questions asking for the minimum TORA. Calculate these in the same way as minimum TODA.

Example: What is the minimum take-off run that must be available if the all engine TORR is 2000 m, and the one engine out TORR is 2400 m?

The answer is the greater of:

2000 m x 1.15 = 2300 m and 2400 m, this is 2400 m.

ACCELERATE-STOP DISTANCE (JAR 25.109)

The accelerate-stop distance on a dry runway is the greater of the following distances:

The sum of the distances necessary to:

i. Accelerate the aeroplane from a standing start with all engines operating to V_{EF} for take-off from a dry runway

ii. Allow the aeroplane to accelerate from V_{EF} to the highest speed reached during the rejected take-off, assuming the critical engine fails at $V_{EF,}$ and the pilot takes the first action to reject the take-off at the V_1 from a dry runway

iii. Come to a full stop on a dry runway from the speed reached as prescribed in sub-paragraph (ii) of this paragraph plus

iv. A distance equivalent to 2 seconds at the V_1 for take-off from a dry runway

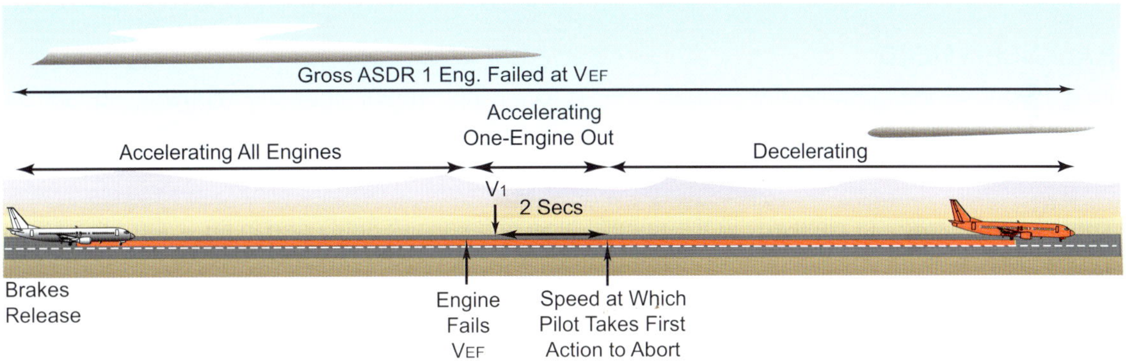

The sum of the distances necessary to:

i. Accelerate the aeroplane from a standing start with all engines operating to the highest speed reached during the rejected take-off, assuming the pilot takes the first action to reject the take-off at the V_1 for take-off from a dry runway; and

ii. With all engines still operating, come to a full stop on a dry runway; plus

iii. A distance equivalent to 2 seconds at the V_1 for take-off from a dry runway.

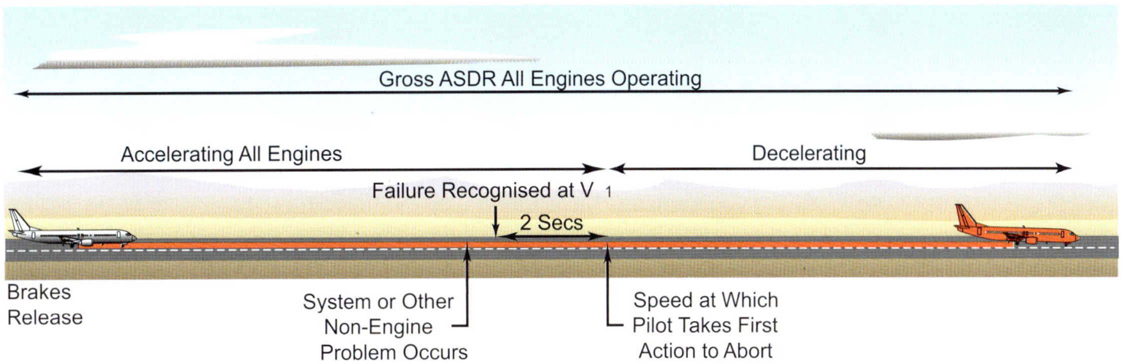

This minimum acceleration stop distance, which must be available, allows for an abort with all engines working and with one engine out. This distance considers only gross performance. There is no safety factor because the probability of a rejected take-off at V_{EF} is less than remote.

The accelerate-stop distance on a wet runway (JAR 25.109) is the same definition as for a dry runway but with allowance for the wet surface. It still allows for the abort with all engines operating or one engine out and is again based on gross distance.

FIELD LENGTH LIMITED TAKE-OFF MASS (FLTOM)

The field length limited take-off mass is the heaviest that the aeroplane can be in the aerodrome conditions to comply with all six distance requirements above for either a dry or wet runway as appropriate. The six requirements are ASDR, TODR, and TODA with all engines working and one engine failed. If the ASDA, TODA, and TORA were of different lengths, this would take a number of graphs and a length of time.

A simpler and quicker method of finding a field length limiting mass relies on a special sort of balanced field.

BALANCED FIELD

In a balanced field, the ASDA equals the TODA. This means that the stopway equals the clearway. Since the clearway is normally longer than the stopway, some of the clearway is ignored for a balanced field, which may restrict the maximum take-off weight.

There is no stopway or clearway in the special type of balanced field used in fig. 4.4 for the MRJT in CAP 698. This means that the field length referred to is TORA, which equals ASDA and TODA. This further restricts the field length take-off mass but simplifies and quickens the determination of the mass.

DETERMINING THE FIELD LENGTH LIMITING TAKE-OFF MASS – FIG. 4.4

Before using fig. 4.4 to determine the balanced field take-off mass, understand how to use the graphs.

RULES FOR USING GRAPHS

Always move vertically or horizontally in graphs, except when between a reference line and a value when moving in proportion with the guidelines. In fig. 4.4 below, the example line has been changed to green when it is horizontal or vertical. Between each reference line and example value, it has been changed to a red line, which moves at an angle to the gridlines in proportion to the guidelines.

Figure 4.4 Take Off Performance Field Limit Graph

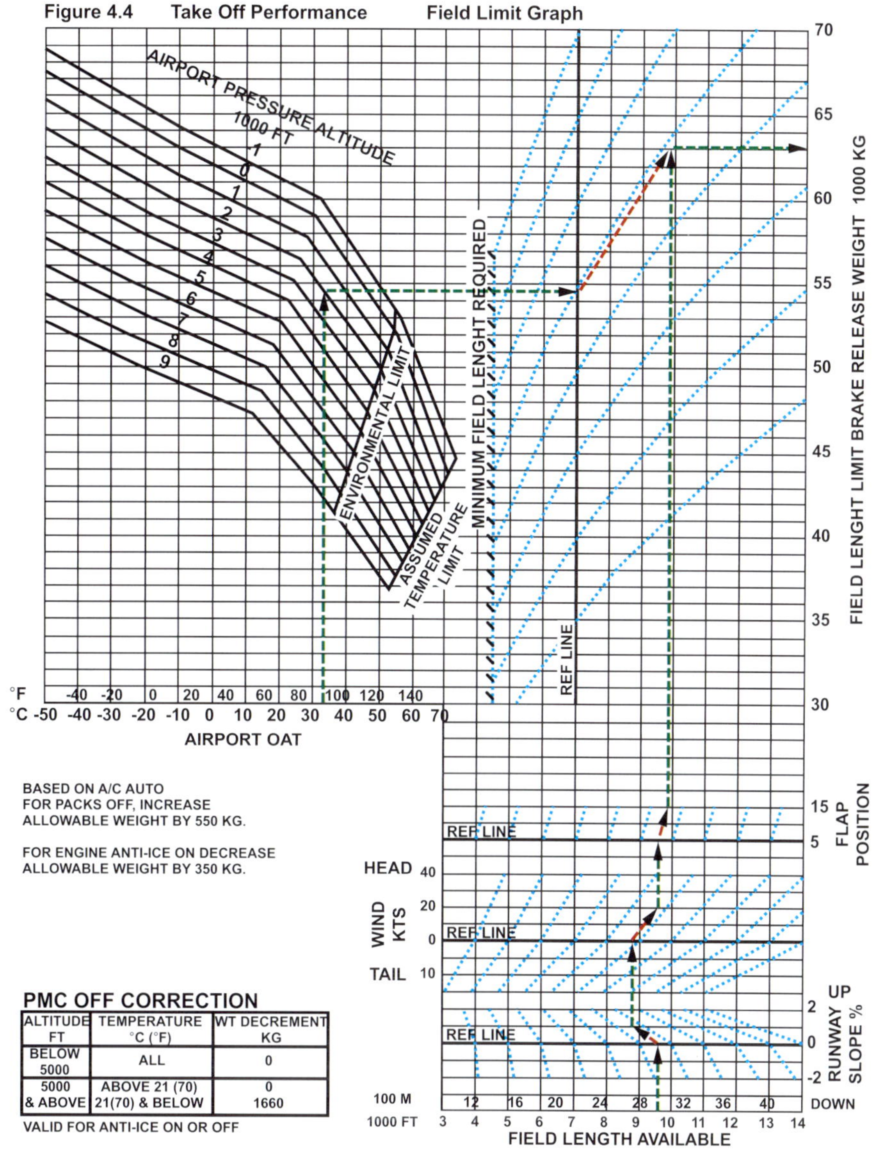

BASED ON A/C AUTO
FOR PACKS OFF, INCREASE ALLOWABLE WEIGHT BY 550 KG.

FOR ENGINE ANTI-ICE ON DECREASE ALLOWABLE WEIGHT BY 350 KG.

PMC OFF CORRECTION

ALTITUDE FT	TEMPERATURE °C (°F)	WT DECREMENT KG
BELOW 5000	ALL	0
5000 & ABOVE	ABOVE 21 (70) 21(70) & BELOW	0 1660

VALID FOR ANTI-ICE ON OR OFF

Guidelines only exist around a reference line. The reference lines have been coloured blue in the above graph. The dashed blue lines are guidelines. The pressure altitude lines to the left of the graph are not guidelines, because they have no reference line associated with them.

When there are guidelines, there must be an example that gives direction. Following the direction of the example, always stop at a reference line and move in proportion to the guidelines until reaching the required value. After the value, again move horizontally or vertically as appropriate.

Example to find the FLTOM using Figure 4.4:

Given the following information, find the field length limiting mass.

Aerodrome pressure altitude 1500 ft, temperature 20°C
Field length available 2000 m, 0.8% upslope, 5 kt tailwind, and flaps 15°

- Start on the left-hand side of the graph at 20°C and move vertically up to 1500 ft pressure altitude (midway between 2000 ft and 1000 ft).
- Move right until reaching the weight reference line. Mark this point and then draw a dashed line parallel to the guidelines.
- Starting at the bottom of the right-hand side of the graph at 2000 m, move vertically up to the slope reference line. Stop and move to the left with the guidelines to 0.8% upslope.
- Move vertically up to the wind reference line and stop. Now move with the guidelines to the value of 5 kt tailwind. Because this value of 5 kt tailwind is lower on the graph than the reference line, this results in a zigzag in the drawn line.
- Move vertically up to the flap reference line. If the flaps had been at 5°, the reference line and value would have coincided and the line would have continued up vertically. However, because the flaps are at 15°, move slightly right with the guidelines to the value of 15°.
- Move vertically up until the dashed weight guideline is met, now turn horizontally and read off the take-off mass from the right-hand scale, which is approximately 54 000 kg.
- When there is no reference to the PMC or ACS packs, it is to be assumed that they are on and no correction is required. It is also assumed that the anti-ice is off.

Figure 4.4 Take Off Performance Field Limit Graph

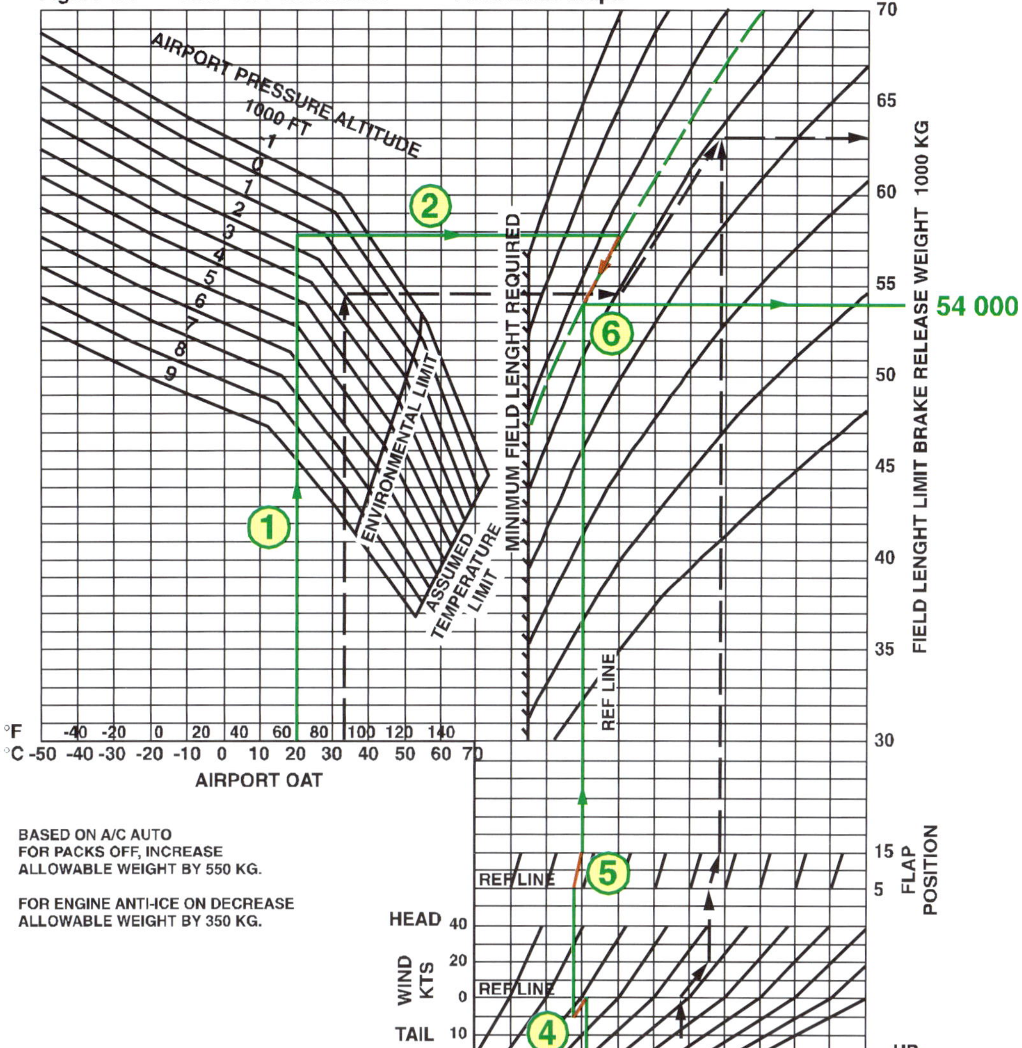

PMC OFF CORRECTION

ALTITUDE FT	TEMPERATURE °C (°F)	WT DECREMENT KG
BELOW 5000	ALL	0
5000 & ABOVE	ABOVE 21 (70) 21(70) & BELOW	0 1660

VALID FOR ANTI-ICE ON OR OFF

CLIMB LIMITED TAKE-OFF MASS – FIG. 4.5

For very long runways, the FLTOM would be very heavy and unlikely to limit the take-off mass. However, the aeroplane must also be able to climb away at a minimum still-air gradient and is likely to be climb limited.

Climb gradient depends on excess thrust divided by aeroplane weight. Since excess thrust depends on air density, the only factors that affect climb gradient are weight, altitude, and temperature. The climb limited mass is also known as a **WAT limited mass** (Weight, Altitude, and Temperature) or **MAT limited mass** (Mass, Altitude, and Temperature).

It is important to recognise that wind does not affect the climb mass, because it is a still air gradient (or free gradient) requirement. The effect of wind on gradient with respect to the ground is needed in Chapter 12 when looking at gradients required to clear obstacles after take-off.

Example to find the climb limited TOM using Figure 4.5:

What is the change in climb limited TOM if the flaps are extended from 5° to 15°? The pressure altitude of the airport is 500 ft and the ambient temperature is 36°C.

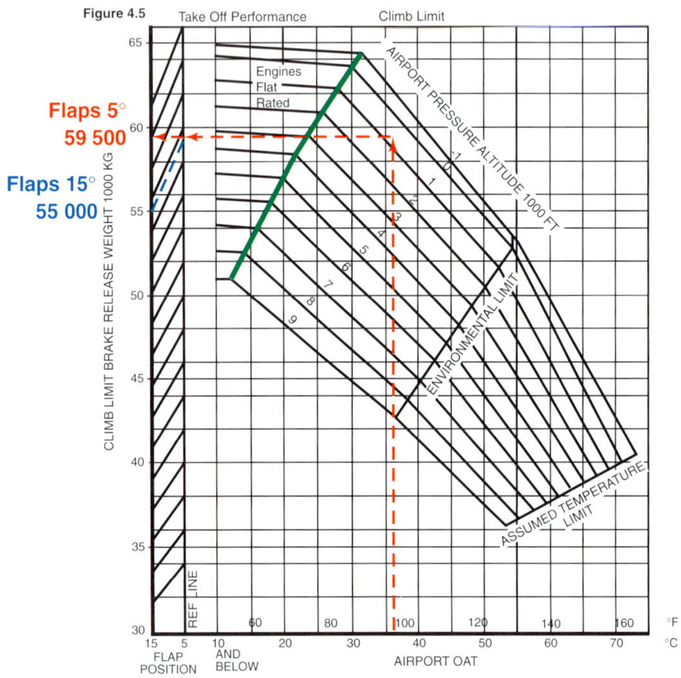

- Enter at the bottom of the graph at a temperature of 36°C and move vertically up to a pressure altitude of 500 ft.
- Move horizontally and stop at the flap reference line. For flaps 5°, continue horizontally, because 5° flap is on the reference line. This is shown by the red line and gives a mass of 59 500 kg.
- The blue line moves with the flap guidelines from the reference line to flaps 15°, giving a mass of 55 000 kg.
- The effect of extending the flaps from 5° to 15° is to reduce the climb limited mass by 4500 kg.

The graph is based on A/C and PMC on and anti-ice off. The notes state the effect on climb mass if otherwise.

The JAR exam questions refer to the **kink** in fig. 4.5. This is shown by the green line and represents the temperature deviation below which the engines are flat rated. Refer to Chapter 4 for further explanation.

TYRE SPEED LIMITED MASS – FIG. 4.6

Fig. 4.6 gives the tyre limited mass for 225 mph rated tyres and 5° flap. The purpose of the graph is to give the maximum mass and the V_{LOF} without exceeding 225 mph groundspeed. The graph compensates for the effect of air density on V_{LOF}, which is a CAS for the given groundspeed of 225 mph. The detrimental effect of a tailwind, which pushes V_{LOF} to a slower CAS for the same groundspeed, is in the notes. The notes also allow for the beneficial effect of flaps 15° and the detrimental effect of 210 mph rated tyres.

Example:

At what TOM would 210 mph tyres become limiting at a pressure altitude of 3000 ft, ambient temperature of 25°C, and 10 kt headwind? Flaps are at 5°.

Figure 4.6 Take-Off Performance Tyre Speed Limit

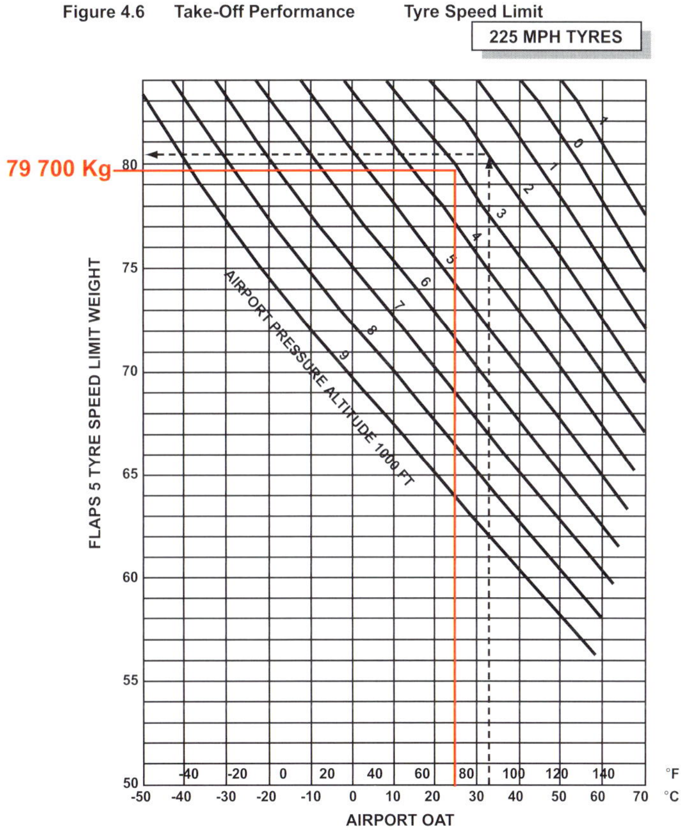

Increase 'flaps 5' tyre speed limit weight by 6600kg for flaps 15 degrees

Decrease 'flaps 5' tyre speed limit weight by 9600kg for 210mph tyres and flaps 5 degrees

Decrease 'flaps 5' tyre speed limit weight by 210mph tyres and flaps 15 degrees

Increase tyre speed limit weight by 400kg per knot of headwind

Decrease tyre speed limit weight by 650kg per knot of tailwind

- Enter at 25°C, move vertically up to the PAlt of 3000 ft and then horizontally to read off the tyre limiting mass of 79 700 kg.
- Because the tyres are only rated to 210 mph and not 225 mph, decrease the mass by 9600 kg (flaps 5°).
- 79 700 – 9600 = 70 100 kg
- Each kt of headwind increases the mass by 400 kg, therefore 10 kt headwind increases the tyre limiting mass to 70 100 + (400 x 10) = 74 100 kg.

DETERMINING THE PERFORMANCE LIMITED TAKE-OFF MASS (PLTOM)

The PLTOM is the lowest of the:

- FLTOM
- Climb Limited Mass
- Tyre Limited Mass
- Obstacle Limited Mass (covered in Chapter 12)

Practically, the tyre limited mass is rarely limiting because hot, high conditions also reduce the climb limited mass. However, taking off with a tailwind in hot, high conditions could result in a tyre limiting mass and must be checked. This situation could also result in an obstacle limiting mass, which is covered in chapter 12.

If there are no significant obstacles to be cleared after take-off, either the FLTOM or climb limited mass normally limits the PLTOM. To ensure that the aeroplane completes its take-off within the field length available, and then climbs at least the minimum required gradient, the PLTOM must be the lighter of these two masses.

However, the pilot has a choice of flap settings. Increasing flap setting increases the FLTOM but reduces the climb limited mass. It is important that the JAA examination candidate can find the best (heaviest) PLTOM and its corresponding flap setting.

Example 1:

The FLTOM for flaps 5°, 10°, and 15° are 58 000 kg, 59 200 kg, and 59 800 kg respectively (shown in red in the table below). If the climb limited mass for flaps 5°, 10°, and 15° are 61 000 kg, 59 600 kg, and 57 900 kg respectively (shown in blue in the table below), what is the maximum take-off mass and at which flap setting?

First, find the lowest of the field length and climb limiting masses for each flap setting. This is the mass underlined in the table below. It is the heaviest TOM at each given flap setting at which it is possible to both complete the take-off in the distance available and climb at a minimum gradient.

Flap setting	5°	10°	15°
FLTOM kg	<u>58 000</u>	<u>**59 200**</u>	59 800
Climb limited TOM kg	61 000	59 600	<u>57 900</u>

Then select the greatest of the underlined values (shown in bold), which is 59 200 kg at flap 10°. The PLTOM is, therefore, 59 200 kg and requires the flaps to be at 10°.

Example 2:
The FLTOM for flaps 5°, 10°, and 15° are 120 000 kg, 123 200 kg, and 126 700 kg, respectively. Before finding the heaviest mass at each flap setting, the masses must be adjusted for wind. There is a tailwind of 5 kt. For each knot of tailwind, the mass reduces by 600 kg.

This means that the: FLTOM at 5° flap is 120 000 kg – (5 x 600 kg) = 117 000 kg
FLTOM at 10° flap is 123 200 kg – (5 x 600 kg) = 120 200 kg
FLTOM at 15° flap is 126 700 kg – (5 x 600 kg) = 123 700 kg

These values are show in red in the following table.

The climb limited mass for flaps 5°, 10°, and 15° are 121 000 kg, 119 500 kg, and 117 900 kg, respectively (shown in blue in the following table). Only the FLTOM needs to be adjusted for wind because wind does not affect the climb limited mass, which only has a still air gradient requirement.

What is the maximum take-off mass and at which flap setting?

Find the lowest of the field length and climb limiting masses for each flap setting. This is the mass underlined in the table below. Then select the most beneficial flap setting that gives the greatest take-off mass.

Flap setting	5°	10°	15°
FLTOM kg	<u>117 000</u>	120 200	123 700
Climb limited TOM kg	121 000	**<u>119 500</u>**	<u>117 900</u>

The PLTOM is 119 500 kg (shown in bold) at 10° flap.

DETERMINING THE ACTUAL TAKE-OFF MASS

The actual take-off mass may be the PLTOM, which means that the take-off is performance limited. However, the actual take-off mass is often less than the PLTOM. This may be because the **maximum structural take-off mass (MSTOM)** is lower than the PLTOM. Alternatively, it could be because the loaded aeroplane is lighter than both the MSTOM and the PLTOM. In both these cases, the aeroplane does not need all the field length available and climbs at an angle steeper than the minimum required.

Example:
Find the maximum take-off mass given a PLTOM of 68 000 kg and a MSTOM of 62 800 kg.

The heaviest the aeroplane can be without performance or structural limitations is the lower of the two masses, which is 62 800 kg. In this case, the aeroplane is not performance limited. However, if the PLTOM had been 59 000 kg, the maximum take-off mass would have been the lower of 59 000 kg and 62 800 kg, which is 59 000 kg. The aeroplane is performance limited. The lower of the PLTOM and MSTOM is the **regulated take-off mass (RTOM)**. The aeroplane's actual take-off mass can be any mass up to and including the RTOM.

DETERMINING THE TAKE-OFF V SPEEDS FOR THE MRJT

Once the actual take-off mass has been determined, the V speeds V_1, V_R, and V_2 are found in pages 63 to 65 in the CAP 698.

First, look at the density sub-graph on page 63, which is reproduced below.

DENSITY SUB GRAPH

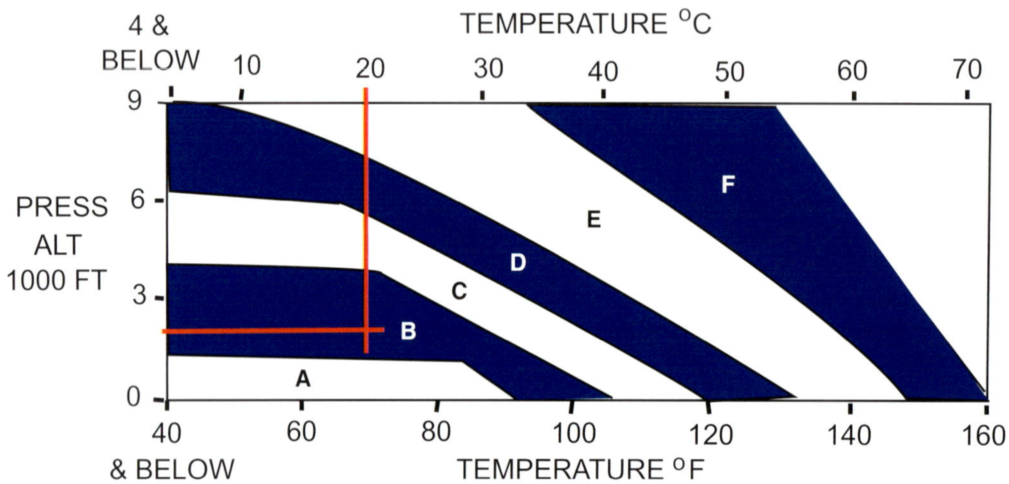

Entering the density sub-graph with the aerodrome pressure altitude and temperature enables an area A to F to be selected. For an aerodrome at 2000 ft pressure altitude and a temperature of 20°C, the area is B.

Now turn to page 64, if taking off using flaps 5°, or page 65 if using flaps 15°. For this example, a take-off mass of 55 000 kg and 5° of flap are used. Because area B from the density sub-graph was selected, look at the main table in the centre of page 64 to find the area B, which is highlighted in yellow.

Select the V speeds by reading across at the actual take-off weight of 55 000 kg. V_1 is 138 kt, V_R is 140 kt, and V_2 is 149 kt. For take-off masses between the weights in the table, the V speeds need to be interpolated to the nearest whole knot.

WT 1000 Kg.	A			B			C		
	V_1	V_R	V_2	V_1	V_R	V_2	V_1	V_R	V_2
70	158	163	168	158	164	169			
65	151	155	161	152	156	162	153	157	162
60	144	148	155	145	148	155	146	149	155
55	137	139	149	138	140	149	138	141	148
50	129	131	142	130	132	142	131	133	142
45	121	123	136	122	124	135	122	125	135
40	113	114	130	113	116	129	113	116	128

WT 1000 Kg.	D			E			F		
	V_1	V_R	V_2	V_1	V_R	V_2	V_1	V_R	V_2
70									
65									
60									
55	140	143	148						
50	132	134	141	133	135	141			
45	124	126	135	125	127	134	128	128	134
40	113	117	128	114	118	127	119	120	126

ADJUSTMENT OF V_1 DUE TO RUNWAY SLOPE AND/OR WIND

If there is runway slope or wind, the value of V_1 gained from the main table on page 64 must be adjusted. This is done by using the small table at the top right hand-side of page 64. This table is reproduced below.

Slope/Wind V_1 adjustment						
Weight 1000 Kg.	Slope%			Wind Kt		
	-2	0	2	-15	0	40
70	-3	0	4	-3	0	1
60	-2	0	2	-3	0	1
50	-2	0	1	-4	0	1
40	-2	0	1	-4	0	1

***V_1 not to exceed V_R**

If the runway has a downslope of -2%, V_1 needs to be reduced by two knots (i.e. the V_1 of 138 kt now becomes 136 kt). However, a tailwind of 5 kt results in the V_1 reducing by approximately one knot.

This table is also useful for theory questions because it states that:

V_1 increases with upslope and headwind

V_1 decreases with downslope and tailwind

CHECKING V_1 FOR V_{MCG}

At low aeroplane weights, all the V speeds are lower. This can cause a problem in that V_1 (the speed from which the pilot can both go and reject a take-off) must not be slower that V_{MCG}. If the V_1 from the main table is less than V_{MCG} in the table at the bottom of page 64, then V_1 must be increased to the value of V_{MCG}.

MINIMUM V_1 (MCG)

Actual OAT		Press Alt. X 1000 ft				
°C	°F	0	2	4	6	8
55	131	104				
50	122	107	103			
40	104	111	107	103	99	94
30	86	116	111	107	104	98
20	68	116	113	111	107	102
10	50	116	113	111	108	104
50	-58	118	115	112	109	105

For A/C packs OFF increase V_1 (MCG) by 2 knots

V_{MBE} AND TAKE-OFF MASS – FIGURE 4.7

V_{MBE} is the maximum CAS at which the brakes could absorb all the energy from a take-off rejected at V_1. V_{MBE} must be equal to or greater than V_1

Figure 4.7 allows the CAS V_{MBE} to be found for the aeroplane's take-off mass in given conditions of air density, slope, and wind. If the value of V_1 obtained from pages 64/65 exceeds $V_{MBE,}$ the TOM must be reduced by 300 kg per kt difference. Re-enter page 64/65 at the new lower TOM.

For the purpose of the theoretical exam questions, figure 4.7 is useful because it states the effect of slope and wind on V_{MBE}.

V_{MBE} increases with upslope and headwind.

V_{MBE} decreases with downslope and tailwind.

ALL FLAPS

CHECK V_{MBE} WITH OUTSIDE SHADED AREA OR WHEN OPERATING WITH TAILWIND OR IMPROVED CLIMB.

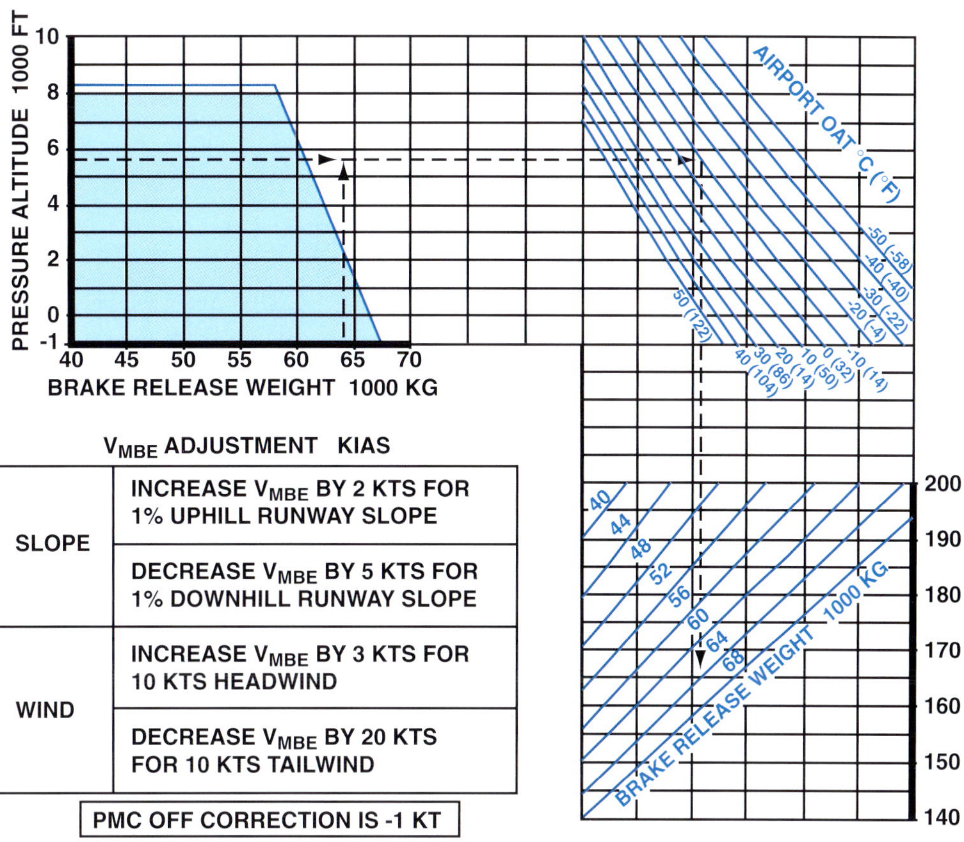

V_{MBE} ADJUSTMENT KIAS

SLOPE	INCREASE V_{MBE} BY 2 KTS FOR 1% UPHILL RUNWAY SLOPE
	DECREASE V_{MBE} BY 5 KTS FOR 1% DOWNHILL RUNWAY SLOPE
WIND	INCREASE V_{MBE} BY 3 KTS FOR 10 KTS HEADWIND
	DECREASE V_{MBE} BY 20 KTS FOR 10 KTS TAILWIND

PMC OFF CORRECTION IS -1 KT

FINDING TAKE-OFF %N_1

The thrust setting for take-off and go around is maximum thrust called **TOGA**, which stands for take-off and go-around. When TOGA is selected, the power management computer (PMC) automatically selects the required %N_1. However, if the PMC is off, the %N_1 for take-off or go-around is found by entering figure 4.10 with the airport temperature and pressure altitude. These figures are valid for system conditions except air conditioning off when an extra 1% needs to be added to the figure in the table.

Figure 4.10 Expanded Maximum Take-off % N_1

Airport OAT		Pressure Altitude Ft.									
°C	°F	-1000	0	1000	2000	3000	4000	5000	6000	7000	8000
54	129	93.3	94.1	93.6							
52	126	93.6	94.2	94.2	93.7						
50	122	93.8	94.3	94.3	94.3	93.9					
48	118	94.0	94.5	94.4	94.4	94.4	94.1				
46	115	94.1	94.7	94.6	94.5	94.5	94.6	94.4			
44	111	94.3	94.8	94.8	94.7	94.7	94.7	94.8	94.6		
42	108	94.5	95.0	95.0	94.9	94.9	94.8	94.9	95.0	94.8	
40	104	94.6	95.2	95.2	95.1	95.0	95.1	95.1	95.2	95.1	94.9
38	100	94.8	95.3	95.4	95.3	95.2	95.3	95.3	95.4	95.3	95.2
36	97	95.1	95.5	95.5	95.5	95.4	95.6	95.6	95.6	95.5	95.4
34	93	95.3	95.7	95.7	95.7	95.6	95.8	95.8	95.8	95.7	95.6
32	90	95.5	95.9	95.9	95.8	95.8	96.0	96.0	95.9	95.9	95.8
30	86	95.2	96.1	96.1	96.0	96.0	96.3	96.2	96.1	96.0	96.0
28	82	94.9	95.8	96.3	96.2	96.2	96.5	96.4	96.3	96.2	96.1
26	79	94.6	95.5	96.0	96.4	96.4	96.6	96.5	96.5	96.4	96.3
24	75	94.2	95.2	95.6	96.1	96.5	96.8	96.7	96.7	96.6	96.5
22	72	93.9	94.8	95.3	95.7	96.2	96.9	96.9	96.9	96.8	96.6
20	68	93.6	94.5	95.0	95.4	95.9	96.6	97.1	97.1	97.0	96.9
18	64	93.3	94.2	94.7	95.1	95.6	96.3	96.8	97.3	97.2	97.1
16	61	93.0	93.9	94.3	94.8	95.2	96.0	96.4	96.9	97.4	97.3
14	57	92.6	93.5	94.0	94.4	94.9	95.6	96.1	96.6	97.0	97.5
12	54	92.3	93.2	93.7	94.1	94.6	95.3	95.8	96.3	96.7	97.2
10	50	92.0	92.9	93.4	93.8	94.2	95.0	95.4	95.9	96.4	96.8
8	46	91.7	92.6	93.0	93.4	93.9	94.6	95.1	95.6	96.0	96.5
6	43	91.3	92.2	92.7	93.1	93.6	94.3	94.7	95.3	95.7	96.2
4	39	91.0	91.9	92.4	92.8	93.2	93.9	94.4	94.9	95.3	95.8
2	36	90.7	91.6	92.0	92.4	92.9	93.6	94.1	94.6	95.0	95.5
0	32	90.4	91.2	91.7	92.1	92.6	93.3	93.7	94.2	94.7	95.1
-2	28	90.0	90.9	91.4	91.8	92.2	92.9	93.4	93.9	94.3	94.8
-4	25	89.7	90.6	91.0	91.4	91.9	92.6	93.0	93.5	94.0	94.4
-6	21	89.4	90.2	90.7	91.1	91.5	92.2	92.7	93.2	93.6	94.1
-8	18	89.0	89.9	90.3	90.7	91.2	91.9	92.3	92.8	93.3	93.7
-10	14	88.7	89.6	90.0	90.4	90.8	91.5	92.0	92.5	92.9	93.4
-12	10	88.3	89.2	89.7	90.0	90.5	91.2	91.6	92.1	92.5	93.0
-14	7	88.0	88.9	89.3	89.7	90.2	90.8	91.3	91.8	92,2	92.6
-16	3	87.7	88.5	89.0	89.4	89.8	90.5	90.9	91.4	91.8	92.3
-18	0	87.3	88.2	88.6	89.0	89.5	90.1	90.6	91.1	91.5	91.9
-20	-4	87.0	87.8	88.3	88.7	89.1	89.8	90.2	90.7	91.1	91.6
-22	-8	86.6	87.5	87.9	88.3	88.7	89.4	89.9	90.3	90.8	91.2
-24	-11	86.3	87.1	87.6	88.0	88.4	89.1	89.5	90.0	90.4	90.8
-26	-15	85.9	86.8	87.2	87.6	88.0	88.7	89.1	89.6	90.0	90.5
-28	-18	85.6	86.4	86.9	87.2	87.7	88.4	88.8	89.3	89.7	90.1
-30	-22	85.2	86.0	86.5	86.9	87.3	88.0	88.4	88.9	89.3	89.7

Valid for PMC 'on', A/C 'auto', engine anti-ice 'on' or 'off'.
For A/C off Add 1.0% N_1
Do not operate engine anti-ice "on" at airport OAT above 10°C (50° F).

Chapter 11
Additional Take-Off Techniques

INTRODUCTION

Having looked at the normal take-off/reject, this chapter discusses four situations where a different technique is beneficial for safety or economic reasons.

INCREASED V_2 PROCEDURE

The increased V_2 procedure is also referred to as the **improved climb technique**. Starting with its two names is useful because they describe:

- Its purpose, which is to improve a climb limited take-off mass.
- How it is done, which is by increasing the V_R and thereby V_2 take-off speeds.

An increased V_2 technique is an option when there is spare runway, and the take-off mass is restricted by a climb or obstacle limiting mass. In Chapter 6, it was determined that:

$$\text{Climb gradient} = \frac{T-D}{W} = \frac{\text{Excess Thrust}}{W}$$

To achieve the required climb gradient when there is little excess thrust results in a low limiting aeroplane weight. However, an increase in the excess thrust enables the same required gradient at a higher aeroplane weight.

Because an engine failure at V_1 must be allowed for, excess thrust cannot be increased by increasing thrust. The remaining engines are already at take-off go-around (TOGA). It may, however, be possible to increase the excess thrust by reducing the drag. If the aeroplane is not field length limited, drag could be reduced by decreasing the flap setting. Drag may be further reduced by climbing at a speed faster than V_2, which is the principle behind the technique.

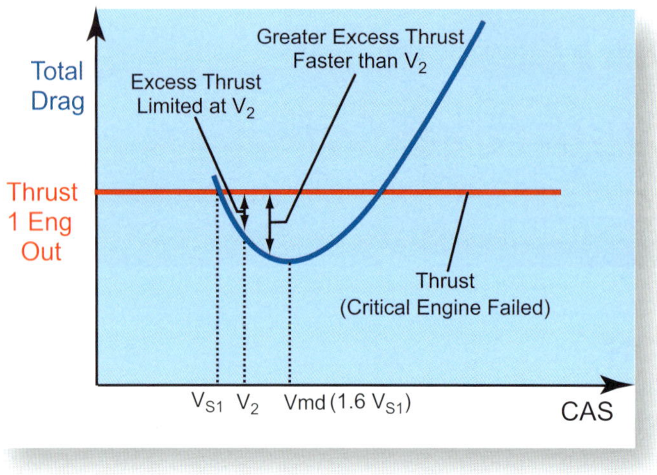

The above graph illustrates that V_2 is a very slow speed, and total drag is high. Since V_2 may be only 20% above the stall speed, and V_{md} for a jet is typically at 1.6 V_S (60% above the stall speed), the aeroplane has very little excess thrust. However, if the aeroplane rotates at a speed faster than the normal V_R, there is less drag and more excess thrust.

This increase in excess thrust now opens up the possibility of increasing aeroplane weight until it is again climb mass limited. This increase in the climb limiting mass results in the total drag curve moving up and to the right. All the V speeds increase as aeroplane mass increases, but V_R and V_2 must increase further to gain the benefit of the reduced induced drag.

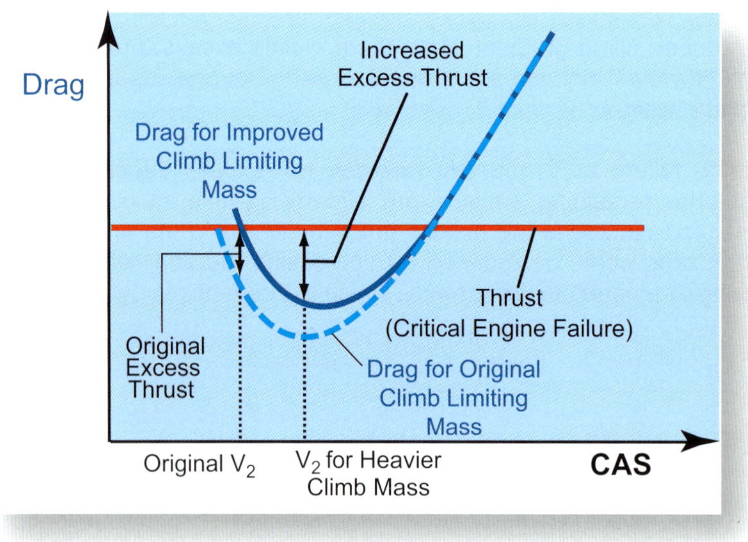

In summary, an increased V_2 technique is possible when the field length mass exceeds the climb or obstacle mass, which itself is limiting the take-off mass.

INCREASED V_2 PROCEDURE EXAMPLE

(Look at pages 74 to 76 in 698 while following through this example.)

Given the following information, what is the maximum take-off mass using the increased V_2 procedure if appropriate?

> Climb mass 55 000 kg
> Field length take-off mass 62 000 kg
> Flaps 5° and tyre limiting mass 80 000 kg

The increased V_2 procedure is beneficial because the aeroplane is climb limited and there is spare runway at the MTOM of 55 000 kg.

Using the flaps 5° graphs at the top of page 75, enter the bottom with 7000 kg (62 000 kg – 55 000 kg). Move vertically up until meeting the diagonal line.

Moving horizontally left, the climb weight improvement of 2750 kg can be read off.

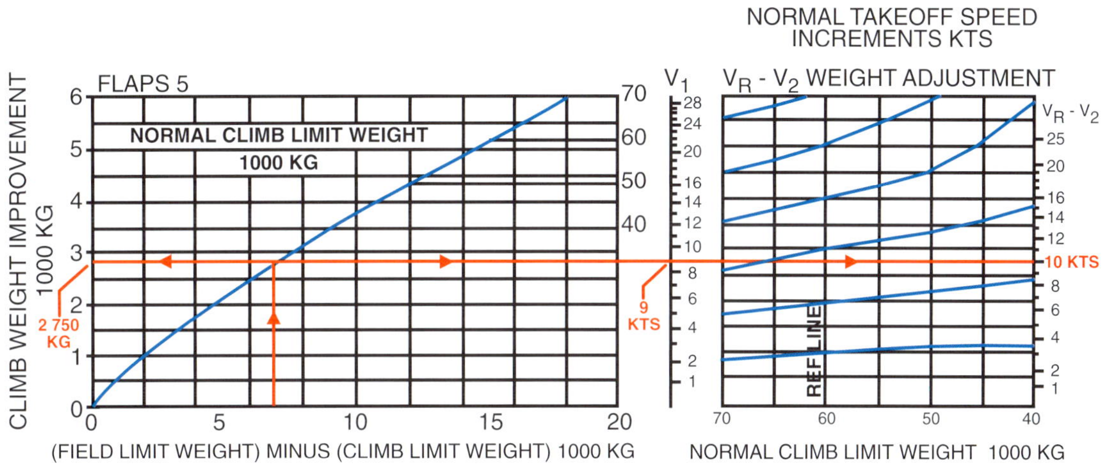

Note: If the V speed increments are required, these are obtained by moving horizontally right from the diagonal line. The V_1 increment is read off first (approximately 9 kt) and then the V_R and V_2 increments by using the right-hand graph. Note that when the horizontal line meets the reference line, it would stop and then move up with the guidelines until reaching the original climb mass of 55 000 kg. To read the V_R and V_2 increments (approximately 10 kt), the line would then move horizontally again.

The process is now repeated on page 76 to check that the V_{TYRES} is not exceeded.

Enter the bottom at 25 000 kg (80 000 kg – 55 000 kg) and move vertically up.

This time the vertical line must stop at the horizontal normal climb limiting mass of 55 000 kg which was reached before the diagonal line 4700 kg is read off.

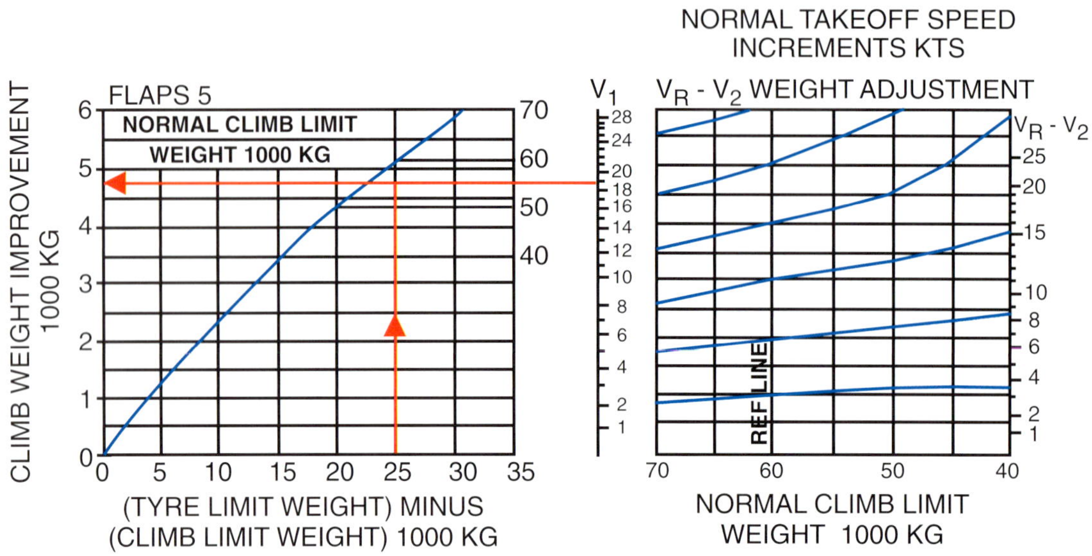

Now, select the lower of the two climb weight improvements, which in this example is 2750 kg.

Add this improvement to the original climb mass to get the new improved climb mass of 55 000 kg + 2750 kg = 57 750 kg.

If the V speeds had been required, the normal V speeds for a mass of 57 750 kg would first be obtained from page 64. The V speed increments from page 75 in this example would then be added to obtain the increased V_2 speeds.

REDUCED THRUST TAKE-OFF

The purpose of a reduced thrust take-off is to improve engine life. It is a very common procedure for smaller or lighter aeroplanes taking off from long runways. In this case, the aeroplane is neither field length nor climb limited. However, reducing the thrust does bring the aeroplane closer to its performance limited condition.

The point at which V_1 is reached is closer to the runway's end because the aeroplane accelerates more slowly along the runway. If stopping from a rejected take-off is likely to cause any problems, the reduced thrust take-off is not permitted. Looking on page 77, a reduced thrust take-off is not permitted with:

- Icy or very slippery runways
- Contaminated runways
- Antiskid unserviceable
- Reverse thrust unserviceable

There is also a restriction that a reduced thrust take-off is not permitted with a PMC off. The reason for the final restriction that a reduced thrust take-off is not permitted with the power management computer off is less obvious until it is understood how to set the take-off thrust.

The value of the reduced thrust is set by entering a hotter than ambient assumed temperature into the flight management system (FMS). The actual ambient temperature is also entered in the FMS initialisation pages. At temperatures hotter than the flat rating cut-off, thrust reduces with increase in air temperature. By entering a hotter assumed temperature, the PMC selects the lower thrust setting that would be available at that hotter temperature.

METHOD TO DETERMINE THE ASSUMED TEMPERATURE

The assumed temperature is the coldest of the temperatures at which the aeroplane would have become performance limited or the temperature at which the engine would have reduced thrust by 25%, which is the maximum thrust reduction permitted.

Example:

Find the assumed temperature for an aeroplane mass 55 000 kg at an aerodrome pressure altitude 1000 ft, ambient temperature 25°C, field length available 7200 ft, level, 20 kt headwind, and flaps 5°.

Determine the temperature at which the aeroplane would be field length limited. This is found by working backward from the mass and up from the field length. Then move left to the pressure altitude and down to read off the field length limiting temperature of 48°C. This is shown in the graph on the next page.

Figure 4.4 Take Off Performance Field Limit Graph

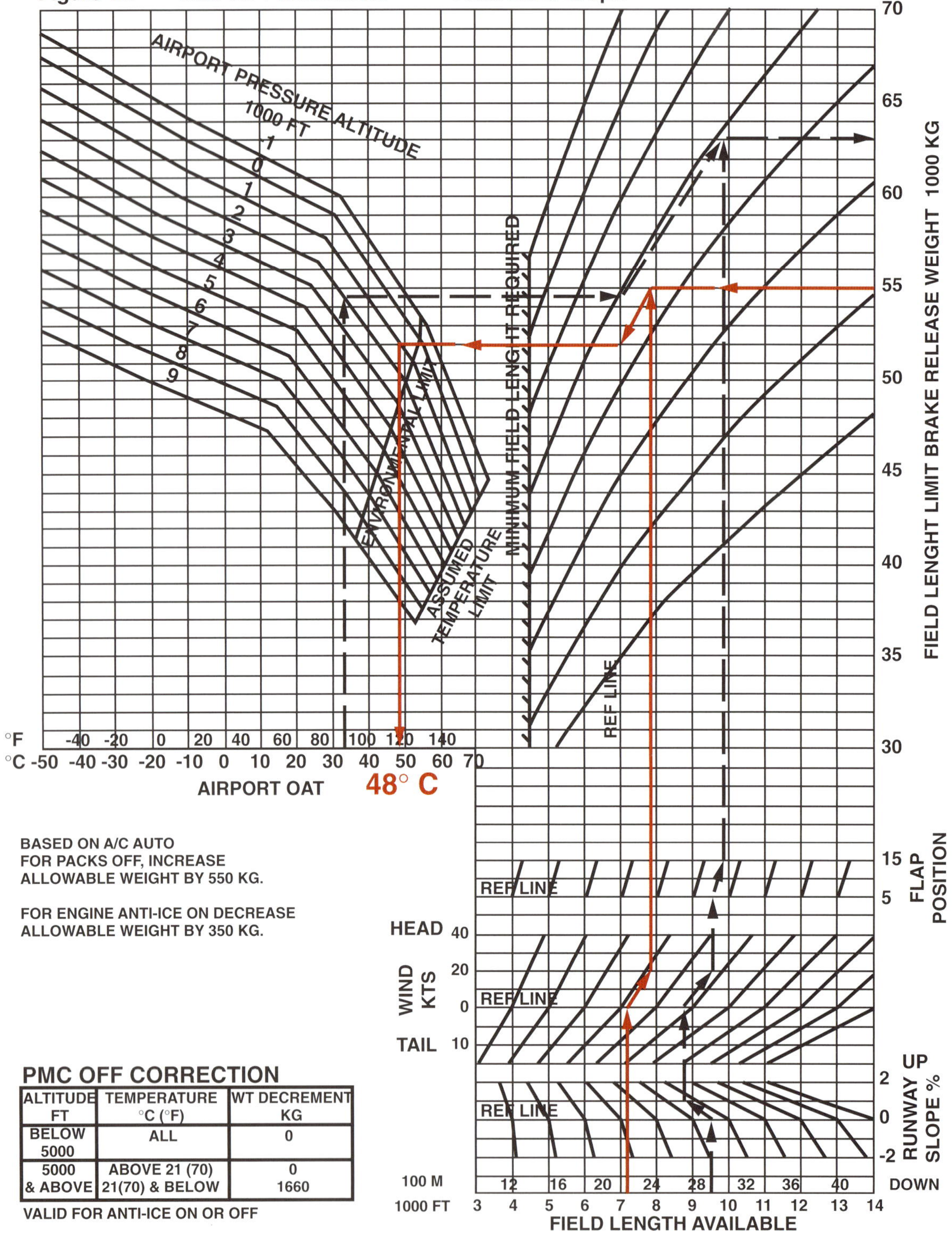

PMC OFF CORRECTION

ALTITUDE FT	TEMPERATURE °C (°F)	WT DECREMENT KG
BELOW 5000	ALL	0
5000 & ABOVE	ABOVE 21 (70) 21(70) & BELOW	0 1660

VALID FOR ANTI-ICE ON OR OFF

Now obtain the temperature at which the aeroplane would become climb limited. Enter fig. 4.5 on the left at a mass of 55 000 kg because flaps 5° is on the flap reference line, continue horizontally to the pressure altitude of 1000 ft. Move vertically down and read off the climb limiting temperature of 44°C.

Figure 4.5

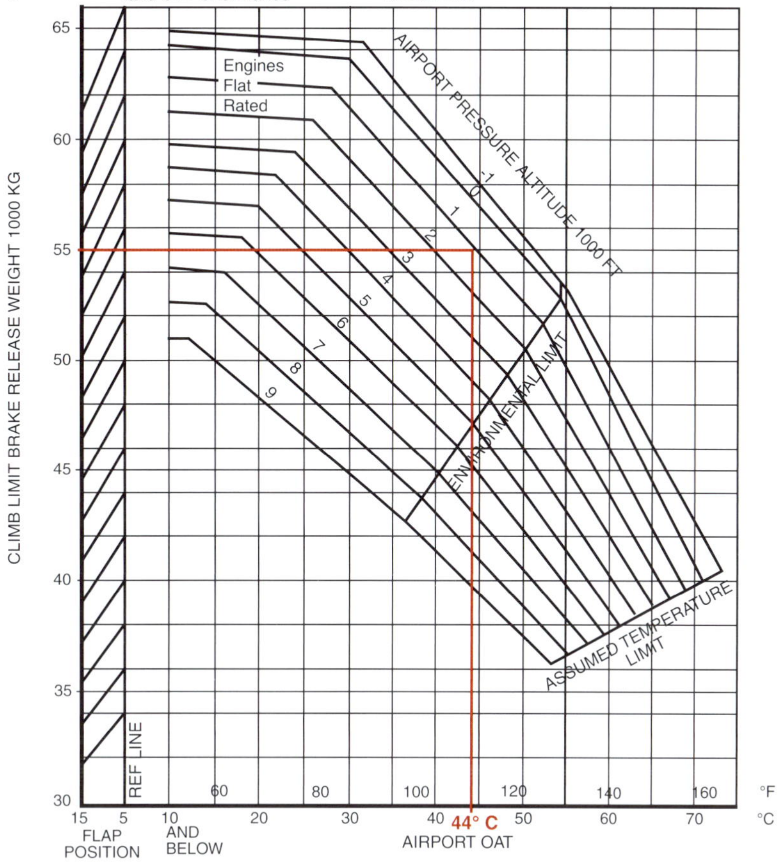

In the same way, find the tyre limiting temperature from figure 4.6 and an obstacle limiting temperature from figure 4.20. Final temperature is the temperature at which the engine would have reduced to 75% of its thrust at the ambient temperature. This is done by entering at the ambient temperature and pressure altitude in figure 4.17 and reading the temperature from within the table, which is 59°C.

Figure 4.17 Assumed Temperature Reduced Thrust

PMC - ON

Assumed temp. $\%N_1$ = Max. Take-off $\% N_1$ minus $\% N_1$ adjustment

Maximum Assumed Temperature*

OAT °C	Press. Alt. 1000 Ft.								
	0	1	2	3	4	5	6	7	8
55	71	71							
50	69	68	68	69	70				
45	67	66	66	67	67	67	68	70	
40	65	64	64	64	64	64	64	66	68
35	63	62	62	62	61	61	62	63	64
30	61	60	60	59	59	59	59	60	61
25	61	59	58	57	56	56	56	57	58
20	61	59	58	57	55	53	54	54	55
15 & below	61	59	58	57	55	53	53	52	52

The assumed temperature is the lowest of the limiting temperatures:

- Climb limiting temperature of 44°C
- Field length limiting temperature of 48°C
- Tyre limiting temperature greater than 60°C
- Obstacle limiting temperature (e.g. 52°C for a given obstacle)
- 75% thrust temperature 59°C

The lowest of these temperatures is 44°C.

This assumed temperature would then be entered into the FMS, which would result in the reduced thrust take-off.

Note that if an engine failure did occur after V_1, it is not necessary to increase the thrust on the remaining engines to the maximum take-off thrust setting. However, the aeroplane is performance limited. It would be prudent, once pilot capacity allowed, to return to maximum take-off thrust.

CONTAMINATED RUNWAYS

JAR OPS define a runway as contaminated when more than 25% of the runway surface area is covered by greater than 3 mm of water or its equivalent depth in slush, wet snow, or compacted snow or ice.

The equivalent water depth is found by multiplying the contamination depth by its specific gravity. This means that slush with a specific gravity of 0.7 that is 5 mm deep has a water equivalent depth of 3.5 mm.

JAR OPS do not preclude operations from contaminated runways provided that the operator has approval and procedures in the Operating Manual. The UK CAA, however, prohibits taking off and landing on a contaminated runway with a tailwind and from runways with greater than 15 mm water, slush, or wet snow and 80 mm of dry snow. They also recommend a 10 kt maximum crosswind.

Operating off contaminated runways is hazardous and is best avoided, if possible. Contamination vastly reduces braking effectiveness which affects both the rejected take-off and landing. Contamination is also thrown from the wheels up onto the aeroplane, causing impingement drag that can be so large that acceleration to V_{LOF} is not possible.

To take off from a contaminated runway, it is necessary to reduce V_1 and take-off mass.

Example:

The normal PLTOM is 60 000 kg at an aerodrome 4000 ft pressure altitude. If there are 6 mm of slush, what is the MTOM and V_1 reduction?

Looking at the 6 mm table in fig. 4.14, the mass and V_1 reductions are 8800 kg and 7 kt respectively. The take-off mass is 60 000 – 8800 kg = 51 200 kg.

0.25 INCH (6MM) SLUSH/STANDING WATER DEPTH

Mass x 1000kg	Mass and V_1 Reductions			
	Press Alt Ft	0	4000	8000
40	1000Kg	3.4	4.0	4.9
	KIAS	19	16	12
44	1000Kg	4.3	5.3	6.3
	KIAS	18	14	10
48	1000Kg	5.3	6.3	7.5
	KIAS	16	12	9
52	1000Kg	6.2	7.2	8.4
	KIAS	13	10	8
56	1000Kg	7.0	8.1	9.1
	KIAS	11	8	7
60	1000Kg	7.9	8.8	9.5
	KIAS	8	7	6
64	1000Kg	8.7	9.4	9.7
	KIAS	7	5	5
68	1000Kg	9.4	9.9	9.7
	KIAS	5	5	5

Field Length Available Ft	$V_1 = V_{MCG}$ Limit Mass 1000Kg		
	Pressure Altitude (Ft)		
	0	4000	8000
5400	40	-	-
5600	43	35	-
5800	47	38	-
6000	50	41	-
6200	53	43	36
6400	56	46	38
6600	59	48	41
6800	63	51	43
7000	66	54	45
7200	70	57	48
7400	-	60	50
7600	-	63	52
7800	-	65	55
8000	-	68	57
8200	-	-	59
8400	-	-	62
8600	-	-	64
8800	-	-	67

If the contamination depth, normal TOM, or aerodrome pressure altitude is between those specified in the tables, interpolation is necessary.

It is useful to note that as the contamination depth increases, the majority of the correction is in the larger take-off mass reduction. The lighter TOM results in all the V speeds reducing with the extra V_1 reduction decreasing as contamination thickness increases.

HYDROPLANING

Hydroplaning is a problem associated with aeroplanes operating from contaminated runways. At speeds above the hydroplaning speed, braking effectiveness is vastly reduced, which poses a considerable problem on landing or potentially in the rejected take-off case.

There are three types of hydroplaning: dynamic, viscous, and reverted rubber.

DYNAMIC HYDROPLANING

Dynamic hydroplaning occurs when the contamination is not displaced from under the tyres fast enough to allow the tyre to make pavement contact over its total footprint area. The tyre rides up on a wedge of water and partial or total hydroplaning occurs. The tyre is no longer in contact with the runway surface area and the wheel can stop rotating, which results in total loss of braking action. For this to occur, the water equivalent depth of the water, slush, or wet snow must exceed the depth of the tyre tread and the aeroplane's speed must exceed V_p.

For a rotating tyre, $V_p = 9\sqrt{P}$ where P is the tyre pressure in pounds per square inch (psi).

When landing on a contaminated runway (in an aeroplane with antiskid), touch down positively and apply the brakes immediately.

Although braking is ineffective above V_p, contamination reduces the braking coefficient of friction at all speeds. However, speeds slower than V_p are potentially lethal in the take-off situation, as slush impingement drag increases as speed increases toward V_p. Once past V_p, the tyre is held off the runway surface by the contamination, and less of the contamination is thrown up onto the aeroplane, reducing the impingement drag.

VISCOUS HYDROPLANING

Viscous hydroplaning can cause complete loss of braking action. It can occur at slower speeds than the dynamic hydroplaning speed, V_p. It also differs from dynamic hydroplaning in that the runway only needs to be wet or very smooth or contaminated with a film of oil, dust, grease, or rubber. It can occur on the touchdown point on a runway where rubber has been laid down on the runway surface. This rubber is burnt off periodically by the airport authority to reduce the problem.

REVERTED RUBBER HYDROPLANING

Rubber reversion hydroplaning is caused when a wheel locks and superheated, high-pressure steam is generated by the friction in the tyre footprint area. The high temperature causes the rubber to revert to its uncured state, resulting in tyre skids.

ANTISKID INOPERATIVE

The final problem to consider is a system failure that is permissible, but reduces the aeroplane's ability to stop. This would typically include antiskid or reverse thrust inoperative. If the antiskid is inoperative, braking effectiveness is reduced considerably. This has performance implications for both the rejected take-off and landing. Reduced thrust take-offs or operations from contaminated runways are not permitted when antiskid is inoperative. However, an aeroplane's Minimum Equipment List (MEL) allows an aeroplane to be dispatched with antiskid inoperative in normal situations, but it is restricted to a much lighter take-off and landing mass for a given distance available.

If the stopping ability of the aeroplane if reduced, the fastest speed from which it can stop, $V_{STOP,}$ is slower. However, to be able to continue the take-off with the critical engine failing at this slower speed results in the necessity to reduce the take-off mass.

Page 80 of CAP 698 shows a method of calculating take-off mass and V speeds if the antiskid is inoperative.

It is a simplified calculation where the take-off mass is reduced by a fixed mass of 7700 kg. The V speeds for this new lighter TOM are then determined from figures 4.8 or 4.9 and V_1 is further reduced by amount shown in fig. 4.18.

Chapter 12
The Initial Take-Off Climb

INTRODUCTION

Following take-off, the aeroplane is in one of two very different situations.

It is normally climbing away enroute to its original destination with all engines still operating. Very occasionally, it has suffered an engine failure during take-off and is climbing to avoid obstacles, before returning to land at the same airport.

First, consider the normal situation in which no engines have failed, and the flight progresses as planned.

NOISE ABATEMENT

If engine failure does not occur during the take-off phase, the excess thrust greatly exceeds that required for obstacle clearance. In this normal situation, some of the excess thrust can be used to accelerate the aeroplane past its flap retraction speeds, allowing the aeroplane to clean up while climbing. However, with all engines at maximum take-off thrust, the excess thrust is still greater than that needed for climbing and accelerating. This allows the thrust to be reduced above 800 ft, which reduces jet noise for those living and working around airports.

Noise abatement procedures which reduce take-off thrust are not advisable in adverse operating conditions such as:

- If the runway surface conditions are adversely affected (e.g. snow, slush, ice, or other contaminants)
- When the horizontal visibility is less than 1.9 km (1 nm)
- When the crosswind component, including gusts, exceeds 15 kt
- When the tailwind component, including gusts, exceeds 5 kt
- When wind shear has been reported or forecast
- If thunderstorms are expected to affect the approach or departure

There are two Noise Abatement Procedures, NADP 1 and NADP2.

NOISE ABATEMENT DEPARTURE PROCEDURE 1 (NADP 1)

This procedure is intended to provide noise reduction for noise sensitive areas in close proximity to the departure end of the runway.

The thrust is reduced at or above 800 ft, but the airspeed is kept constant at the initial climbing speed, which must not be less than V_2 + 10 kt. By 3000 ft, the angle of climb is reduced, allowing the aeroplane to accelerate for flap/slat retraction.

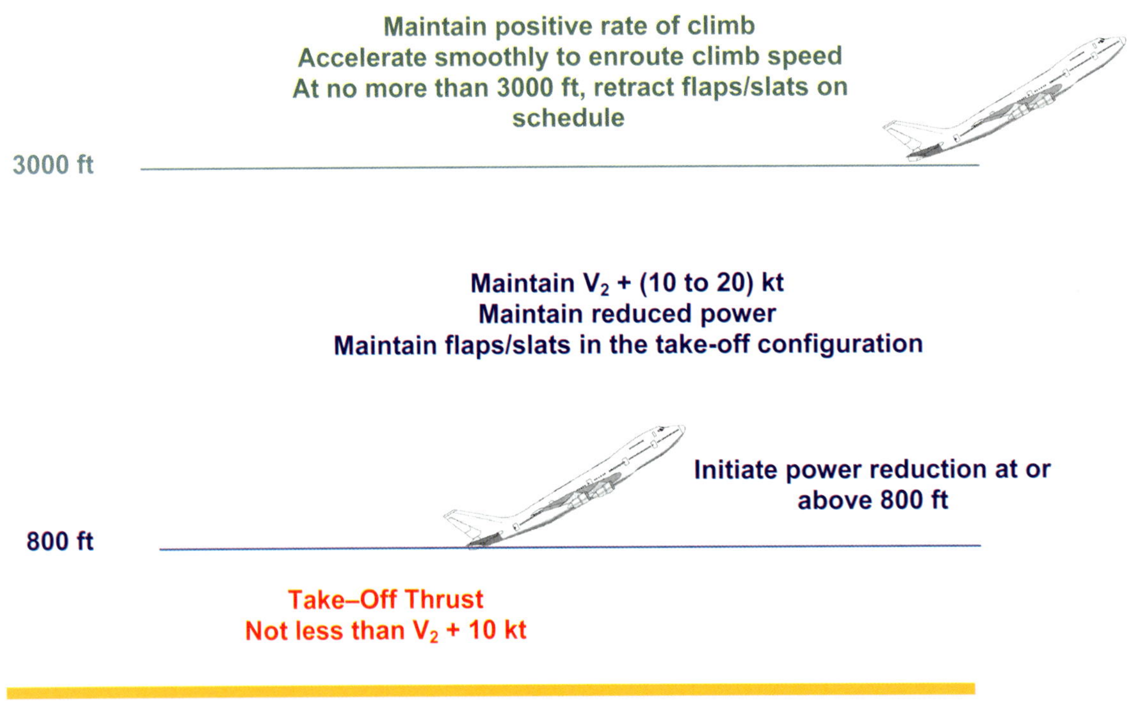

NOISE ABATEMENT DEPARTURE PROCEDURE 2 (NADP 2)

This procedure is used when the noise sensitive area is distant from the aerodrome. The procedure differs in that the thrust is not reduced on reaching 800 ft but at a greater height, either when flap/slat retraction is initiated or completed. By delaying the reduction in thrust, the aeroplane can both climb steeply and accelerate toward V_{ZF} (the minimum safe manoeuvring speed with zero flap). The aeroplane is now clean and higher when it reduces the thrust over the more distant noise sensitive area.

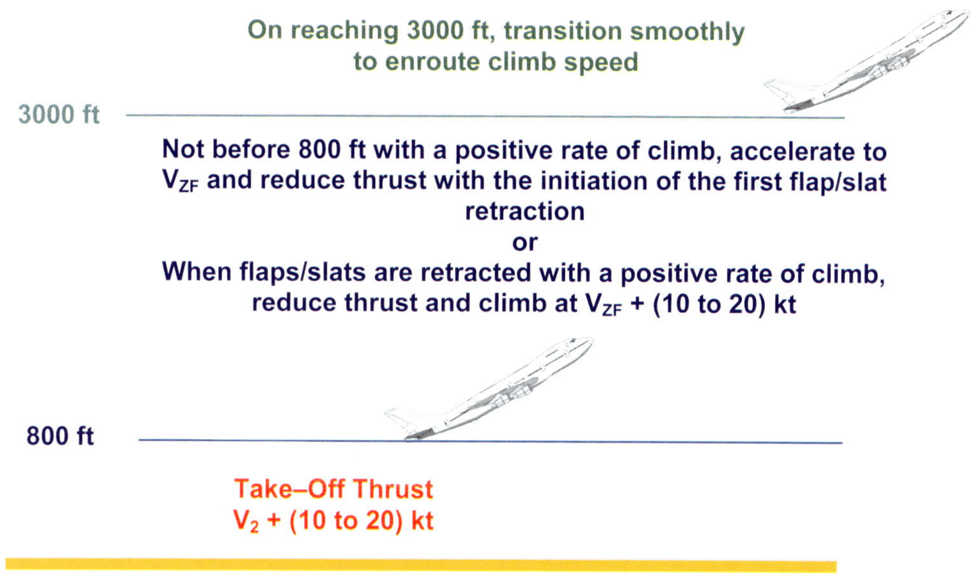

However, in the situation where an engine has failed, there is considerably less excess thrust. The aeroplane is not able or required to conform to noise abatement procedures, and the take-off mass must be limited so that the engine out net take-off flight path clears obstacles by no less than 35 ft. Now consider this much less common and very different situation of the one engine out net take-off flight path.

THE NET TAKE-OFF FLIGHT PATH

When an engine fails at or after V_1, the reduction in excess thrust means that obstacle clearance after take-off may become critical. Consider the net climb performance during the initial climb because the probability of an engine failure at or after V_1 is sufficiently high together with the very low probability of survival after hitting an obstacle. That is not to say that a net all engine obstacle gradient is not also considered. It is just that it is extremely unlikely to be the cause of an obstacle limited take-off mass.

The net take-off flight path (NTOFP) begins at the screen and extends to approximately 1500 ft above aerodrome level. JAR-OPS 1.495(a) specifies that the NTOFP, determined from the data provided in the Aeroplane Flight Manual, must clear all relevant obstacles by a vertical distance of 35 ft.

This vertical clearance distance is increased to 50 ft if the aeroplane needs to turn in the NTOFP. However, the clearance is reduced to only 15 ft when taking-off on a wet or contaminated runway, and an engine failure occurs at V_{1WET}. When a runway is wet or contaminated, the operator and pilots should exercise special care with respect to obstacle assessment, especially if a take-off mass is obstacle limited and the obstacle density high.

The vertical profile of the NTOFP is shown below. It is divided into a number of segments each with different requirements.

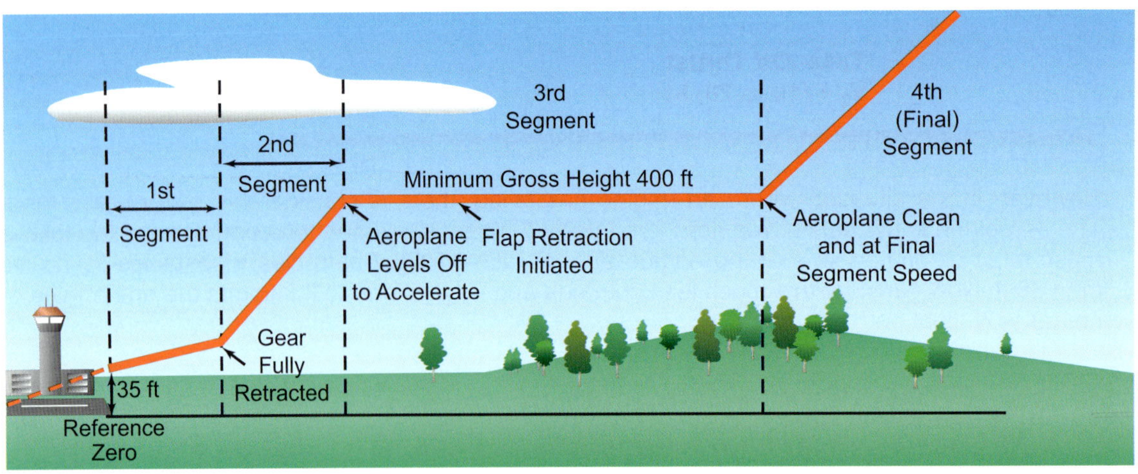

Segment	Gear	Flap	Thrust (from operating engines)	Speed
1st	Down or traveling	Take-off setting	Maximum take-off thrust	At least V_2
2nd	Up	Take-off setting	Maximum take-off thrust	At least V_2
3rd	Up	Reduced in stages from take-off to up	Maximum take-off thrust	Increasing from V_2 to final segment speed
4th (Final)	Up	Up	Maximum continuous	Final segment speed

GRADIENT REQUIREMENTS

From the previous page, it is known that for the probability of passenger death to be remote or less, obstacle clearance must be based on a net gradient. The size of the safety margin is, however, relatively small. First, determine the gross gradient for each segment, assuming that the critical engine failed at V_1 on the take-off run. Then obtain the net gradient by reducing the gross gradient by:

- 0.8% for a 2-engine aeroplane
- 0.9% for a 3-engine aeroplane
- 1.0% for a 4-engine aeroplane

It is the net take-off flight path that is used to determine the obstacle limited mass, which provides a minimum obstacle clearance of 35 ft.

The diagram below shows the average, gross gradient in green and a lower net gradient in red. It also shows that if the decision is to go at V_1 (having suffered an engine failure) and the aeroplane achieves a gross (average) climb gradient, the minimum obstacle clearance actually increases from 35 ft with distance from reference zero. This should give some comfort as 35 ft is extremely close, but stresses the importance of using correct techniques, especially if the obstacles are close and/or the runway wet.

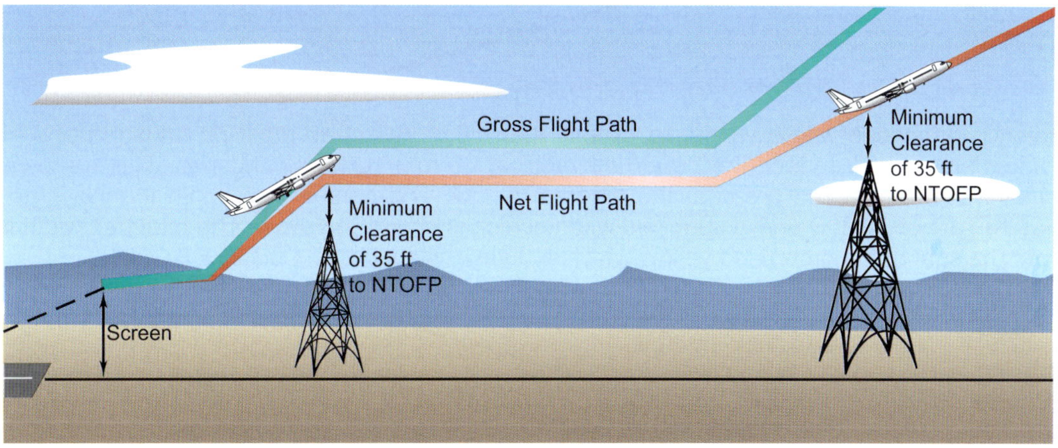

OBSTACLE CLEARANCE AND THE DOMAIN

JAR-OPS 1.495 specifies that the operator must ensure that the net take-off flight path clears all obstacles:

- By a vertical distance of at least 35 ft, or
- By a horizontal distance of at least 90 m plus 0.125 x D, where D is the horizontal distance the aeroplane has travelled from the end of the take-off distance available.

This means that the aeroplane only needs to climb over obstacles that are likely to be in the way. The purpose of the domain is to define which obstacles are "in the way" and need to be cleared vertically.

DOMAIN DIMENSIONS

The dimensions of the domain are shown below. Note that it gets wider the further the aeroplane flies from reference zero, which is at the bottom of the screen at the end of TODA. This is to allow for some drift from the extended centre line, due to crosswinds and slight flying inaccuracies.

Domain widths are normally described in terms of their semi or half widths, which extend outward on both sides of the extended runway centre line. The initial half or semi-width is 90 m, and this is coloured green. The domain then diverges from the extended centerline, with the half width increasing at the rate of 0.125D until it reaches a specified maximum width. This component of the half width is coloured yellow. The whole of the half width is therefore the sum of the green and yellow distances, which is 90 m + 0.125D.

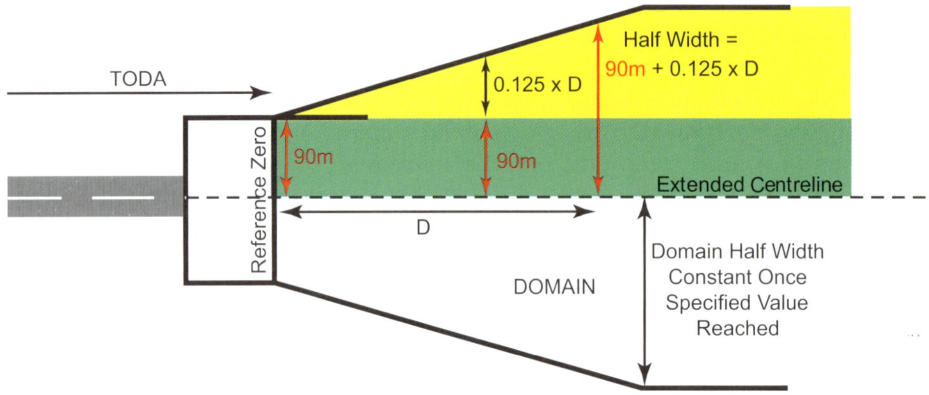

Alternately, aeroplanes with a wingspan of less than 60 m (which is most jet transport and all other aeroplanes), may reduce the initial half width to 60 m + half the wingspan. This narrower initial half width is coloured green in the diagram below. The domain half width then diverges again at the rate of 0.125D until a specified width, which is shown in yellow. The total half width is therefore the sum of the green and yellow which is 60 m + wingspan/2 + 0.125 x D.

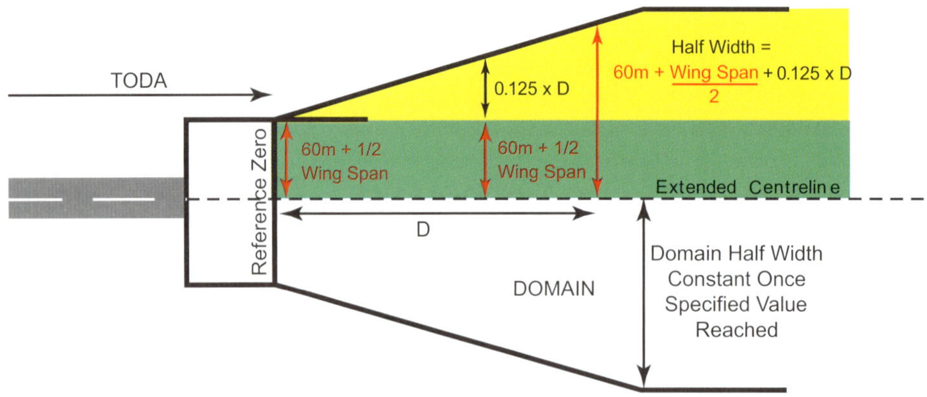

The domain half width at a specified distance, D, from reference zero is often examined in the JAR ATPL, and, therefore, learn the equations for calculating domain half width.

Example:

What is the minimum domain half width at a distance (D) of 800 m if the aeroplane's wingspan is 32 m?

Use the following equation to obtain the minimum half width.

$$\text{Domain half width} = 60\text{ m} + \frac{\text{wingspan}}{2} + 0.125D$$

$$= 60\text{ m} + \frac{32\text{ m}}{2} + (0.125 \times 800\text{ m})$$

$$= 176\text{ m}$$

TURNS IN THE NTOFP

When there is a single limiting obstacle on the edge of the domain, it may not be necessary to reduce the obstacle TOM to clear it vertically if, by turning, the obstacle falls outside of the domain centered around the turning extended centerline.

However, because of the reduced climb performance when turning, there are additional requirements:

- The turn must not be commenced below 50 ft or half of the aeroplane's wingspan, whichever is greater.
- The angle of bank must not exceed 15° below 400 ft, and above this for Class A aeroplanes only may be increased to not exceed 25°.
- The obstacle clearance, and therefore screen height, increases to 50 ft, which requires additional field length.
- The flight manual states whether the minimum speed in the first two segments needs to be increased, which would require additional field length.
- The flight manual includes an additional gradient decrement for the NTOFP.

MAXIMUM DOMAIN WIDTH

It was stated that the domain does not keep widening with distance from reference zero but parallels off at a specified value. This specified value depends on the navigational accuracy and whether there is a turn in the flight path.

Where the intended flight path does not require track changes of more than 15°, an operator need not consider those obstacles which have a lateral distance greater than:

- 300 m if the pilot is able to maintain the required navigational accuracy through the obstacle accountability area, or
- 600 m for flights under all other conditions.

Where the intended flight path does require track changes of more than 15°, an operator need not consider those obstacles which have a lateral distance greater than:

- 600 m if the pilot is able to maintain the required navigational accuracy through the obstacle accountability area, or
- 900 m for flights under all other conditions.

DETERMINING THE OBSTACLE LIMITING MASS

The obstacle limiting mass determined from fig. 4.20 (flaps 5°) and fig. 4.21 (flaps 15°) ensures the minimum required obstacle clearance for both all engines and one engine out at V_1 or later.

The graph is entered with each significant obstacle height and distance. Obtain the obstacle limiting mass by working up the graph correcting for ambient temperature, aerodrome pressure altitude, and 50% of the reported headwind component or not less than 150% of the reported tailwind.

Note: As in all graphs in CAP 698, the wind is factored by the slope of the wind guidelines. Therefore, enter with the actual wind and let the graph factor it.

Chapter 13
Enroute

CLIMB SCHEDULES

After fulfilling a standard departure or other ATC requirements, the pilot wants to climb to increase the aeroplane's specific range. The climb occurs at the appropriate speed in the climb schedule.

A climb schedule states a climb CAS and Mach number, such as 240 kt/0.74 M. At lower altitudes, the aeroplane climbs at the given CAS, and the angle of attack remains constant. This results in the TAS and the Mach number increasing.

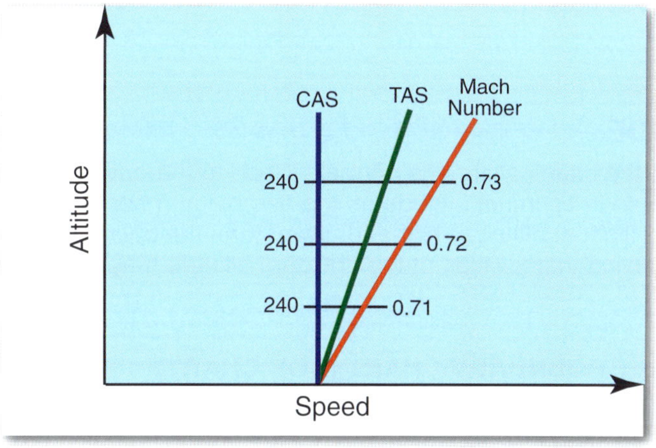

The diagram below shows that at a particular altitude, the Mach number has increased to the Mach number in the climb schedule. This is the change-over altitude, above which the climb continues at a constant Mach number. As the climb is now at a constant Mach number, the CAS is decreasing and the angle of attack is increasing.

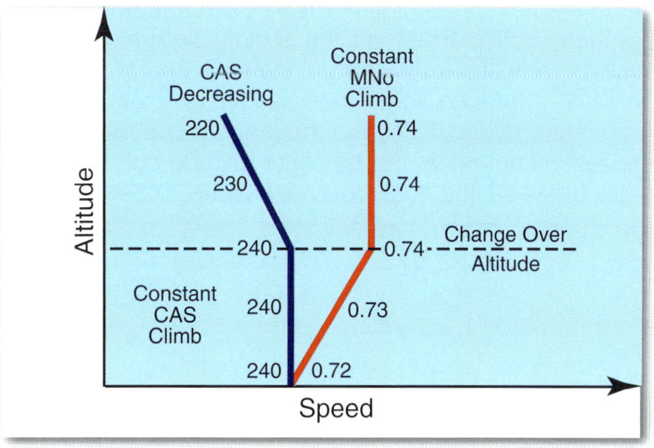

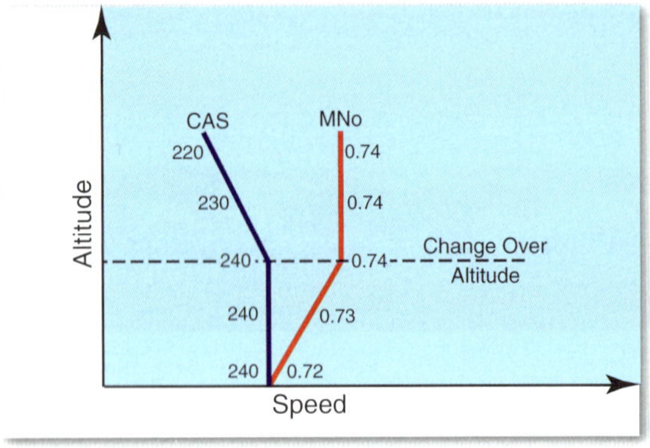

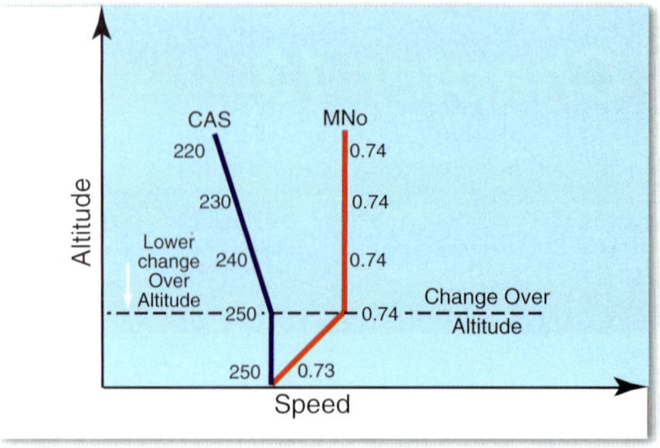

However, the change-over altitude varies if the climb schedule is changed. The diagrams above show the original climb at the schedule 240 kt/0.74 M on the left and another climb with a new climb schedule 250 kt/0.74 M on the right. The increase in the climb schedule CAS results in a greater Mach number at the same altitude. This means that the change-over altitude is lower.

Whenever the climb schedule CAS increases or Mach number reduces, the change-over altitude is lower. Conversely, the change-over altitude is higher if the climb schedule changes to a slower CAS or greater Mach number.

CRUISE

CRUISE ALTITUDE

To reduce fuel burn, the cruise altitude is normally close to the optimum altitude. As explained in Chapter 8, the increase in optimum altitude as the aeroplane mass reduces results in a cruise or step climb. However, flight at altitudes higher or lower than the optimum may be beneficial if there is a more favourable wind there. Flight at the optimum altitude may also be impossible due to the onset of stall buffet.

THE BUFFET ONSET BOUNDARY CHART (BOB CHART)

Buffet from the turbulent airflow that has separated from the wing occurs before both the low and shock stall. The Mach numbers at which this buffet occurs, for different altitudes, aeroplane masses, CG positions, and load factors, is shown in the BOB chart for a particular aeroplane. Sometimes, the BOB chart is drawn for a single load factor of 1.3 g, which allows for limited manoeuvring and turbulence.

A BOB Chart is drawn on the next page. It is normally used to determine the Mach number of the low and shock (high-speed) buffet. Enter on the bottom right-hand side with appropriate load factor (e.g. 1.3) and move vertically to the aeroplane's weight. Move horizontally to the %MAC value and then to the MAC reference line. Finally, move horizontally left to cross the pressure altitude curves at two Mach numbers, which are the Mach numbers for the high- (shock) and low-speed buffet. If the horizontal line meets the pressure altitude curve at its highest point, it means that there is no margin between the high and low-speed buffet, and the aeroplane is at its aerodynamic ceiling.

MEDIUM RANGE JET TRANSPORT

CRUISE MANOEUVRE CAPABILITY (Clean Aircraft)

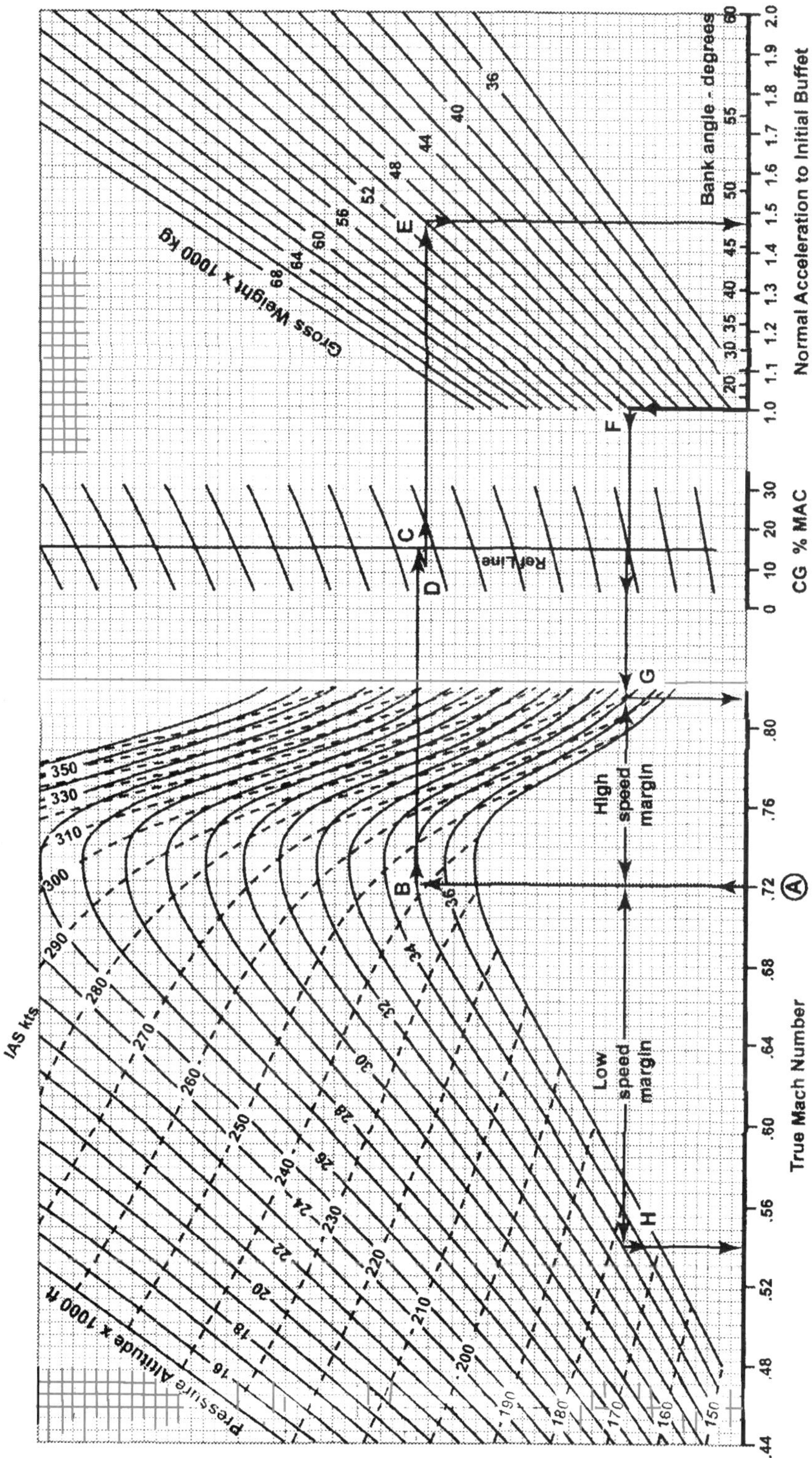

CRUISE SPEED

Although the speed in the cruise is a Mach number, it is based either on a TAS or directly on a Mach number. Cruise Mach numbers determined by TAS vary depending on the balance between fuel costs and time constraints.

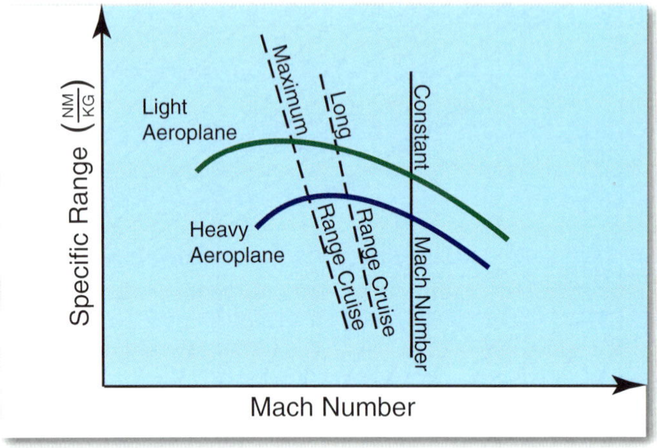

If only fuel costs determine the cruise speed, the Mach number corresponding to the maximum range TAS is used. However, long-range cruise and a cruise based on a cost index greater than zero are at faster true air speeds and corresponding Mach numbers. When time is the main consideration, a faster, constant Mach number is used. These are shown in the above diagram.

ENGINE FAILURE IN THE CRUISE

If an engine fails in the cruise, the thrust on the remaining engines is insufficient to maintain speed in straight-and-level flight, and the aeroplane needs to descend. In chapter 6, you learned that angle of descent depends on the excess drag, and that the minimum angle of descent is close to V_{MD}.

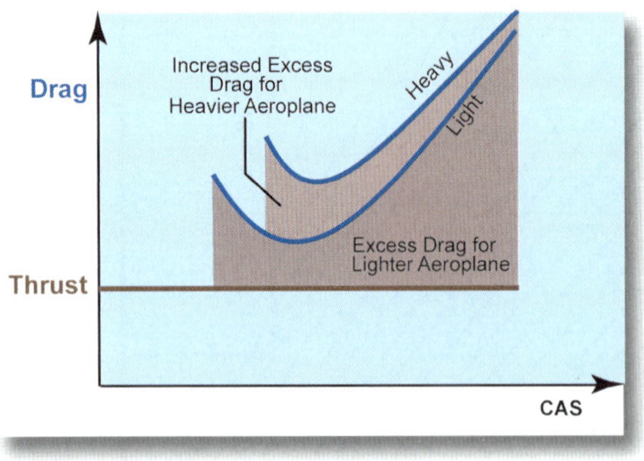

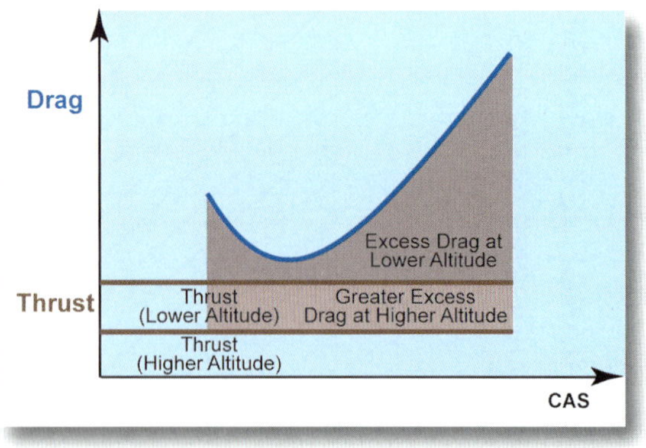

The above graphs show that the excess drag, and hence angle of descent, is greatest when the aeroplane is:

- Heavy and, therefore, has more drag
- High and, therefore, thrust on the remaining engines is less

The angle of the descent together with planned altitude and aeroplane mass are critical when considering enroute obstacle clearance. To ensure sufficient safety, now consider the JAR OPS enroute performance requirements.

ENROUTE GRADIENT MARGIN

In assessing enroute obstacle clearance, base the gradients on net performance. The margin by which the gross gradients reduce varies.

For one engine inoperative, the margins are:

- 1.1% for 2-engine aeroplanes
- 1.4% for 3-engine aeroplanes
- 1.6% for 4-engine aeroplanes

For two engines inoperative, the margins are:

- 0.3% for 3-engine aeroplanes
- 0.5% for 4-engine aeroplanes

These adjusted net gradients are used to determine the JAR-OPS enroute performance requirements for obstacle clearance.

ENROUTE (ONE ENGINE INOPERATIVE) — JAR-OPS 1.500

The operator must ensure that with one engine inoperative, the net flight path either:

- Clears vertically, by at least 2000 ft, all terrain and obstructions along the route within 9.3 km (5 nm) on either side of the intended track or

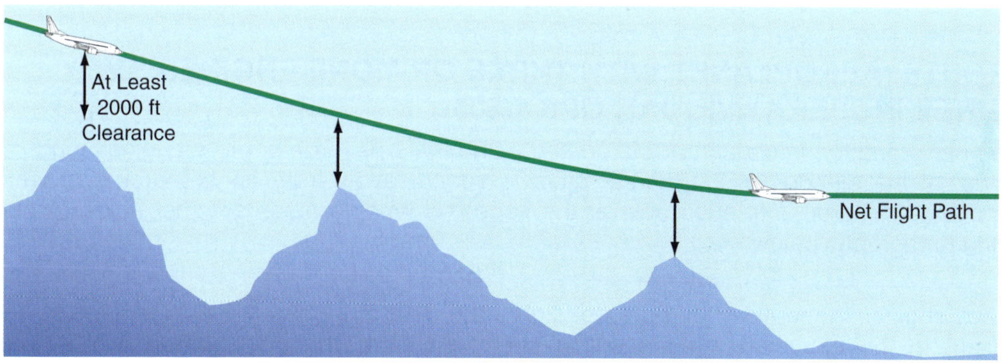

- That the gradient of the net flight path must be positive at least 1000 ft above all terrain and obstructions along the route within 9.3 km (5 nm) on either side of the intended track.

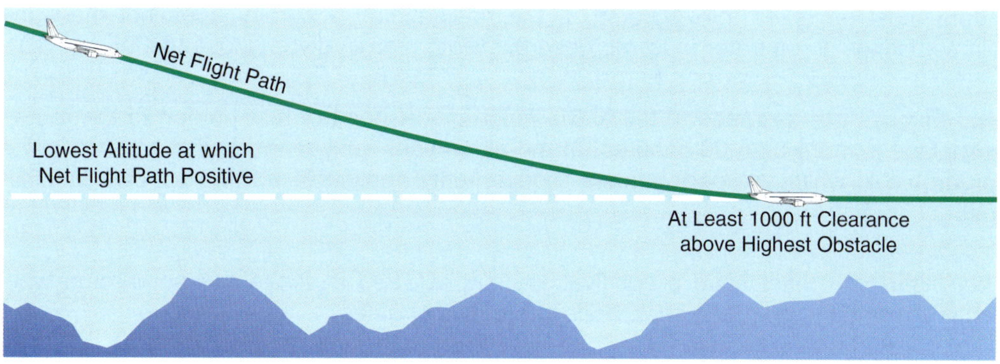

In addition to at least one of the above:

- The aeroplane must have a positive gradient at 1500 ft above the aerodrome where the landing is assumed to be made after engine failure.

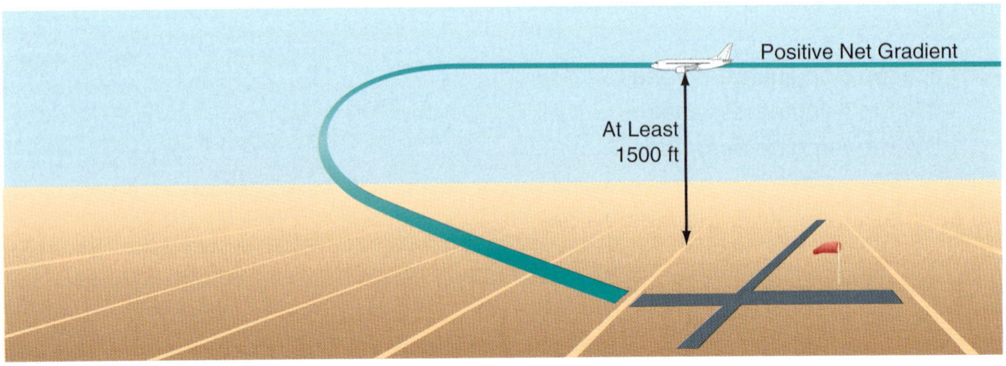

In assessing the compliance of the drift-down requirement (of at least 2000 ft obstacle clearance):

- The engine is assumed to fail at the most critical point along the route.
- Account is taken of the effects of winds on the flight path.
- Fuel jettisoning is permitted. In this case, the fuel is jettisoned as soon as possible once the fuel required to reach the alternate has been calculated.
- The aerodrome where the aeroplane is assumed to land after engine failure must meet the landing requirements.

ENROUTE (AEROPLANES WITH THREE OR MORE ENGINES, TWO ENGINES INOPERATIVE) JAR-OPS 1.505

At no point along the intended track is an aeroplane that has three or more engines more than 90 minutes, at the all-engines long-range cruising speed, away from an aerodrome at which the performance requirements applicable at the expected landing mass are met unless it complies with the paragraphs below.

The two engines inoperative, enroute net flight path data must permit the aeroplane to continue the flight in the expected meteorological conditions from the point where two engines are assumed to fail simultaneously to an aerodrome at which it is possible to land and come to a complete stop when using the prescribed procedure for a landing with two engines inoperative. The net flight path must clear vertically, by at least 2000 ft, all terrain and obstructions along the route within 9.3 km (5 nm) on either side of the intended track. At altitudes and in meteorological conditions requiring ice protection systems to be operable, the effect of their use on the net flight path data must be taken into account. If the navigational accuracy does not meet the 95% containment level, an operator must increase the width margin given above to 18.5 km (10 nm).

The two engines are assumed to fail at the most critical point of that portion of the route where the aeroplane is more than 90 minutes, at the all-engines long-range cruising speed, away from an aerodrome at which the performance requirements applicable at the expected landing mass are met.

The net flight path must have a positive gradient at 1500 ft above the aerodrome where the landing is assumed to be made after the failure of two engines.

Fuel jettisoning is permitted to an extent consistent with reaching the aerodrome with the required fuel reserves if a safe procedure is used.

The expected mass of the aeroplane at the point where the two engines are assumed to fail must not be less than that which would include sufficient fuel to proceed to:

- An aerodrome where the landing is assumed to be made,
- To arrive there at least 1500 ft directly over the landing area, and
- To fly level for 15 minutes.

EXTENDED RANGE TWIN OPERATIONS (ETOPS)

Normally, a twin-engine aeroplane must be within 60 minutes of a suitable alternate aerodrome at all points of its intended route. However, an aeroplane may be given approval for this time interval to be increased. An ETOPS of 120 minutes means that the aeroplane must remain within 120 minutes flying time of a suitable alternate assessed using the still air, single-engine cruise speed.

CAP 698 AND ENROUTE ENGINE FAILURE

DETERMINING OPTIMUM DRIFT-DOWN SPEED

Fig 4.22 allows the optimum drift-down speed to be determined at different aeroplane weights. It is useful to note that the optimum drift-down speed is slower when the aeroplane is lighter, because the drag curve has moved down and to the left.

DRIFTDOWN SPEED/LEVEL OFF

Weight 1000 Kg.		Optimum Driftdown Speed KIAS	Level Off Altitude Ft.		
Start Driftdown	Level Off		IAS + 10° C & Below	IAS + 15° C	IAS + 20° C
70	67	245	14200	12900	11400
65	62	237	16700	15500	14200
60	57	228	19200	18200	17000
55	52	218	21900	20900	19800
50	48	209	24800	23800	22800
45	43	198	27700	26900	26000
40	38	187	30700	30100	29300
35	33	175	33900	33400	32700

DETERMINING THE AEROPLANE MASS FOR REQUIRED NET LEVEL-OFF ALTITUDE

Fig. 4.23 determines the heaviest aeroplane mass at point of engine failure, allowing for 1000 ft vertical clearance above the highest obstacle on track to the appropriate alternate aerodrome.

Enter the left-hand side with the pressure altitude of the highest obstacle plus 1000 ft. Move horizontally to the appropriate ISA deviation and down to read off the maximum gross weight at point of engine failure.

Note: The air conditioning can be turned off below 17 000 ft, which has a beneficial effect.

CIVIL AVIATION AUTHORITY
PERFORMANCE-AEROPLANE

DATA SHEET
MRJT1

1 ENGINE INOP.

Figure 4.34 Net Level-Off Altitude

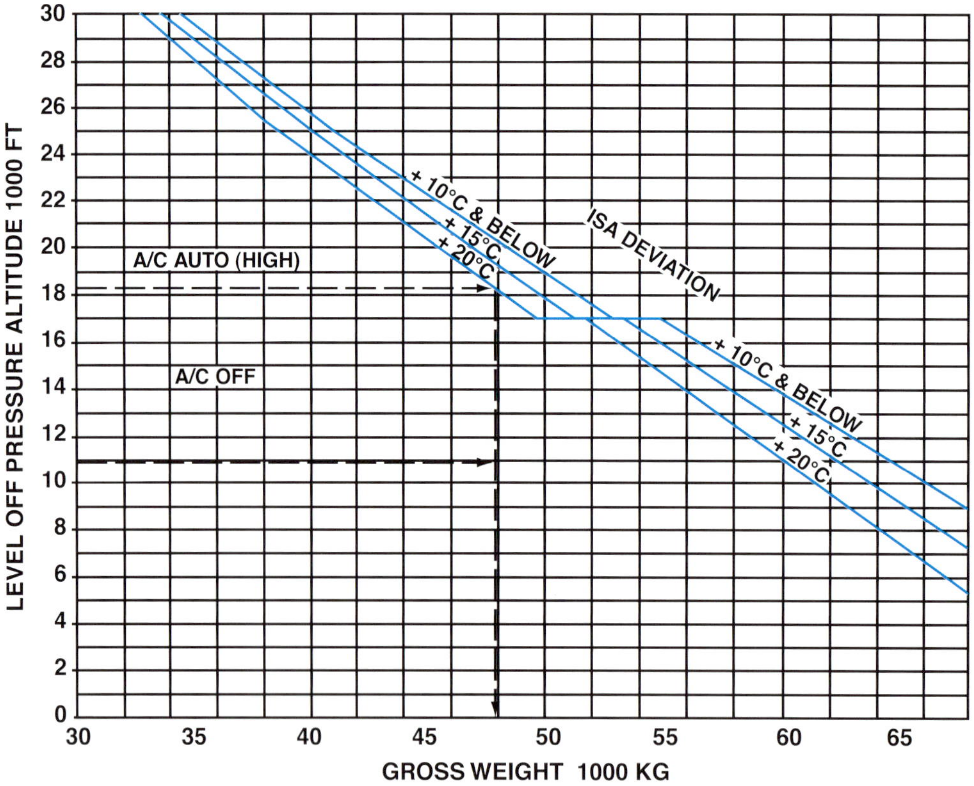

DETERMINING THE NET FLIGHT PATH DRIFT-DOWN PROFILE

Figures 4.24 to 4.27 inclusive allow the net drift-down profiles to be established for different weights and aeroplane masses and winds. Check each obstacle for at least 2000 ft vertical clearance.

The effect of air density on the thrust from operating engines is allowed for by using the appropriate figure for the planned flight level. Figure 4.24 is shown below, which is for an engine failure at FL370.

There are two interesting points relating to these graphs:

- The effect of temperatures above ISA + 10°C is allowed for by increasing the gross weight to a heavier equivalent weight in a sub-graph in the top right-hand corner.
- At lighter masses, the drift-down does not begin immediately. This is because altitude is held until the aeroplane has decelerated to its slower drift-down speed.

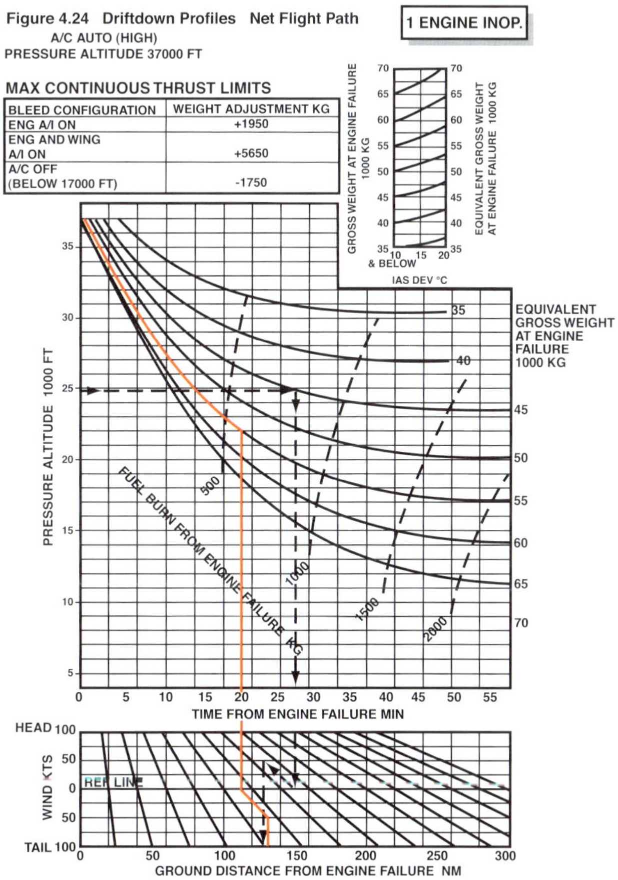

Example:

What is the ground distance to descend 15 000 ft from FL370, mass 55 000 kg, ISA + 5°C and a 50 kt tailwind?

Worked Answer:

At ISA +5°C, no increase is required so the equivalent gross weight is also 55 000 kg.

Follow the 55 000 kg profile down to FL220 (37 000 minus 15 000 ft). Stop at the wind reference line and move with the guideline to 50 kt wind. Move vertically down to read off a ground distance of just over 130 nm.

Chapter 14
Landing

LANDING REQUIREMENTS AT DESTINATION AND ALTERNATE AERODROMES

The performance requirements at alternate aerodromes are the same as for at the destination. The maximum landing mass is the most restrictive (lowest) of:

- The climb-limited mass
- The field-length limited mass
- The structural maximum landing mass

THE CLIMB-LIMITED MASS

The climb-limited mass for Class A aeroplanes allows for both the landing climb and discontinued approach climb requirements outlined below. For aeroplanes using decision heights below 200 ft, an additional discontinued instrument approach climb requirement is needed.

LANDING CLIMB

The maximum mass at which a gradient of 3.2% can be achieved is with:

- All engines operating at the power available after 8 seconds from the initiation of movement of the thrust control from the minimum flight idle position to the TOGA position
- The aeroplane in the landing configuration
- Expected air density for the aerodrome altitude and ambient temperature expected at the time of landing
- A climb speed not less than 1.13 V_{SR0} or V_{MCL}, or more than 1.23 V_{SR0}

DISCONTINUED APPROACH CLIMB (BAULKED CLIMB)

The maximum mass at which the following gradient can be achieved:

- 2.1% for 2-engine aeroplanes
- 2.4% for 3-engine aeroplanes
- 2.7% for 4-engine aeroplanes

With:

- The critical engine inoperative and the remaining engines at TOGA
- The normal approach speed but no greater than 1.41 $_{VSR0}$
- Landing gear retracted and flaps in the approach configuration
- Expected air density for the aerodrome altitude and ambient temperature expected at the time of landing

DISCONTINUED INSTRUMENT APPROACH CLIMB

For instrument approaches with decision heights below 200 ft, an operator must verify that the approach mass of the aeroplane, taking into account the take-off mass and the fuel expected to be consumed in flight, allows a missed approach gradient of climb with the critical engine failed and with the speed and configuration used for go-around of at least 2.5%, or the published gradient, whichever is the greater.

DETERMINING THE CLIMB LIMITED MASS

Figure 4.29 in CAP 698 allows the climb limited mass to be determined. Like the take-off climb mass graph, figure 4.5, the gradient is with respect to the air. This means that the landing climb mass is not affected by the wind.

Figure 4.29 Landing Performance Climb Limit

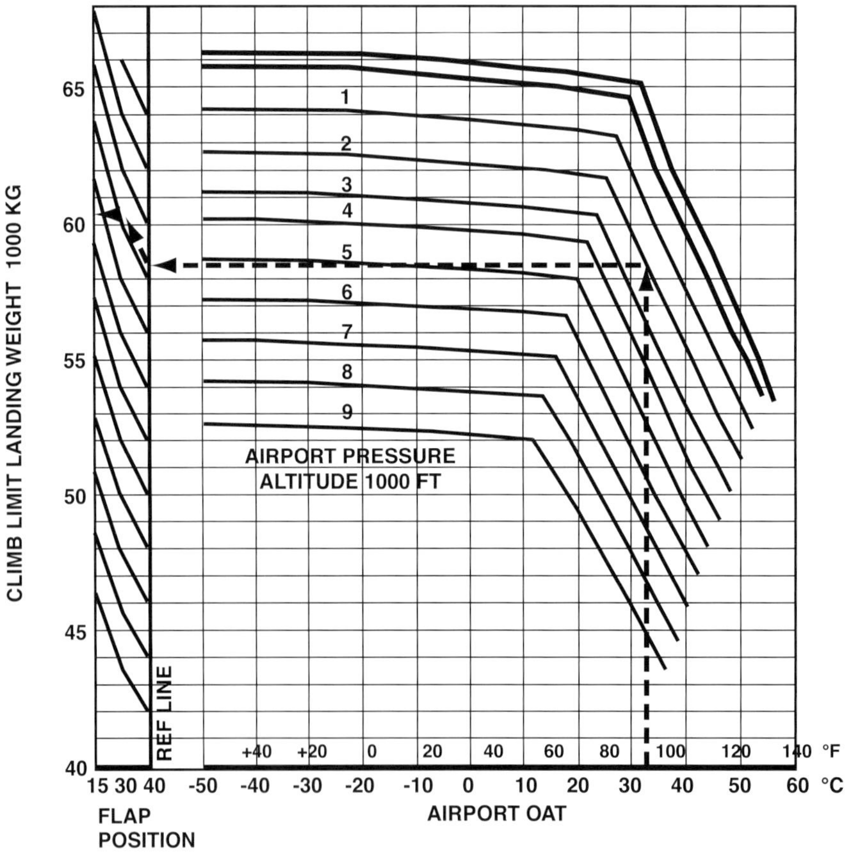

LANDING DISTANCE REQUIREMENTS (JAR-OPS 1.515)

The landing mass for the estimated time of landing at the destination aerodrome and at any alternate aerodrome must be such as to allow a full stop landing from 50 ft above the threshold:

- Within 60% of the landing distance available for turbojet powered aeroplanes.

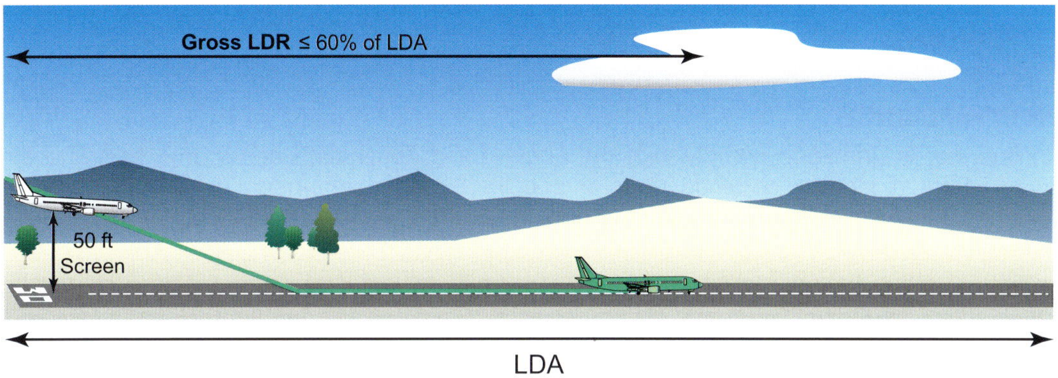

This means that the LDR ≤ 0.6 LDA, or, rearranging the formulae, the LDR x 1.67 ≤ LDA or

- Within 70% of the landing distance available for turbo-propeller powered aeroplanes.

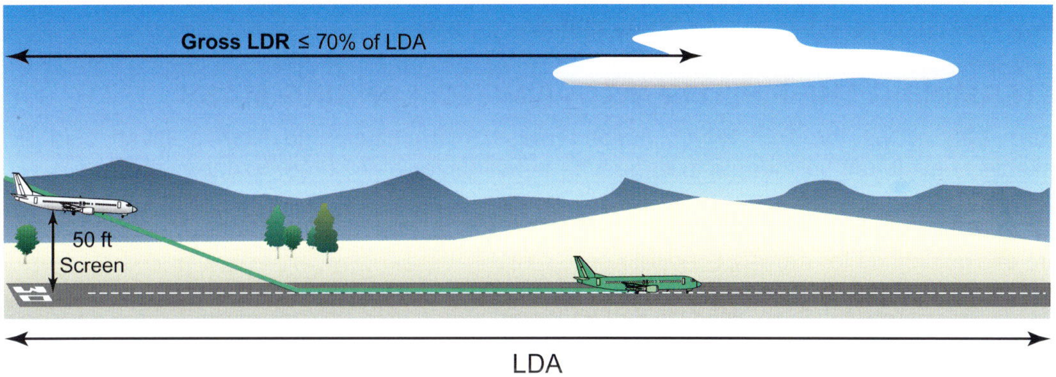

This means that the LDR ≤ 0.7 LDA, or, rearranging the formulae, the LDR x 1.43 ≤ LDA.

For steep approach procedures, the Authority may approve the use of landing distance data based on a screen height of less than 50 ft but not less than 35 ft.

When showing compliance with the above, an operator must take account of the following:

- The reference speed at the screen (V_{REF}) not less than 1.23 V_{SR0}
- The aeroplane in the landing configuration
- The altitude at the aerodrome
- The standard day temperature
- Not more than 50% of the headwind component or not less than 150% of the tailwind component
- The runway slope in the direction of landing if greater than ± 2%

RUNWAY SELECTION

Landing must be considered in both still air and factored forecast conditions.

- In still air, the aeroplane uses the most favourable runway.
- Using the forecast wind, the aeroplane lands on the runway most likely to be assigned, considering the probable wind speed and direction and the ground handling characteristics of the aeroplane and considering other conditions such as landing aids and terrain.

NON COMPLIANCE

If an operator is unable to comply with the above for a destination aerodrome having a single runway where a landing depends upon a specified wind component, an aeroplane may be dispatched if two alternate aerodromes are designated that permit compliance.

If the forecast wind at the destination means that the operator cannot comply with the above conditions, the aeroplane may still be dispatched. This may be done if the conditions at one alternate are such that the rules for landing are complied with.

WET RUNWAY

If the runway is forecast to be wet at the estimated time of arrival, the LDR must be increased by 15%.

This means that the dry, gross LDR must be multiplied by 1.92 (1.67 x 1.15) for a turbojet and 1.64 (1.43 x 1.15) for a turbo-propeller aeroplane.

DETERMINING THE FIELD LENGTH LIMITED LANDING MASS

Figure 4.28 allows the field length limiting mass to be calculated from a given field length available or minimum field length that must be available for a given aeroplane mass.

Note that the graph, like all the other CAP MRJT data, has already been adjusted to net, and there are guidelines for runway condition.

The effect of antiskid inoperative is incorporated in the figure by the second set of pressure altitude lines on the right. Unless stated in a question that antiskid is inoperative, the left-hand set of pressure altitude lines is to be used.

Example 1:

Determine the field length limiting landing mass at an aerodrome at a pressure altitude of 4000 ft with 5000 ft field length available, 20 kt headwind, wet surface, and flaps 30°.

Figure 4.28 Landing Performance Field Length Limit

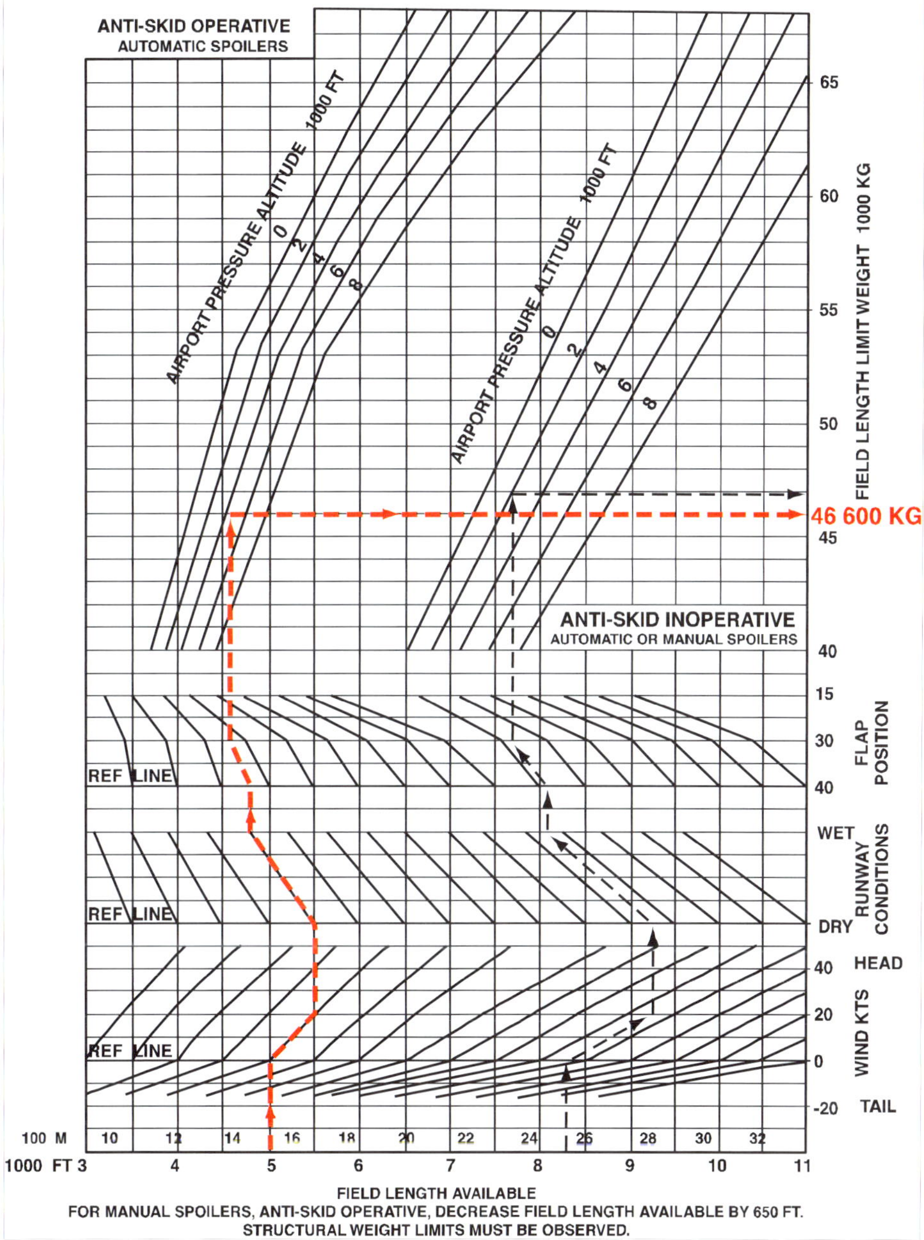

Worked Answer 1:

The red line on figure 4.28 starts at the bottom at the field length available of 5000 ft. As you are moving in the direction of the example arrows, stop at each of the reference lines and then move with the guidelines to the given value before continuing vertically to the next reference line. Because the question does not state that antiskid is inoperative, use the left set of pressure altitude lines turning horizontally to read off a field length limiting landing mass of 46 600 kg.

Example 2:

Determine the minimum field length that must be available if antiskid is not working at a unidirectional, dry runway with a tailwind of 10 kt. The aeroplane mass at landing is 43 500 kg, and the aerodrome pressure altitude is 2000 ft.

Figure 4.28 Landing Performance Field Length Limit

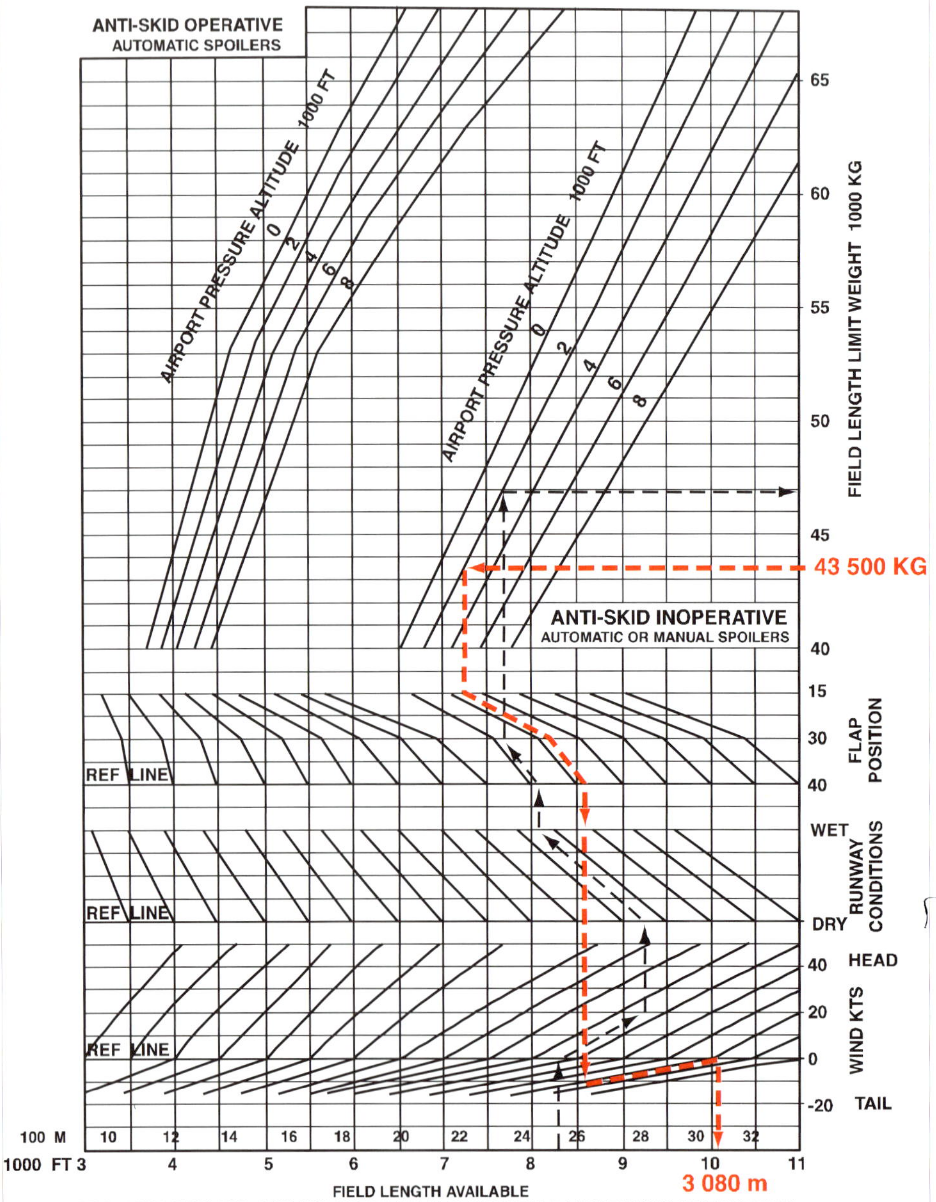

FOR MANUAL SPOILERS, ANTI-SKID OPERATIVE, DECREASE FIELD LENGTH AVAILABLE BY 650 FT.
STRUCTURAL WEIGHT LIMITS MUST BE OBSERVED.

Worked Answer 2:

Enter the right-hand side with the landing mass of 43 500 kg and move left horizontally to the right-hand set of pressure altitude lines, which are for antiskid inoperative. Then move vertically down through the flap position, runway condition, and wind guidelines noting that you are moving in the opposite direction to the printed example. This means that when an area of guidelines is reached, the line must continue vertically until the value and then move with the guidelines to the reference line. The answer is approximately 3080 m or 10 100 ft.

Chapter 15
JAR Performance Class B Aeroplanes

PERFORMANCE CLASS B

Propeller-driven aeroplanes with a maximum approved passenger seating configuration of 9 or less and a maximum take-off mass of 5700 kg or less are operated in accordance with JAR-OPS, Subpart H–Performance Class B.

GENERAL (JAR OPS 1.525)

A single-engine aeroplane cannot be:

- Operated at night, or
- In IMC unless under SVFR.

Where a two-engine Class B aeroplane does not meet the climb requirements, detailed later, it must be treated as a single-engine aeroplane.

TAKE-OFF CLIMB

ALL ENGINES OPERATING

All single and twin piston-engine aeroplanes must have a steady gradient of climb after take-off of at least 4% with:

- Take-off power on each engine
- The landing gear extended except that, if the landing gear can be retracted in not more than 7 seconds, it may be assumed to be retracted
- The wing flaps in the take-off position
- A climb speed not less than the greater of 1.1 V_{MC} and 1.2 V_{S1}

ONE ENGINE INOPERATIVE

In addition, at an altitude of 400 ft above the take-off surface, twin-engine aeroplanes that can be operated in IMC must have a steady gradient of climb that can be measurably positive with:

- The critical engine inoperative and its propeller in the minimum drag position
- The remaining engine at take-off power
- The landing gear retracted
- The wing flaps in the take-off position(s)
- A climb speed equal to that achieved at 50 ft

The steady gradient of climb must be not less than 0.75% at an altitude of 1500 ft above the take-off surface with:

- The critical engine inoperative and its propeller in the minimum drag position
- The remaining engine at not more than maximum continuous power
- The landing gear retracted
- The wing flaps retracted
- A climb speed not less than 1.2 V_{S1}

LANDING CLIMB

ALL ENGINES OPERATING

The steady gradient of climb must be at least 2.5% with:

- Not more than the power or thrust that is available 8 seconds after initiation of movement of the power controls from the minimum flight idle position
- The landing gear extended
- The wing flaps in the landing position
- A climb speed equal to V_{REF}

ONE ENGINE INOPERATIVE

Twin-engine aeroplanes which can be operated in IMC must have a steady gradient of climb not less than 0.75% at an altitude of 1500 ft above the landing surface with:

- The critical engine inoperative and its propeller in the minimum drag position
- The remaining engine at not more than maximum continuous power
- The landing gear retracted
- The wing flaps retracted
- A climb speed not less than 1.2 V_{S1}

TAKE-OFF (JAR OPS 1.530)

The operator must ensure that the take-off mass does not exceed the maximum take-off mass specified in the Aeroplane Flight Manual, taking account of the following.

GROSS TO NET SAFETY FACTORS

The operator uses the unfactored, gross take-off distance specified in the Aeroplane Flight Manual to ensure that it does not exceed:

When multiplied by a factor of 1.25, the take-off run available, or

When stopway and/or clearway is available, the longest of the following:

- The take-off run available
- When multiplied by a factor of 1.15, the take-off distance available and
- When multiplied by a factor of 1.3, the accelerate-stop distance available.

AERODROME AIR DENSITY

The pressure altitude and ambient temperature at the aerodrome must be allowed for as they affect the air density. Low air density results in longer distances required or lower take-off weights for a given take-off distance available.

RUNWAY SURFACE

The take-off distance from the aeroplane flight manual is for a hard, dry surface. This distance must be adjusted if the surface is wet or grass. Grass affects the take-off roll because of increased rolling resistance. The factors to be applied are in the table below:

Surface Type	Condition	Factor
Grass up to 20 cm long	Dry	1.20
	Wet	1.30
Paved	Wet	1.00

Problems can occur when an aeroplane is using grass runways:

- Care should be taken in assessing the rate of acceleration.
- If the take-off is rejected on short wet grass, the surface may be slippery. In this case, the distance may be increased substantially.

RUNWAY SLOPE

Any runway upslope in the direction of take-off must be taken into account:

- Upslope up to 2%, take-off distance to be increased by 5% for each 1% of upslope
- Upslope >2%, corrections for runways with an upslope of more than 2% require the approval of the authority.
- Any advantage of downslope is ignored for the purpose of calculating take-off mass distance.

WIND

Not more than 50% of the reported headwind component or not less than 150% of the reported tail-wind component can be factored into the take-off distance.

CONTAMINATED RUNWAYS

Taking-off from a runway contaminated with water, slush, or snow is inadvisable. Take-off should be delayed until the runway is cleared.

TAKE-OFF OBSTACLE CLEARANCE

There is no obstacle clearance requirement for single-engine aeroplanes. In the VMC conditions required for operation, the pilot is expected to see and avoid any obstacles after take-off. Class B twin-engine aeroplanes do have an obstacle requirement, which is covered in the following section.

TAKE-OFF OBSTACLE CLEARANCE – MULTI-ENGINE AEROPLANES (JAR OPS 1.535)

The operator ensures that the take-off flight path of an aeroplane with two or more engines clears all obstacles:

- By a vertical margin of at least 50 ft, or
- By a horizontal distance of at least 90 m plus 0.125 x D, where D is the horizontal distance travelled by the aeroplane from the end of the take-off distance available or the end of the take-off distance if a turn is scheduled before the end of the take-off distance available.

Note: For aeroplanes with a wingspan of less than 60 m, a horizontal obstacle clearance of half the aeroplane wingspan plus 60 m, plus 0.125 x D may be used.

TAKE-OFF FLIGHT PATH – VISUAL COURSE GUIDANCE NAVIGATION

In order to allow visual course guidance navigation, an operator must ensure that the weather conditions prevailing at the time of operation including ceiling and visibility are such that the obstacle and/or ground reference points can be seen and identified.

The Operations Manual must specify the minimum weather conditions for the aerodrome concerned that enable the flight crew to continuously determine and maintain the correct flight path with respect to ground reference points to provide a safe clearance with respect to obstructions and terrain as follows:

- The procedure must be well-defined with respect to ground reference points, so that the track to be flown can be analysed for obstacle clearance requirements.
- The procedure must be within the capabilities of the aeroplane with respect to forward speed, bank angle, and wind effects.
- A written and/or pictorial description of the procedure must be provided for crew use.
- The limiting environmental conditions must be specified (e.g. wind, cloud, visibility, day/night, ambient lighting, obstruction lighting).

SAFE OPERATION IN CONDITIONS OF LIMITED VISIBILITY

Unlike the Performance Class A airworthiness requirements already studied, performance Class B does not necessarily provide for engine failure in all phases of flight. It is accepted that performance accountability for engine failure need not be considered until a height of 300 ft is reached.

The weather minima given in Appendix 1 to JAR-OPS 1.430 up to and including 300 ft imply that if a take-off is undertaken with minima below 300 ft, a one engine inoperative flight path must be plotted starting on the all-engine take-off flight path at the assumed engine failure height. This path must meet the vertical and lateral obstacle clearance specified. Should engine failure occur below this height, the associated visibility is taken as the minimum which would enable the pilot to make, if necessary, a forced landing broadly in the direction of the take-off. At or below 300 ft, a circle and land procedure is extremely inadvisable.

If the assumed engine failure height is more than 300 ft, the visibility must be at least 1500 m. To allow for manoeuvring, the same minimum visibility should apply whenever the obstacle clearance criteria for a continued take-off cannot be met. To comply with the above, it is assumed that:

- The take-off flight path begins at a height of 50 ft above the surface at the end of the take-off distance required and ends at approximately 1500 ft above the surface.
- The aeroplane is not banked before the aeroplane has reached a height of 50 ft above the surface.
- The angle of bank does not exceed 15° after this point.
- Failure of the critical engine occurs at the point on the all-engine take-off flight path where visual reference for the purpose of avoiding obstacles is expected to be lost (i.e. cloud base).
- The gradient of the take-off flight path from 50 ft to the assumed engine failure height is equal to the average all-engine gradient during climb and transition to the enroute configuration multiplied by a factor of 0.77.
- The gradient of the take-off flight path from the height reached above to the end of the take-off flight path is equal to the one engine inoperative enroute climb gradient shown in the Aeroplane Flight Manual.

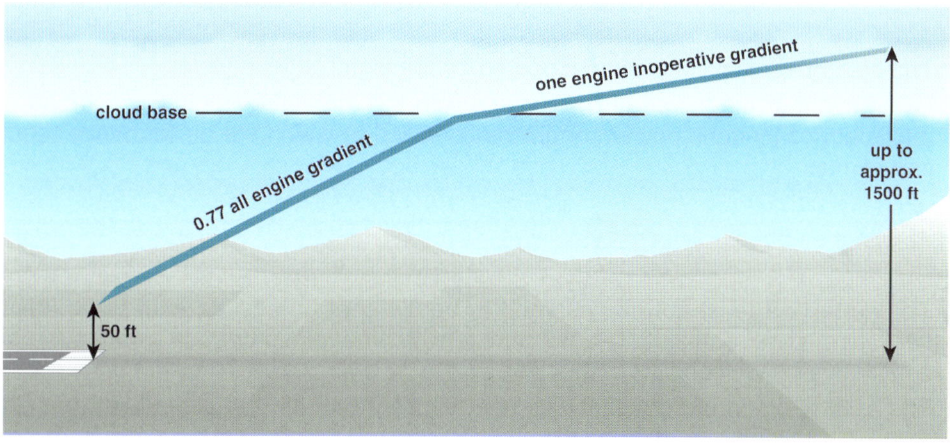

OBSTACLE AREA OR DOMAIN

Where the intended flight path does not require a track change of more than 15°, an operator need not consider obstacles which have a lateral distance from the extended runway centre line greater than:

- 300 m if the flight is conducted under conditions allowing visual course guidance navigation, or if navigational aids are available enabling the pilot to maintain the intended flight path with the same accuracy, or
- 600 m for flights under all other conditions.

Where the intended flight path requires track changes of more than 15°, an operator need not consider those obstacles which have a lateral distance from the extended runway centre line greater than:

- 600 m for flights under conditions allowing visual course guidance navigation.
- 900 m for flights under all other conditions.

To comply with the above, an operator must take account of the following:

- The mass of the aeroplane at the commencement of the take-off run
- The pressure altitude at the aerodrome
- The ambient temperature at the aerodrome
- Not more than 50% of the reported headwind component or not less than 150% of the reported tailwind component

ENROUTE

MULTI-ENGINE AEROPLANES (JAR-OPS 1.540)

The operator ensures that the aeroplane is capable of continuing flight at or above the relevant minimum altitudes for safe flight stated in the Operations Manual to a point 1000 ft above an aerodrome. The following are taken into account:

- The meteorological conditions expected for the flight
- In the event of the failure of one engine with the remaining engines operating within the maximum continuous power conditions specified at which the performance requirements can be met

To comply with the above:

- The aeroplane must not be assumed to be flying at an altitude exceeding that at which the rate of climb equals 300 ft per minute with all engines operating within the maximum continuous power conditions specified.
- The assumed enroute gradient with one engine inoperative shall be the gross gradient of descent or climb, as appropriate, correspondingly increased by a gradient of 0.5% or decreased by a gradient of 0.5%.

The altitude at which the rate of climb equals 300 ft per minute is not a restriction on the maximum cruising altitude at which the aeroplane can fly in practice. It is merely the maximum altitude from which the drift-down procedure can be planned to start.

Aeroplanes may be planned to clear enroute obstacles assuming a drift-down procedure, having first increased the scheduled enroute one engine inoperative descent data by 0.5% gradient.

SINGLE-ENGINE AEROPLANES (JAR-OPS 1.542)

The operator has to ensure that the aeroplane, in the meteorological conditions expected for the flight, and in the event of engine failure, is capable of reaching a place at which a safe forced landing can be made.

To comply with the above:

- The aeroplane must not be assumed to be flying, with the engine operating within the maximum continuous power conditions specified, at an altitude exceeding that at which the rate of climb equals 300 ft per minute.
- The assumed enroute gradient shall be the gross gradient of descent increased by a gradient of 0.5%.

In the event of an engine failure, single-engine aeroplanes have to rely on gliding to a point suitable for a safe forced landing. Such a procedure is clearly incompatible with flight above a cloud layer, which extends below the relevant minimum safe altitude.

The altitude at which the rate of climb equals 300 ft per minute is not a restriction on the maximum cruising altitude at which the aeroplane can fly in practice; it is merely the maximum altitude from which the engine-inoperative procedure can be planned to start.

The above statements require an operator to ensure that in the event of an engine failure, the aeroplane should be capable of reaching a point from which a successful forced landing can be made. Unless otherwise specified by the Authority, this point should be 1000 ft above the intended landing area.

LANDING

DESTINATION AND ALTERNATE AERODROMES (JAR-OPS 1.545)

The landing mass of the aeroplane must not exceed the maximum landing mass specified for the altitude and the ambient temperature expected for the estimated time of landing at the destination and alternate aerodrome.

GROSS TO NET SAFETY FACTOR (JAR-OPS 1.550)

An operator shall ensure that the landing mass of the aeroplane determined for the estimated time of landing allows a full stop landing from 50 ft above the threshold within 70% of the landing distance available at the destination aerodrome and at any alternate aerodrome.

The Authority may approve the use of landing distance data factored in accordance with this paragraph based on a screen height of less than 50 ft but not less than 35 ft. Short landing operations may also be approved.

To comply with the above, the following have to be taken into account:

- The altitude at the aerodrome
- Not more than 50% of the head-wind component or not less than 150% of the tail-wind component
- The runway surface condition and the type of runway surface
- The runway slope in the direction of landing

To dispatch an aeroplane in accordance with the above, it must be assumed that:

- The aeroplane will land on the most favourable runway in still air
- The aeroplane will land on the runway most likely to be assigned considering:
    - The probable wind speed and direction
    - The ground handling characteristics of the aeroplane
    - Other conditions such as landing aids and terrain

If an operator is unable to comply with the above rules for the destination aerodrome, the aeroplane may be dispatched if an alternate aerodrome is designated that complies.

RUNWAY SLOPE

The landing distances required should be increased by 5% for each 1% of downslope except that correction factors for runways with slopes in excess of 2% need the acceptance of the Authority. There is no correction for upslope of 2% or less.

SURFACE

Unless otherwise specified, the following safety factor for grass must be applied:

Grass (on firm soil up to 20 cm long) Dry distance x 1.15

WET AND CONTAMINATED RUNWAYS

The operator ensures that when the appropriate weather reports or forecasts indicate that the runway at the estimated time of arrival may be wet, the landing distance available must be equal to or exceed the required wet landing distance.

When landing on very short grass that is wet, the surface may be slippery, in which case the distances may increase by as much as 60% (1.60 factor). However, it is not possible for a pilot to determine accurately the degree of wetness of grass therefore a factor of 1.15 is to be used. The dry landing distance calculated is multiplied by a factor of 1.15 to gain the wet landing distance required.

Chapter 16
Single-Engine Piston (SEP1)

INTRODUCTION

This chapter uses the CAP 698 to obtain aeroplane data for the single-engine piston Class B aeroplane. The previous chapter looked at the JAR regulations that apply to public transport using Class B aeroplanes. However, class B aeroplanes are normally used for private and instructional uses, which do not require the same level of safety as public transport. The graphs for Class B aeroplanes are normally drawn to provide gross values, which must be factored for public transport.

The data for the single-engine piston (SEP1) aeroplane is contained in the CAP 698 in the green pages of Section II. The following pages show worked examples using these graphs and data.

TAKE-OFF DISTANCE REQUIRED

Figures 2.1 and 2.2 enable determination of the gross take-off distance required. The figures differ only in the take-off flap position. Figure 2.1 is for flaps up and figure 2.2 is for flaps extended in the approach setting.

Both graphs allow for the variables of aeroplane weight and aerodrome temperature, pressure altitude, and wind component when moving through the graph. However, the figure determined is the gross distance required for a paved, level, and dry runway. To allow for public transport, slope, and wet/dry grass factor the figure determined by the values stated in the CAP.

Always factor winds to allow for a lull in a headwind and a gust in a tailwind. Use 50% of a headwind and 150% of a tailwind. However, the wind guidelines in all the figures in the CAP 698 factor the wind. Therefore, enter with the forecast or reported wind, not the factored wind.

The data on page 6, section 2.1a and b, may still be incorrect and is awaiting revision. As a precaution, use the factors on page 19, section 2.1a and b, which relate to the multi-engine Class B aeroplane and are correct.

Example 1:

Determine the gross take-off distance for the SEP1 aeroplane given the following:

> Aerodrome pressure altitude 1000 ft, temperature 20°C, aeroplane weight 3300 lb, flaps up, and 15 kt reported headwind.

Worked example 1:

Enter at the left-hand side with 20°C and move vertically up to 1000 ft (halfway between sea level and 2000 ft). Move horizontally right and stop at the weight reference line, then move down and right with the guide lines to the weight value of 3300 lb, before moving horizontally again to the wind reference line. The different gradients of the head and tailwind guidelines factor the wind. Therefore, follow the guideline down and right to 15 kt headwind before moving horizontally to the screen reference line. As the take-off distance ends at the screen (50 ft for class B), the line must move in proportion to the guidelines up and right across the whole width of the obstacle height guidelines. An answer of 1550 ft (plus or minus no more than 100 ft) should be achieved.

TAKE-OFF DISTANCE-FLAPS UP

ASSOCIATED CONDITIONS:

POWER .... TAKE-OFF POWER SET BEFORE BRAKE RELEASE
MIXTURE .... FULL RICH
FLAPS .... UP
LANDING GEAR .... RETRACT AFTER POSITIVE CLIMB ESTABLISHED
COWL FLAPS .... OPEN
RUNWAY .... PAVED, LEVEL, DRY SURFACE

EXAMPLE:

OAT .... 15°C
PRESSURE ALTITUDE .... 5653 FT
TAKE-OFF WEIGHT .... 3650 LBS
HEAD WIND COMPONENT .... 10 KST

GROUND ROLL .... 1900 FT
TOTAL DISTANCE OVER 50-FT OBSTACLE ... 3475 FT
TAKE-OFF SPEED AT
ROTATION .... 73 KTS
50-FT .... 84 KTS

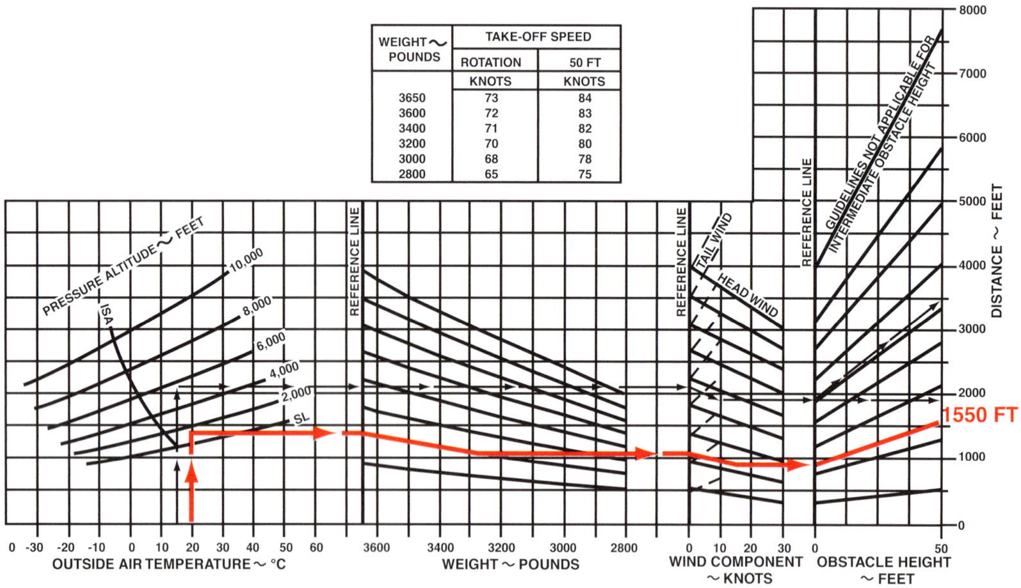

WEIGHT ~ POUNDS	TAKE-OFF SPEED	
	ROTATION KNOTS	50 FT KNOTS
3650	73	84
3600	72	83
3400	71	82
3200	70	80
3000	68	78
2800	65	75

Example 2:

Given a take-off distance required of 2000 ft from figure 2.1, what is the minimum take-off distance required for public transport if the runway is short, dry grass and has no stopway or clearway and a 1.2% upslope?

Worked example 2:

If the gross TODR is 2000 ft, the net TODR required must be 2000 ft x 1.25 = 2500 ft. However, this is for a paved surface. Multiply the TODR by 1.2 = 3000 ft to allow for the increased rolling resistance of grass. Finally, for each 1% of upslope, increase the distance by 5%. Therefore, the distance must be increased by 1.2 x 5% = 6%. The final answer is 3000 ft x 1.06 = 3180 ft.

The order of applying the factors does not affect the answer, but they are cumulative. It is not the same as 2000 ft x 1.51.

FIELD LENGTH TAKE-OFF MASS

Use figures 2.1 and 2.2 to also determine the maximum take-off mass for a given field length and conditions. As mass is in the centre of the graph, it is obtained by working forward from the temperature and backward from the field length available. The intersection of the two lines determines the maximum take-off mass. The intersection method would also be required to find a minimum headwind or maximum tailwind.

Example 1:

Using figure 2.2, find the maximum take-off mass for a public transport flight given the following:

Temperature -2°C, pressure altitude 2000 ft, 20 kt headwind, and 2275 ft of level, wet grass runway.

Worked example 1:

Because the field distance is gross, paved, level, and dry, the graph cannot be entered at 2275 ft, which is the take-off distance available. First, divide it by 1.25 (to find the gross distance) = 1820 ft and then 1.3 for the wet grass = 1400 ft.

Enter the figure on the right-hand side and work backward as shown by the blue line. Remember that because working backward, stop at the value and then move to the reference line with the guide lines, and not visa versa. Stop at the weight reference line and now work from left to right as shown by the red line. Enter at -2°C, move vertically to 2000 ft pressure altitude, and then stop at the weight reference line. Now descend with the weight guide lines until the intersection of the red and blue lines is found at 3420 lb.

TAKE-OFF DISTANCE-FLAPS UP

ASSOCIATED CONDITIONS:

POWER .... TAKE-OFF POWER SET BEFORE BRAKE RELEASE
MIXTURE .... FULL RICH
FLAPS .... UP
LANDING GEAR .... RETRACT AFTER POSITIVE CLIMB ESTABLISHED
COWL FLAPS .... OPEN
RUNWAY .... PAVED, LEVEL, DRY SURFACE

EXAMPLE:

OAT .... 15°C
PRESSURE ALTITUDE .... 5653 FT
TAKE-OFF WEIGHT .... 3650 LBS
HEAD WIND COMPONENT .... 10 KST

GROUND ROLL .... 1900 FT
TOTAL DISTANCE OVER 50-FT OBSTACLE ... 3475 FT
TAKE-OFF SPEED AT
ROTATION .... 73 KTS
50-FT .... 84 KTS

WEIGHT ~ POUNDS	TAKE-OFF SPEED	
	ROTATION KNOTS	50 FT KNOTS
3650	73	84
3600	72	83
3400	71	82
3200	70	80
3000	68	78
2800	65	75

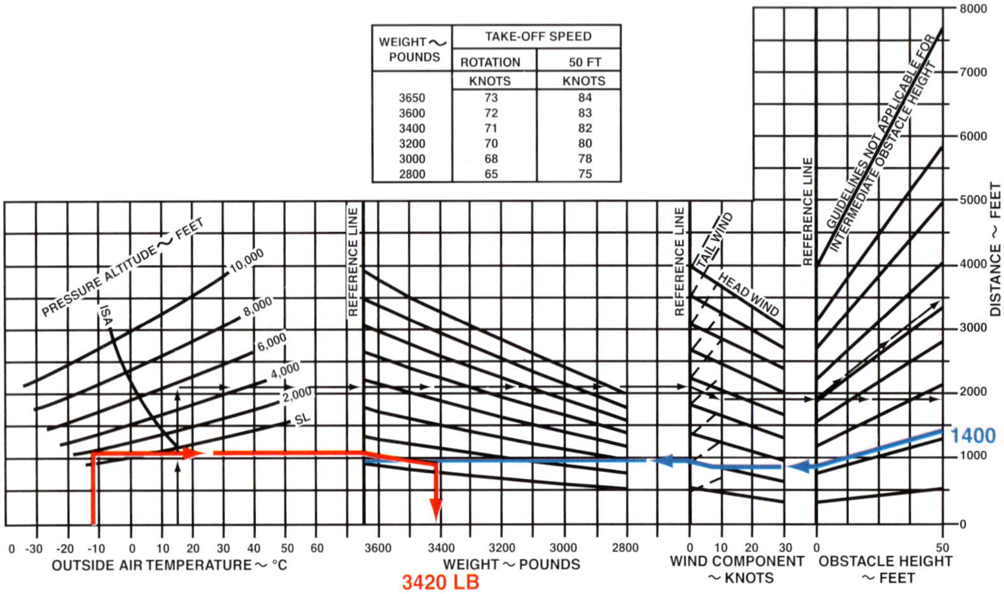

CLIMB LIMITED MASS

Use figure 2.3 to find a climb limited mass, a climb gradient, or rate of climb.

The red line on the figure below shows that the 4% climb gradient after take-off can be achieved at maximum take-off mass at airfields up to around 10 000 ft pressure altitude. This aeroplane is, therefore, unlikely to become climb limited.

Although there is no legal obstacle clearance requirement after take-off in a class B single-engine aeroplane, use figure 2.3 to determine a climb gradient and check obstacle clearance. The blue line shows that at a temperature of 20°C and a pressure altitude of 1000 ft, an aeroplane mass of 3500 lb would climb at a gradient of 10.2% and have a rate of climb of 1200 fpm.

Use figure 2.3 to determine the maximum planned altitude for enroute terrain clearance. For this aeroplane, the altitude where the rate of climb is 300 fpm is well above 10 000 ft.

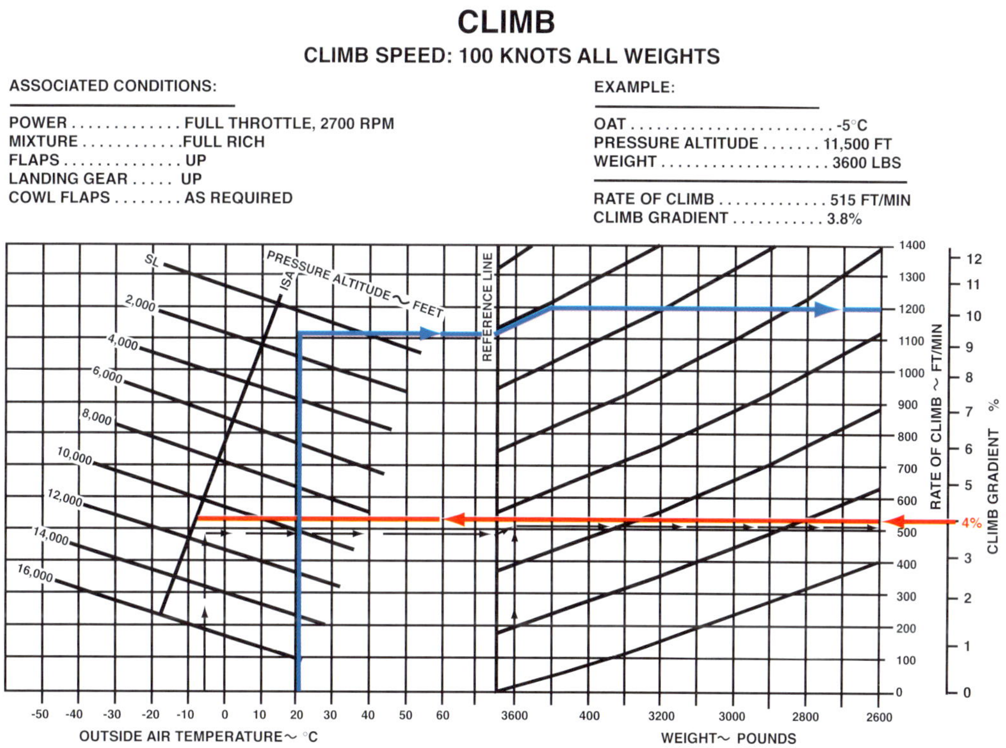

CALCULATING OBSTACLE CLEARANCE

If the climb gradient and distance/height of an obstacle is known, it is possible to calculate the amount by which the lowest part of the aeroplane will clear the obstacle.

Example 1:

Calculate the obstacle clearance over an obstacle 725 ft high and 1½ from the end of TODA for a Class B single-engine aeroplane climbing at 8.6%.

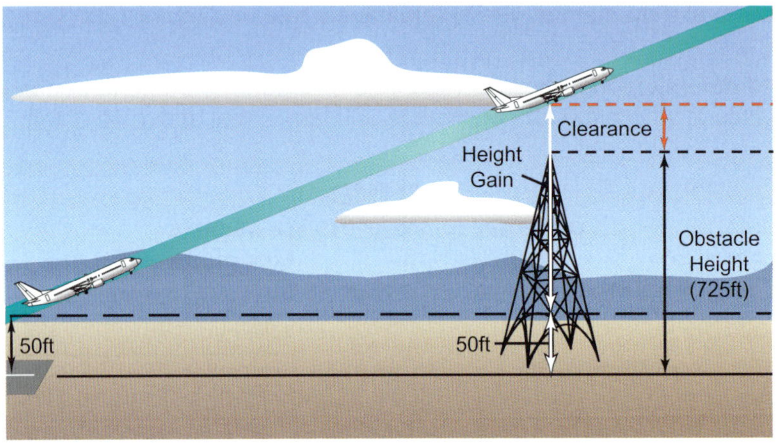

Worked Answer 1:

At the screen, a Class B aeroplane is at 50 ft. If this screen height is added to the height gained in $1^1/_2$ climbing at 8.6%, find the height of the aeroplane using the following equation:

$$\% \text{ gradient} = \frac{\text{height gain}}{\text{horizontal distance}} \times 100, \text{ and rearranging}$$

$$\text{Height gain} = \frac{\% \text{ gradient} \times \text{horizontal distance}}{100}$$

$$\text{Height gain} = \frac{8.6 \times 9120}{100} = 785 \text{ ft}$$

Note: There are 6080 ft in 1 . Therefore, the obstacle is 6080 x 1½ = 9120 ft from the screen.

The aeroplane is at 785 + 50 = 835 ft

As the obstacle is 725 ft high, it is cleared by (835 - 725 ft) = 110 ft

LANDING FIELD LENGTH REQUIRED

Figure 2.4 enables determination of the gross landing distance required. The graphs allow for the variables of aeroplane weight, aerodrome temperature, pressure altitude, and wind component when moving through the graph. However, the figure determined is the gross distance required for a paved, level, and dry runway. To allow for public transport, slope, and wet/dry grass, factor the figure determined by the values stated in the CAP on page 14.

Factor winds to allow for a lull in a headwind and a gust in a tailwind. Use 50% of a headwind and 150% of a tailwind. Remember that the wind guidelines in the CAP 698 factor the wind. When planning, take both the still air and factored forecast into account for landing. In this case, the still air situation is normally the most limiting, unless a runway is unidirectional. However, in the JAA exam, use the given winds as if overhead the landing aerodrome.

Chapter 17
Multi-Engine Piston (MEP1)

INTRODUCTION

This chapter uses the CAP 698 to obtain aeroplane data for a multi-engine piston Class B aeroplane. Chapter 15 looked at the JAR regulations that apply to public transport using Class B aeroplanes. The multi-engine graphs are again gross, which means they must be factored for public transport.

The data for the multi-engine piston (MEP1) aeroplane is contained in the CAP 698 in the blue pages of Section II. Use the majority of the graphs in the same way as for the single-engine piston. The following pages show the main differences on take-off and landing.

TAKE-OFF DISTANCE REQUIRED

Use figures 3.1 and 3.3 to determine the gross take-off distance required. The figures differ only in the take-off flap position. Figure 3.1 is for flaps up and figure 3.3 is for flaps 25°.

Both graphs allow for the variables of aeroplane weight, aerodrome temperature, pressure altitude, and wind component when moving through the graph. However, the figure determined is the gross distance required for a paved, level, and dry runway. To allow for public transport, slope, and wet/dry grass, factor the figure determined by the values stated in the CAP.

Always factor winds to allow for a lull in a headwind and a gust in a tailwind. Use 50% of a headwind and 150% of a tailwind. However, the wind guidelines in all the figures in the CAP 698 factor the wind. Enter with the forecast or reported wind, not the factored wind.

Although there is no requirement to be able to stop within the ASDA from the lift-off speed, this is prudent. Use graphs 3.2 and 3.4 to check this for flaps up and flaps 25°.

DETERMINING THE TODR AND ASDR

Example 1:

Determine the TODR and ASDR (from the lift-off speed) for an aeroplane mass 4400 lb, flaps up, 2000 ft pressure altitude, 14°C and, 10 kt headwind.

NORMAL PROCEDURE TAKEOFF

ASSOCIATED CONDITIONS:

2800 RPM AMD 40 INCHES MAP
PAVED, LEVEL, DRY RUNWAY LIFTOFF AT 79 KIAS
BARRIER AT 79 KIAS FLAPS 0° COWL FLAPS 1/2 OPEN

EXAMPLE:

OAT .... 21°C
PRESSURE ALTITUDE .... 2000 FT
GROSS WEIGHT .... 3969 LBS
HEADWIND .... 9 KNOTS
TAKEOFF GROUND ROLL .... 1350 FT
TAKEOFF DISTANCE OVER 50 FT
BARRIER......................... 3260 FT

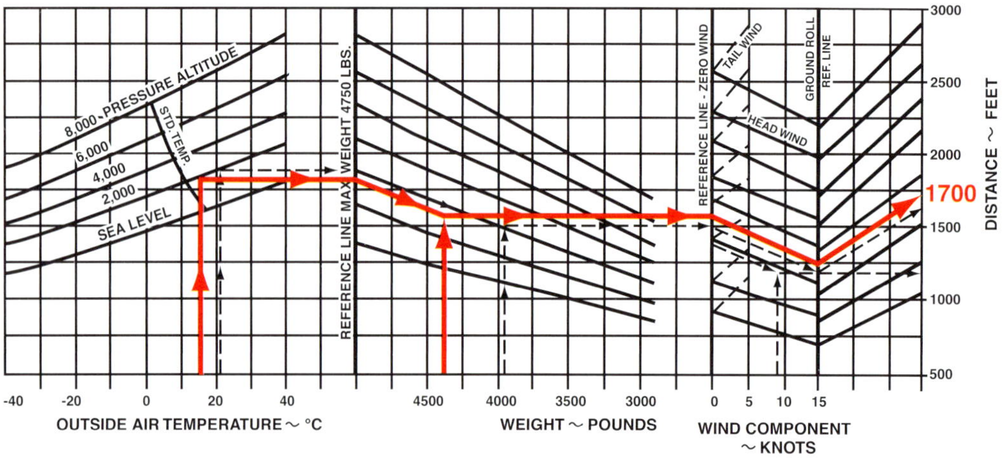

Worked Example:

For flaps up, the TODR is determined from figure 3.1 and the ASDR from figure 3.2. To determine the TODR, enter at 14°C at the bottom left-hand side moving vertically to 2000 ft and then moving horizontally to the weight reference line. Move with the weight guide lines to the aeroplane weight of 4400 lb, then horizontally again to the wind reference line. Move with the wind guide lines to 10 kt headwind and then horizontally again to the screen reference line. Follow the guide lines up to read off the TODR of approximately 1700 ft.

Now find the ASDR from figure 3.2. Again, enter at the temperature of 14°C and move vertically to the pressure altitude of 2000 ft. Move horizontally to the aeroplane weight reference line and then move with the weight guidelines to the aeroplane weight of 4400 lb. Move horizontally to the wind reference line. Then move with the wind guidelines to the 10 kt headwind, before moving horizontally again to obtain the ASDR of approximately 3550 ft.

Example 2:

Given a take-off distance required of 2200 ft from figure 3.1, what is the minimum take-off distance required for public transport if the runway is wet grass, has no stopway or clearway, and has a downslope of 0.8%?

ACCELERATE AND STOP DISTANCE

ASSOCIATED CONDITIONS:

STANDARD WHEELS, TIRES AND BRAKES
FULL POWER BEFORE BRAKE RELEASE
0° WING FLAPS ABORT SPEED 79 KIAS
BOTH THROTTLES CLOSED AT ENGINE FAILURE
MAXIMUM BRAKING PAVED, LEVEL, DRY RUNWAY
COWL FLAPS 1/2 OPEN

EXAMPLE:

OAT .... 21°C
PRESSURE ALTITUDE .... 2000 FT
TAKE-OFF WEIGHT .... 3969 LBS
HEAD WIND .... 9 KNOTS
ACCELERATE & STOP DISTANCE ... 3260 FT

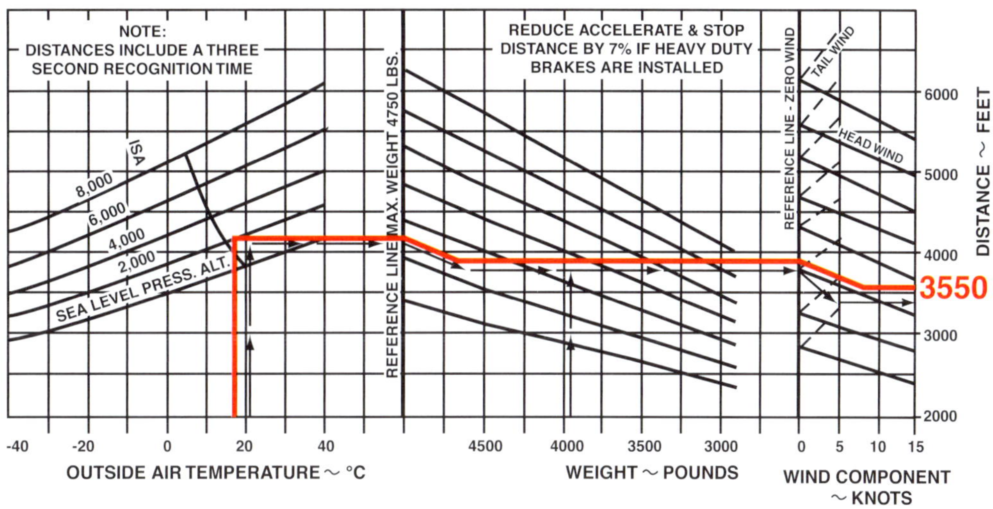

Worked example 2:

If the gross TODR is 2200 ft, the net TODR required must be 2200 ft x 1.25 = 2750 ft. However, this is for a paved surface. To allow for the increased rolling resistance of wet grass, multiply the TODR by 1.3 = 3575 ft. There is no correction for downslope. The final answer is, therefore, 3575 ft.

The order of applying the factors does not affect the answer.

CLIMB LIMITED MASS

With all engines operating, all Class B aeroplanes must have a steady gradient of climb after take-off of at least 4%. In addition, with one engine inoperative the aeroplane must have a positive climb gradient at 400 ft (maximum take-off power but flaps in take-off position) and 0.75% at 1500 ft (maximum continuous power and flaps up).

These three requirements are found in figures 3.5, 3.6, and 3.7. However, it is only possible to find the rate of climb directly from these graphs and the gradient would need to be calculated. The relationship between rate of climb and climb gradient is below.

$$\%\text{ gradient} = \frac{\text{vertical speed}}{\text{horizontal speed}} \times 100\%$$

$$= \frac{\text{rate of climb}}{\text{TAS}} \times 100\%$$

Because rate of climb is measured in feet per minute and TAS in nautical miles per hour, these units must be converted to be the same, with feet per hour being the simplest.

$$\%\text{ gradient} = \frac{\text{fpm} \times 60}{\text{TAS} \times 6080} \times 100\%$$

$$= \frac{\text{fpm} \times 6000\%}{\text{TAS} \times 6080}$$

Example

Is the aeroplane climb limited at an aerodrome with 9000 ft pressure altitude and a temperature of +18°C using fig 3.5?

Worked Answer

Figure 3.5

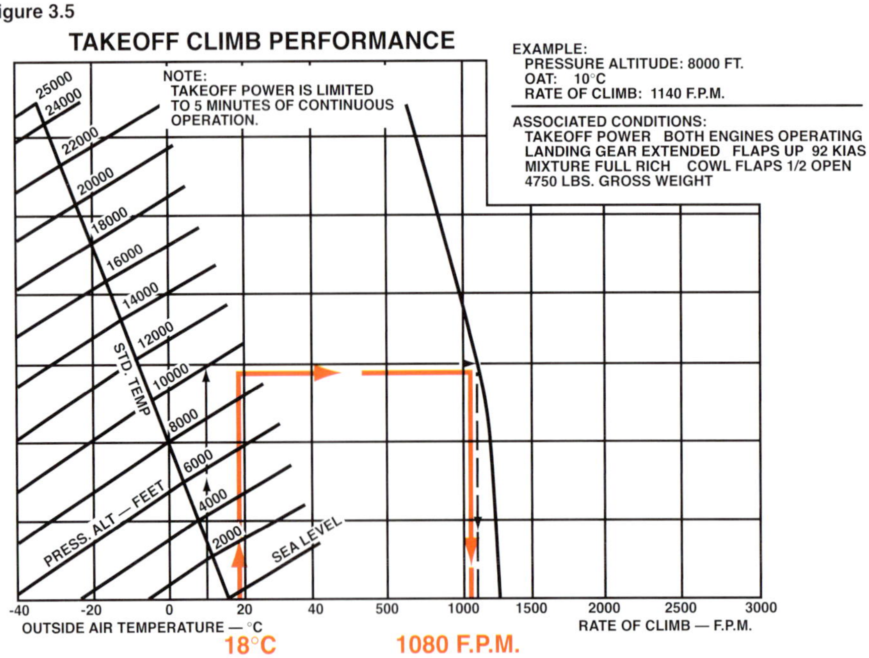

In the above graph, enter at the temperature of 18°C and move vertically up to the pressure altitude of 9000 ft. Now move horizontally to the single weight line and down to read the rate of climb at 1080 fpm. The graph is drawn for a climb IAS of 92 kt, which is a TAS of 110 kt.

Now calculate the climb gradient:

$$\% \text{ gradient} = \frac{1080 \times 6000\%}{110 \times 6080}$$

$$= 9.69\%$$

This gradient of 9.69% exceeds the minimum required gradient of 4% and the aeroplane is not climb limited. It is also possible to see that at normal aerodrome altitudes and temperatures this aeroplane will not be take-off climb limited.

THE NET TAKE-OFF FLIGHT PATH AND OBSTACLE CLEARANCE

Class B multi-engine aeroplanes have an obstacle clearance requirement. This is based on 0.77 of the all-engine climb gradient, up to the cloud base, at which the critical engine is assumed to fail. Above the cloud base, the aeroplane is assumed to be flying at the gross one engine out gradient. Using this profile the aeroplane must clear all obstacles by at least 50 ft.

Figure 3.6 determines both the all engines operating, and one engine out rates of climb.

Example

Calculate the planned flight clearance of an obstacle 640 ft high, 2 nm from reference zero. The aeroplane's take-off mass is 4750 lb, flaps are at 0°, aerodrome pressure altitude is 4000 ft, and the temperature is 22°C. The cloud base is at a height of 500 ft and there is a 10 kt headwind component.

Worked Answer

Figure 3.6

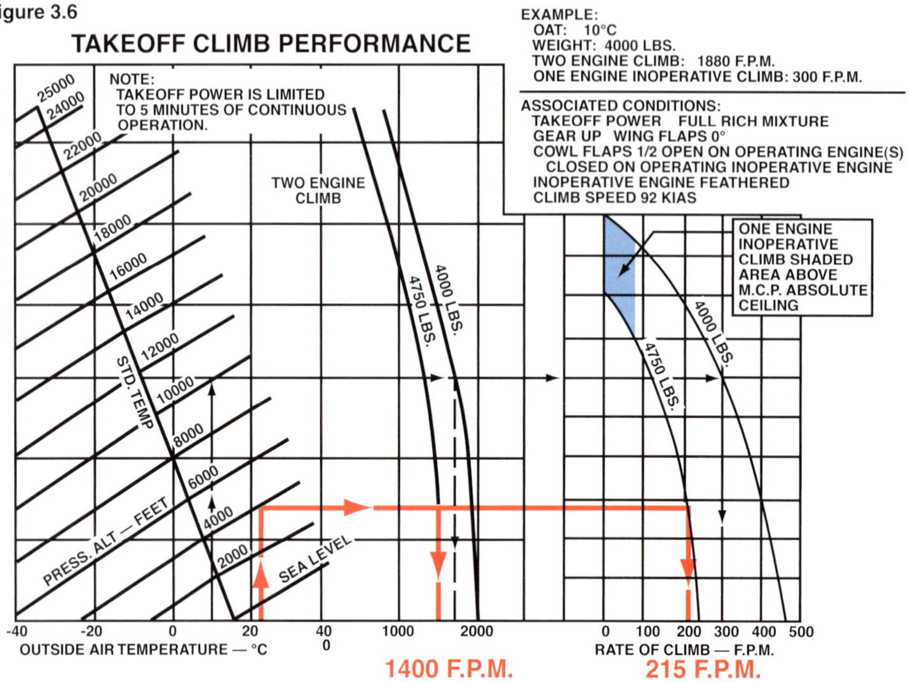

Enter figure 3.6 at 22°C and work vertically to the pressure altitude of 4000 ft. Move horizontally to the two-engine climb 4750 lb line, and then turn to move vertically down, to read off the two-engine gradient of 1400 ft. By continuing across to the one-engine weight line of 4750 lb, move vertically down to read off the one engine out rate of climb of 215 fpm.

Because the cloud base is at 500 ft, the two-engine gradient must first be calculated and then multiplied by 0.77 to get a net all engine gradient. Remember that the aeroplane will be at the screen height of 50 ft at reference zero, and will therefore only need to climb 450 ft to be at the cloud base.

To find the gross two-engine gradient, it is first necessary to find the groundspeed for 92 kt IAS at 4000 ft, 22°C and with a 10 kt headwind component. This TAS is 100 kt and therefore, the groundspeed is 90 kt. Using the equation:

$$\% \text{ Gradient} = \frac{\text{fpm} \times 6000\%}{\text{GS} \times 6060}$$

$$= \frac{1400 \times 6000\%}{90 \times 6080}$$

$$= 15.35\%$$

This gives us the gross gradient, which must be reduced by 0.5% to get the net gradient of 14.85% (15.35 – 0.5 = 14.85%).

Now the horizontal distance to climb to the cloud base can be calculated by rearranging the equation:

$$\% \text{ Gradient} = \frac{\text{height gained} \times 100\%}{\text{horizontal distance}}, \text{ to become}$$

$$\text{Horizontal distance} = \frac{\text{height gained} \times 100\%}{\% \text{ gradient}}$$

$$= \frac{(500 \text{ ft} - 50 \text{ ft}) \times 100\%}{14.85\%}$$

$$= 3030 \text{ ft}$$

Since the obstacle is at 2 nm which is 2 x 6080 ft = 12 120 ft, the horizontal distance to the obstacle above the cloud base is (12 120 – 3030 ft) = 9090 ft.

Using the one-engine rate of climb, the gross one-engine climb can be calculated.

$$\% \text{ Gradient} = \frac{\text{fpm} \times 6000}{\text{GS} \times 6060}$$

$$= \frac{215 \times 6000}{90 \times 6080}$$

$$= 2.36\%$$

Now calculate the vertical distance climbed in the horizontal distance 9090 ft, from the equation:

$$\% \text{ Gradient} = \frac{\text{height gained} \times 100\%}{\text{horizontal distance}}$$

$$\text{Height gained} = \frac{\% \text{ gradient} \times \text{horizontal distance}}{100}$$

$$= \frac{2.36 \times 9090}{100}$$

$$= 214.5 \text{ ft}$$

After 2 nm, the aeroplane will be at a height of 714.5 ft (50 ft + 450 ft + 214.5 ft = 714.5 ft). Since the obstacle is 640 ft high, the clearance will be 74.5 ft (714.5 – 640 ft = 74.5 ft).

LANDING FIELD LENGTH REQUIRED

Use figures 3.9 and 3.10 of CAP 698 to determine the gross landing distance required for normal and short field technique. The graphs allow for the variables of aeroplane weight, aerodrome temperature, pressure altitude, and wind component when moving through the graph. However, the figure determined is the gross distance required for a paved, level, and dry runway. To allow for public transport, slope, and wet/dry grass, factor the figure determined by the values stated in the CAP on page 38/39.

Chapter 18
JAR Performance Class C Regulations

INTRODUCTION

Performance Class C aeroplanes are rare today. Class C includes any multi-engine piston propeller aeroplane with either a take-off mass exceeding 5700 kg or 10 or more passenger seats. It is unlikely they would be used for public transport flight, and exam questions concerning Class C aeroplanes are very rare. It is worth noting, however, that the majority of the regulations are very similar to Class A, with provision for all engines and engine failure during the take-off and enroute.

GENERAL (JAR-OPS 1.560)

The operator must ensure that the approved performance data in the Aeroplane Flight Manual is supplemented, as necessary, with other data acceptable to the Authority if the approved performance data in the Aeroplane Flight Manual is insufficient.

TAKE-OFF (JAR-OPS 1.565)

An operator shall ensure that the take-off mass does not exceed the maximum take-off mass specified in the Aeroplane Flight Manual for the pressure altitude and the ambient temperature at the aerodrome at which the take-off is to be made.

An operator shall ensure that for aeroplanes that have take-off field length data contained in their Aeroplane Flight Manuals that do not include engine failure accountability, the distance from the start of the take-off roll required by the aeroplane to reach a height of 50 ft above the surface with all engines operating within the maximum take-off power conditions specified, when multiplied by a factor of either:

- 1.33 for aeroplanes having two engines
- 1.25 for aeroplanes having three engines and
- 1.18 for aeroplanes having four engines

does not exceed the take-off run available at the aerodromes at which the take-offs are to be made.

An operator shall ensure that, for aeroplanes that have take-off field length data contained in their Aeroplane Flight Manuals that account for engine failure, the following requirements are met in accordance with the specifications in the Aeroplane Flight Manual:

- The accelerate-stop distance must not exceed the accelerate-stop distance available.
- The take-off distance must not exceed the take-off distance available with a clearway distance not exceeding half of the take-off run available.
- The take-off run must not exceed the take-off run available.
- Compliance with this paragraph must be shown using a single value of V_1 for the rejected and continued take-off.
- On a wet or contaminated runway, the take-off mass must not exceed that permitted for a take-off on a dry runway under the same conditions.

To comply, the operator must take account of the following:

- The pressure altitude at the aerodrome
- The ambient temperature at the aerodrome
- The runway surface condition and the type of runway surface
- The runway slope in the direction of take-off
- Not more than 50% of the reported headwind component or not less than 150% of the reported tailwind component
- The loss, if any, of runway length due to alignment of the aeroplane prior to take-off

TAKE-OFF OBSTACLE CLEARANCE (JAR-OPS 1.570)

The take-off flight path with one engine inoperative must clear all obstacles by:

- A vertical distance of at least 50 ft plus 0.01 x D, or
- A horizontal distance of at least 90 m plus 0.125 x D,

where D is the horizontal distance the aeroplane has travelled from the end of the take-off distance available. For aeroplanes with a wingspan of less than 60 m, a horizontal obstacle clearance of half the aeroplane wingspan plus 60 m, plus 0.125 x D may be used.

The take-off flight path must begin at a height of 50 ft above the surface at the end of the take-off distance and end at an approximate height of 1500 ft above the surface.

The following must be taken into account:

- The mass of the aeroplane at the commencement of the take-off run
- The pressure altitude at the aerodrome
- The ambient temperature at the aerodrome
- Not more than 50% of the reported headwind component or not less than 150% of the reported tail-wind component

Track changes shall not be allowed up to that point of the take-off flight path where a height of 50 ft above the surface has been achieved. Up to a height of 400 ft, it is assumed that the aeroplane is banked by no more than 15°. Above 400 ft height, bank angles greater than 15° but not more than 25° may be scheduled. Adequate allowance must be made for the effect of bank angle on operating speeds and flight path including the distance increments resulting from increased operating speeds.

For cases that do not require track changes of more than 15°, an operator need not consider those obstacles which have a lateral distance greater than:

- 300 m if the pilot is able to maintain the required navigational accuracy through the obstacle accountability area, or
- 600 m for flights under all other conditions.

For track changes of more than 15°, an operator need not consider those obstacles that have a lateral distance greater than:

- 600 m if the pilot is able to maintain the required navigational accuracy through the obstacle accountability area, or
- 900 m for flights under all other conditions.

ENROUTE

ONE ENGINE INOPERATIVE (JAR-OPS 1.580)

In the event of any one engine becoming inoperative at any point on the route or on any planned diversion and with the other engine or engines operating within the maximum continuous power conditions specified, the aircraft must be capable of continuing the flight from the cruising altitude to an aerodrome where a landing can be made clearing obstacles within 9.3 km (5 nm) either side of the intended track by a vertical interval of at least:

- 1000 ft when the rate of climb is zero or greater, or
- 2000 ft when the rate of climb is less than zero.

The flight path shall have a positive slope at an altitude of 450 m (1500 ft) above the aerodrome where the landing is assumed to be made after the failure of one engine.

The available rate of climb of the aeroplane shall be taken to be 150 ft per minute less than the gross rate of climb specified.

If the navigational accuracy does not meet the 95% containment level, then the above figures are increased to 18.5 km (10 nm).

Fuel jettisoning is permitted to an extent consistent with reaching the aerodrome with the required fuel reserves if a safe procedure is used.

TWO ENGINES INOPERATIVE (JAR-OPS 1.585)

At no point along the intended track will an aeroplane having three or more engines be more than 90 minutes at the all-engine long-range cruising speed at standard temperature in still air, away from an aerodrome at which the performance requirements applicable at the expected landing mass are met.

The two-engines inoperative flight path shown must permit the aeroplane to continue the flight in the expected meteorological conditions, clearing all obstacles within 9.3 km (5 nm) either side of the intended track by a vertical interval of at least 2000 ft to an aerodrome where the performance requirements are met.

The two engines are assumed to fail at the most critical point of that portion of the route where the aeroplane is more than 90 minutes at the all engines long-range cruising speed at standard temperature in still air to an aerodrome where the performance requirements are met.

The expected mass of the aeroplane at the point where the two engines are assumed to fail must not be less than that which would include sufficient fuel to proceed to an aerodrome where the landing is assumed to be made and to arrive there at an altitude of a least 450 m (1500 ft) directly over the landing area and thereafter to fly level for 15 minutes.

The available rate of climb of the aeroplane shall be taken to be 150 ft per minute less than that specified.

If the navigational accuracy does not meet the 95% containment, the above distances must be increased to 18.5 km (10 nm).

Fuel jettisoning is permitted to an extent consistent with reaching the aerodrome with the required fuel reserves if a safe procedure is used.

LANDING (JAR-OPS 1.590)

DESTINATION AND ALTERNATE AERODROMES

The landing mass of the aeroplane must not exceed the maximum landing mass specified in the Aeroplane Flight Manual for the altitude and, if accounted for in the Aeroplane Flight Manual, the ambient temperature expected for the estimated time of landing at the destination and alternate aerodrome.

LANDING DISTANCES

The landing mass of the aeroplane for the estimated time of landing must allow a full stop landing from 50 ft above the threshold within 70% of the landing distance available at the destination and any alternate aerodrome.

The following must be taken into account:

- The altitude at the aerodrome
- Not more than 50% of the headwind component or not less than 150% of the tail-wind component
- The type of runway surface
- The slope of the runway in the direction of landing

For dispatching an aeroplane, assume that:

- The aeroplane will land on the most favourable runway in still air.
- The aeroplane will land on the runway most likely to be assigned, considering the probable wind speed and direction and the ground handling characteristics of the aeroplane and considering other conditions such as landing aids and terrain.
- If an operator is unable to comply with the above for the destination aerodrome, the aeroplane may be dispatched if an alternate aerodrome is designated which permits full compliance.

LANDING DISTANCE CORRECTION FACTORS

Unless otherwise specified in the Aeroplane Flight Manual, use the following correction factor:

Grass (on firm soil up to 13 cm long) hard landing distance x 1.20

LANDING RUNWAY

Two considerations in determining the maximum permissible landing mass at the destination and alternate aerodromes are used.

The aeroplane mass is such that on arrival, the aeroplane can be landed within 70% of the landing distance available on the most favourable, normally the longest, runway in still air. Regardless of the wind conditions, the maximum landing mass for an aerodrome/aeroplane configuration at a particular aerodrome cannot be exceeded.

Consider anticipated conditions and circumstances. The expected wind or ATC and noise abatement procedures may indicate the use of a different runway. These factors may result in a lower landing mass than that permitted. In this case, dispatch should be based on this lesser mass.

WET AND CONTAMINATED RUNWAYS (JAR-OPS 1.600)

When the appropriate weather reports or forecasts indicate that the runway at the estimated time of arrival may be wet, the landing distance available is equal to or exceeds the required landing distance determined by a factor of 1.15.

When the appropriate weather reports or forecasts, or a combination thereof, indicate that the runway at the estimated time of arrival may be contaminated, the landing distance determined by using data acceptable to the Authority for these conditions does not exceed the landing distance available.